SYNESIUS OF CYRENE

The Transformation of the Classical Heritage

Peter Brown, General Editor

JAY BREGMAN

SYNESIUS
OF CYRENE

PHILOSOPHER-BISHOP

UNIVERSITY OF CALIFORNIA PRESS
Berkeley   Los Angeles   London

University of California Press
Berkeley and Los Angeles, California

University of California Press, Ltd.
London, England

© 1982 by
The Regents of the University of California

Printed in the United States of America

1 2 3 4 5 6 7 8 9

Library of Congress Cataloging in Publication Data

Bregman, Jay.
  Synesius of Cyrene, philosopher-bishop.

  (The transformation of the classical heritage; 2)
  Bibliography: p.
  Includes index.
  1. Synesius, of Cyrene, Bishop of Ptolemaïs.
I. Title.   II. Series: Transformation of the classi-
cal heritage; 2.
BR1720.S9B72   186'.4   81-10293
ISBN 0-520-04192-5   AACR2

For Robert, Alexandra, Rachel, my mother,
and in memory of my father and Uncle Albert

Contents

Acknowledgments

This book is part of an ongoing study of the religious attitudes of the Greco-Roman aristocracies of late antiquity. I hope that it will contribute to our knowledge of an important subject: the relationship between the transformation of classical civilization and the history of Western religious thought.

I am grateful to many scholars for their support, help, and encouragement. Special thanks are due Professor Ramsay MacMullen of Yale, who first suggested this work and made many valuable suggestions. The guidance of Professor Gerhart Ladner, Emeritus, the University of California at Los Angeles, was very important at a crucial stage of my research. The advice and criticism of Professor Milton Anastos, also at Los Angeles, led me to frame basic questions more precisely. The late Professor Paul Alexander of the University of California, Berkeley, was always helpful, warm, and encouraging, especially at times when I had doubts about the value of this work.

I am much indebted to Professor Kees Bolle of the University of California, Los Angeles, for showing me the way in the serious and systematic investigation of religious phenomena and for first bringing this manuscript to the attention of the University of California Press.

Professor Gerard Caspary of the University of California, Berkeley, has made his great learning available to me and has given invaluable aid in the careful interpretation of early Christian sources. The difficult field of Neoplatonism would have been nearly impossible to deal with but for the patient assistance of Professor John Dillon of Trinity College, Dublin, who was also kind enough to read the manuscript several times and to make sure that the translations of original texts were rendered and interpreted accurately. His many suggestions contributed much to the improvement of the entire manuscript. I owe a great deal to Professor Peter Brown of Berkeley, the editor of this series, who worked carefully with me on both the details and the current theories of late antiquity. His scholarship and original vision of the late Roman world made it possible for me to understand Synesius in the context of his time.

It has been a pleasure to work with the editorial staff of the University of California Press. Ms. Doris Kretschmer and Ms. Marilyn Schwartz have displayed tact and insight in their suggestions for the style of the final copy. Dr. Pericles Georges did a thorough job of copy editing and made it possible for me to clarify the meaning of several ambiguous passages.

I must also thank Ms. Eva Meyn for a first-rate job typing a difficult manuscript. All final decisions with respect to content and style are my responsibility.

Orono, Maine

Note on Abbreviations

Full references to ancient and modern works cited in abbreviated form will be found in the bibliography. In addition, the following abbreviations have been used:

LSJ   A *Greek-English Lexicon*. Compiled by H. G. Liddell and R. Scott. Revised by Sir H. S. Jones. 9th ed. Oxford, 1968.

OCD   *The Oxford Classical Dictionary*. 2nd ed. Oxford, 1970.

PG   *Patrologiae Cursus Completus, Series Graeca*. Edited by J. P. Migne. Paris, 1857–1880.

PL   *Patrologiae Cursus Completus, Series Latina*. Edited by J. P. Migne. Paris, 1844–1864.

RE   *Realencylopädie der classischen Altertumswissenschaft*. Edited by A. Pauly, G. Wissowa, and W. Kroll. Stuttgart, 1894–.

Primary reference to Synesius' works in the text and notes is by column number to volume 66 of *PG* and by chapter and column number to N. Terzaghi's edition of Synesius' *Hymni et Opuscula*.

All translations are my own unless otherwise specified.

Introduction

i

In the second half of the fourth century A.D. the last important battles between Hellenism and Christianity were fought. They were marked on both sides by memorable conversions, great religious controversies, and brilliant polemic. Some of the works that emerged from this struggle gained a lasting and deserved value; on the other hand, the struggle of religions often deteriorated to the level of mere slander, mob violence, and a general viciousness of spirit and action. Against this background the outstanding figures are easy to recognize, for they shine like beacons in a world grown dark and increasingly chaotic. One of these, a representative intellectual member of the local pagan aristocracy in the East who became a Christian bishop, is Synesius of Cyrene.

During the late fourth and early fifth centuries some pagans became Christians, while others remained loyal to the religion of their forefathers. Many in both camps were members of the curial order in the cities and were, because of their urban ideals, education, and social position, the people most familiar with the traditions of classical antiquity. They comprised that group which M. I. Rostovtzeff designated as the city bourgeoisie and identified as the last possessors of the higher culture of antiquity.[1] Many people from other classes and stations in life also found Christianity attractive. They had a need for acceptance, a need to feel they belonged to something lasting and important. But conversions on a mass scale, although lacking the dramatic aspects of the more spectacular individual changes of religion, were due also to the success of many Christian emperors in defeating barbarians and usurpers in times of crisis.[2]

---

1. *SEHRE*[2] xvi and 533–541. This monograph is based on the author's dissertation for the Ph.D. in history (Yale University, 1974).

2. As one example among many see, e.g., Sozomen *HE* 8.1. Armenia and the Eastern provinces were at this time overrun by the Huns. "Rufinus, Prefect of the East, was suspected of having clandestinely invited them to devastate the Roman territories, in fur-

The most impressive conversions to the new religion, however, must have been those of people like Augustine, who, after trying all the philosophical and religious systems of the day, from Neoplatonism to Manichaeanism, became true, believing Christians. They were haunted by Christianity; their increasing sense of sinfulness and worthlessness built to a crisis, during which all the old creeds were found wanting. At that point they totally rejected all past life and values and found a spiritual rebirth in the new religion. All was attributed to the seeming miracle of divine grace. Just when everything seemed lost, and hope abandoned, God came to the rescue, as it were, and they were saved. This total dependence on God and His grace, this insistence that reason and even mystical intuition can only go so far, is emphasized in the Judaeo-Christian tradition—as opposed to a philosophical religion such as Neoplatonism. True, some Hellenes also believed in the efficacy of the gods and were turning to such sacramental systems as theurgy when their spiritual crisis deepened. The doctrines of the theurgists implied an idea of grace, but they never put forth a doctrine as all-encompassing as that of ultimate dependence on divine grace and salvation once and for all (*hapax, ephapax, semel*) through the Crucifixion and Resurrection of Jesus Christ.[3]

An important indication of the historical direction the world was taking in the late fourth and early fifth centuries is the conversion of Synesius of Cyrene. Though he did not possess the spiritual capacities of St. Augustine, nor was his conversion so spectacular, he was a learned

therance of his own ambitious designs; for he was said to aspire to tyranny. This suspicion led to his being soon after slain; for on the return of the troops from the conquest of Eugenius, the emperor Arcadius, according to custom, went forth from Constantinople to meet them; and the soldiers took the opportunity to massacre Rufinus. *These circumstances tended greatly to the extension of religion* [ital. J. B.]. The emperors attributed to the piety of their father the ease with which the tyrant had been vanquished, and the insidious and ambitious schemes of Rufinus arrested; and they confirmed all the laws which had been enacted by their predecessors in favour of religion, and bestowed upon the Church fresh tokens of their own zeal and devotion. Their subjects profited by their example; so that even the pagans were converted without difficulty to Christianity, and the heretics united themselves to the Catholic Church" (tr. Edward Walford, Bohn's Ecclesiastical Library, London 1905). Cf. Socrates, *HE* 5.1; Philost. *HE* 11.3.

  3. For a discussion of the concept of grace developed by the theurgic Neoplatonists, see Wallis, *Neoplatonism*, 118–123; later Neoplatonists thought that union with the divine could be achieved only through theurgy, and not, as Plotinus, through pure philosophy. For them the soul had fallen completely into the material world and no part remains in the Intelligible—another Plotinian doctrine they rejected. Consequently, theurgic union with the gods depended upon a kind of grace; however, this was conceived as operative through the structure of the cosmos, not in supernatural terms, as Christian grace. For a view of the deep impersonality of the Platonic religious world in all periods, see Trexler, *Studies in the Renaissance* 19.36–37; these pages are excellent on the magical side of Ficino and its differences from popular Christianity of the time.

man deeply and seriously involved in matters speculative and religious, who tried to understand the world and live according to the truth. He received a philosophical education under Hypatia, daughter of the philosopher Theon, and high priestess of Alexandrian Neoplatonism. Synesius' speculative abilities were not of the first rank, but he understood, accepted, and meditated on the traditional problems of ancient metaphysics, and his works throughout reflect his dedication to the principal doctrines of Hellenic philosophy. What makes him significant is his role as a representative and interpreter of the traditional Greco-Roman aristocracy: even though Synesius lived at a time when the Late Antique transformation had already gone far, he remains important in determining the direction and nature of social change in the Empire, for he achieved both a philosophical and a social rapprochement with the Church. Surely one of the reasons that Theophilus, the bishop of Alexandria, sought Synesius for the episcopate so zealously, in spite of the latter's reservations concerning certain dogmas, was thereby to add to the prestige of the Church: if the leaders of traditional Hellenism could be recruited for the Church, then who of substance would remain to oppose it?

Synesius is also important for special historical reasons because in him are united the diverse strands of the entire culture of antiquity from beginning to end. He was a Hellene to the core and as loyal to the ancient city-state of Cyrene as he was to the Roman Empire. He was of Dorian lineage and traced his ancestry back to Eurysthenes the Heraclid, who first brought the Dorians into Sparta. "Such a pure and illustrious pedigree of seventeen hundred years, without adding the royal ancestors of Hercules, cannot be equalled in the history of mankind," says Gibbon.[4] Synesius was thoroughly familiar with Homer and the other classical authors and quoted them frequently, if at times imperfectly.[5] His personal life as a retiring country gentleman, whose favorite pursuits were riding, hunting, and meditation, reminds us of Xenophon's retirement to his estate in the Peloponnesus—though Synesius is a Neoplatonic Xenophon with a mystical sensibility foreign to the latter. Synesius was also a Hellenistic man who became a citizen of the *Oikoumene* when he went to study at Alexandria. There he became familiar with a doctrine representing essentially a new synthesis of Platonic, Aristotelian, and Stoic thought, namely Neoplatonism. This philosophy comes at the end of a long school tradition which has its roots in late classical and early Hellenistic thought. In Alexandria, one of its centers of development, were

4. *Decline and Fall* 1.667 n. 117.

5. For an index, in Greek, of quotations from classical authors by Synesius compared with their original sources in facing columns, see Crawford, Appendix D, 522–579.

brought together the cultural riches of East and West. There lived Hellenes, Jews, Egyptians, Phoenicians, and others, along with exponents of every cult and philosophy from the Platonic Judaism of Philo and the Platonic Christianity of Clement and Origen, to Christian Gnosticism and Neoplatonism, not to mention the Chaldaean Oracles and the Hellenic "Gnosticism" of the *Hermetica*.

Besides being the inheritor of Classical and Hellenistic Greece, Synesius was a man of the Roman Empire. As a member of the curial order he went to Constantinople about the year 399 to request favors for his native city before Emperor Arcadius. He cultivated the friendship of Aurelian, Praetorian Prefect of the East and head of the anti-Gothic party at court. During the crisis in which the Goth Gaïnas became a major threat to the Eastern Empire, Synesius delivered his bold oration *On Kingship*, in which he called for a Platonic philosopher-emperor and a return to the ideals of the age of the Antonines. His work *On Providence* is regarded in part as a political allegory of the events of 399–401 at Constantinople, in which the tale of a conflict between Osiris and his brother Typho is a thinly disguised account of the conflict between Aurelian (Osiris) and his brother Caesarius (Typho).[6] Synesius' entry into the Christian episcopate completes the picture of the ancient world transforming itself into the medieval world in the life of a single figure. Thus, strangely, the life of Synesius, one man of late antiquity, both recapitulates and anticipates all the major themes of antiquity.

The works of Synesius tell us a great deal about his philosophical, political, and religious attitudes. He has left us several works in different genres which, taken together, give us a fairly good picture of the man and his activities. It is especially enlightening to read his prose and his correspondence together, as his 157 letters often supply the key to his more abstract thought. For example, *Ep.* 105, written on the eve of his election to the episcopate, contains a clear statement of his views on philosophy as opposed to Christian dogma.

Not unlike Julian, Synesius was as much a man of letters and a rhetorician as a philosopher. Although he preferred to think of himself as a philosopher, many scholars have judged him (as they have Julian) to be basically a rhetorician who studied philosophy and was familiar with its basic tenets.[7] At any rate, Synesius held literature and the cultivation of a

6. There is a question whether Typho represents Caesarius or Gaïnas. For a discussion of scholarly opinion on this and other matters pertaining to the *De Providentia*, see Fitzgerald, *Essays and Hymns* 2.409–413.

7. Cf. Marrou in *Conflict*, ed. Momigliano, 131.

literary style in high regard. He complained bitterly of those who would sacrifice good prose style on the altar of metaphysical speculation.[8]

Synesius painted his own portrait as a man of diverse interests who avoided all forms of excess, whether Greco-Roman or Christian. Yet study of his works and conflicts reveals a troubled soul seeking to reconcile his historical position with his need to know and to experience the truth. A striking contrast divided the public man—his civic spirit, broad interests, and philosophic attitudes—from the inner man, whose yearning for the life of the soul and spiritual transcendence found expression in some of the best metaphysical poetry of late antiquity.[9]

Some scholars believe they discern a slow drift toward Christian belief in the thought of Synesius, finally culminating in an acceptance of Christian dogma. Others leave the case of Synesius without having resolved all its conflicts and ambiguities. I intend to demonstrate that Synesius was a Platonic "philosopher-bishop" whose acceptance of Christianity was provisional and remained secondary to his commitment to Neoplatonism.

The full range of traditional controversy, leaving until later a commentary on individual points, can be seen in the dozen chief interpreters of Synesius' conversion. Even in summary they reveal the complexity and ambiguity of our subject.

Ancient scholars writing after the death of Synesius, mostly Christians of the early medieval period, tend to assert that because of his sterling character he was given the light of grace, which enabled him to resolve the serious philosophical doubts he held with respect to orthodox doctrine. Evagrius, the Church historian, believed that the conversion of Synesius was completed by the action of grace.[10] The Byzantine *Pratum Spirituale* depicts Synesius convincing a learned pagan named Evagrius of the very dogma he himself called into doubt.[11] Following Portus, Pétau tries to demonstrate that the *Hymns* actually show a systematic development toward Christian orthodoxy, his main thesis being that the works of the Holy Spirit brought Synesius closer, step by step, to the one true revelation through the invisible action of grace.[12] Much doubt has been cast on this view by Wilamowitz: he points out that Synesius' *Hymns* were

---

8. *Ep*. 154, 1553A–1556A; cf. also *Ep*. 101, 1472D. For a discussion of the philosopher as a well-rounded man rather than a complete ascetic, see Glover, 339f.

9. Cf. Misch, V. 2.593–599; orig. *Gesch. d. Autobiog*. For a thorough and accurate treatment of the dating and authenticity of the *Hymns*, see Lacombrade, *Synésios* 170–198; see Wilamowitz, 295 ad fin. See now also *Les Hymnes*, ed. Lacombrade.

10. Evagrius *HE* 1.15.   11. *Pratum Spirituale*, Cap. 195.

12. *PG* 66.1021–1026.

similar in inspiration to the pagan *Hymns* of Proclus. His generally accepted rejection of *Hymn* X—the most Christian of the lot—as spurious has also created serious difficulties for the plausibility of such views as Pétau's.

Gibbon, ever glad to find allies of enlightenment and rationalism in religion, draws us a picture of Synesius as a nonbeliever who entered the church for social and political reasons.[13] Gardner believes that after the pagan temples closed Synesius was able to fulfill his religious needs in churches and that he identified (according to long-standing orthodoxy) the gods with angels, ceasing to view them as objects of worship in themselves.[14] This scheme is logical, but whether Synesius really made these accommodations is questionable.

Among the moderns, Wilamowitz sees Synesius more as a political than as a religious convert—as having never abandoned his basic Neoplatonic tenets although he accommodated himself to Christianity in some respects. He reconciled himself only with those aspects of Christianity close to his philosophical notions (e.g., he understood the doctrine of the Trinity well because it was based on Neoplatonism, as was most Christian theology). "But the teaching, life and death of Jesus were without significance for him"; nor did the entire Jewish inheritance of Christianity, including Paul, exist for him. The Christ near to him in his living presence was the Demiurge active in the creation and in whom the World Soul and human soul had their being. Even as a bishop he relied more on metaphysics than on the gospel. According to Wilamowitz, Theophilus needed Synesius for the sake of the Pentapolis; for this reason his philosophical heterodoxy could be tolerated. Though Wilamowitz makes many valid points, he does not draw a complete picture of Synesius' intellectual development. For instance, he does not deal with Synesius' blending of Chaldaean with Christian theological doctrines in the *Hymns*.[15]

Geffcken believes that Synesius moved from Hellenism to Christianity without a drastic act of conversion. He unified the two confessions, Neoplatonic and Christian, which, according to Geffcken, were extremely close as long as both sides were flexible enough to avoid dogmatic quibbling. Synesius was atypically active and practical and "did not live in the everyday world as a sexless Neoplatonic dreamer." His going over to Christianity did not follow the pattern of a true conversion; as a Hellene he was no enemy of the Christians, but only shook his head at visions of the Christian life which the man of culture in him could not acknowledge.

13. *Decline and Fall* 1.667–668.   14. Gardner, 111.
15. Wilamowitz, 272ff; see esp. 286 and 295.

Christianity never became a living force for him as it did somewhat earlier for Marius Victorinus; "thus for us Synesius is neither a noted philosopher, nor one of the eminent Bishops of his age." Like Wilamowitz, Geffcken presents a good review of the evidence and reaches many sound conclusions, but he does not go far enough in discussing the method and significant implications of Synesius' spiritual development.[16]

Fitzgerald sees Synesius as a practical mind and not a "mystic" like the other Neoplatonists: he was a doer more than a thinker, a soldier, a Lacedaemonian, and a man of action. He was by his very objective and contemplative nature, however, an idealist and a dreamer, prepared to make a transition that seems to us extraordinary. If we could go back to Alexandria where philosophic and religious currents crossed, where friend and foe were often indistinguishable, we would better understand how Synesius became a Christian. His position vis-à-vis Christian doctrine is much like that of certain modernists in the Church, who, besides attempting to accommodate the views of science, have incorporated many Neoplatonic views; they also see great similarities between Plato, Paul, the Fourth Gospel, and so on. "What is really disconcerting to the student of Synesius is not so much his mingling of pagan imagery with Christian theology as his apparent ignorance or studied neglect of Christian theology, and his silence in reference to any of the works of the Greek Fathers of the Church." Fitzgerald's description of the atmosphere at Alexandria is helpful, as are his extensive introduction and notes to his translations, but his distorted view of Neoplatonism causes him to draw a false picture of the conversion of Synesius. In addition, since much research on the Chaldaean Oracles was completed after he wrote, he often mistakes Chaldaean conceptions for those of Valentinian and Basilidean Gnosis.[17]

Theiler attempts to demonstrate how the Chaldaean Oracles influenced Synesius in the composition of his *Hymns* and helped him toward a Christian conception of the Trinity.[18] Hadot elaborates this theme by trying to illustrate how Marius Victorinus and Synesius were able to move from Neoplatonism to a position close to orthodox Trinitarianism by means of a Porphyrian interpretation of the Oracles.[19] Both scholars have gone far in tracing the path by which those Neoplatonists mentioned by St. Augustine in *Ep*. 118 reached Christianity, while others, according to

16. Geffcken, 215–221; see esp. 215 and 221.
17. Fitzgerald, *Essays and Hymns* 20–102, see esp. 99; and *Letters* 11–69.
18. Theiler, *Orakel* 1–41.
19. Hadot, *Porphyre et Victorinus* 461–474.

St. Augustine, descended to theurgy and magic. I intend to demonstrate that a Porphyrian interpretation of the Oracles was the basis for Synesius' general method for resolving not only the problem of the Trinity, but nearly all theological issues as well.[20]

Lacombrade sees the case of Synesius as a kind of "pilgrim's progress." He moved systematically toward Christianity but did not have time to arrive at full conversion. Thus his case cannot be finally decided. Helpful in organizing our study of Synesius is Lacombrade's presentation of three hypotheses which might explain his conversion. The first theory, which follows Druon, suggests that Synesius moved from paganism into the Christian Church by means of a slow and regular evolution. The second, according to Wilamowitz, puts Synesius' Christianity in such close contact with Greek philosophy that Christ and the Demiurge are in every way assimilated. The third, since Synesius affirms that his philosophy and religion are complementary, asserts a trust in his statements and speaks of an exceptional but real unity of culture. Lacombrade himself favors the third alternative. But we will see that the second is closer to the truth.[21]

Marrou studies Synesius in the context of Alexandrian Neoplatonism. Like Lacombrade, he sees him slowly moving in a Christian direction; however, for him Synesius is a transitional figure who lived in an age when orthodoxy was not yet firmly fixed: efforts such as his will not bear fruit until the great synthesis of Neoplatonism and Christian orthodoxy is accomplished by the sixth-century Christian Neoplatonists of Alexandria.[22] Like Lacombrade, Marrou neglects the central importance of the Oracles to Synesius' method of synthesis. Lemerle thinks that Synesius never really was converted, but remained a narrow pagan of his time, like Symmachus, who did not understand the new age.[23] The evidence demonstrates that this is far too narrow a view of Synesius' personality and religious sensibility. Kurt Treu says that the evidence allows for diametrically opposite views. Strictly speaking, this may be true, but if we are to understand Synesius and his age, we must make enough sense of the sources to escape suspension of judgment in a skeptical *epoché*.[24]

There is thus a different Synesius for every scholar. Let us trace his spiritual development to clarify, if possible, its nature, meaning, and significance, both for Synesius and for his Greco-Roman world.

20. On the *Commentaries on the Oracles*, see Theiler, above, p. 7.
21. Lacombrade, *Synésios* 274–280.
22. Marrou, in *Conflict* 128–150; see also *REG* 65.474–484. The opinions of Marrou will be fully discussed in the section on *Ep.* 105 (below pp. 155ff).
23. Lemerle, *Rev. de Phil.* 79.228–230.
24. Treu; cf. esp. p. 26 n. 3, and p. 54 (comm. on 245, 12–15).

ii

The traditional view of the relationship between Hellenic thought and Christian doctrine does not provide an appropriate framework for an interpretation of Synesius' religious position.

Christians discussed the relationship of Greek philosophy to their religion, at least from the time of Justin Martyr and Clement of Alexandria in the second century A.D. In the tradition of the Fourth Gospel, Justin believed that Christ was the Logos of whom all men partook. Those who have lived according to the Logos are Christians. Thus even pre-Christian Greek philosophers such as Socrates and Heraclitus could be claimed as "proto-Christians."[25] Clement, the first Christian philosopher, believed that philosophy could serve as a preparation for perfection in Christ.[26]

But Clement and his followers were also critical of Greek philosophy. A Christian could philosophize, but Christ the Logos was still the measure of truth. In his *Protrepticus*, Clement criticizes the pre-Socratics' confusion of physical principles with divinity as remaining close to idolatry; e.g., Thales' substrate of physical reality, water, is little better than Poseidon.[27] Some philosophers are recognized for attempting to adduce a higher principle than a physical *arche*: Anaximander's *to apeiron* is mentioned and Anaxagoras is cited for placing *nous* above all principles. He rejects Stoic hylozoistic pantheism as abhorrent and criticizes Aristotle for turning the World Soul into God and denying that Providence extends to the sublunary realm: this is self-contradictory, since Aristotle thought that the World-Soul descends to the sublunary; thus Aristotle is found to deny that divine Providence is coextensive with itself.

Clement considers Plato an exception among the Greek philosophers.[28] He cites the *demiourgos* of the *Timaeus* and the *Basileus of Epp*. VII and II in order to demonstrate his essential monotheism. The Hellenes are not without hope. But Plato, who derived his wisdom from many places, admits barbarian wisdom is superior to Greek (*Phaedo*). In fact, his idea of God comes from Moses and the Hebrews. Clement goes on to cite other examples from Greek philosophy and poetry that can be harmonized with Christian monotheism. Indeed, the Logos Himself educated the Greeks in philosophy. Thus Hellenic philosophy is part of the

25. Justin Martyr, *Apology* 11.13.   26. Clement, *Stromateis*, PG 8.816A.
27. Clement, *Protrepticus*, PG 8.164B; for this section in general cf. PG 8.163B–176B and 180B–185C; *Stromateis*, PG 8.816B–817B.
28. Clement, *Protrepticus*, PG 8.172B–176B; *Stromateis*, PG 8.912B–913B.

preparatio evangelica and contains much that is worthwhile. A good Christian could philosophize as long as he realized that Christianity determined the truth.

Clement is here building on a tradition that began with Philo Judaeus, if not earlier. Philo interpreted the Septuagint in Greek philosophical terms and justified his claim that he was adhering to Judaism on the grounds that Plato, Pythagoras, and the other Greeks derived their wisdom from Moses. The Philonic tradition became so strong that, by the second century A.D., the pagan Middle Platonist Numenius of Apamea could say that Plato was "Moses speaking Attic." The best in Greek philosophy was already part of Christian tradition. A Christian could think philosophically as well as praise those Greeks who were in agreement with his doctrine.

Clement's successor Origen was a great systematic thinker. In his hands Christianity assumes the character of a philosophical system (at least in the *De Principiis*). He also attempts to refute the philosophical critique of Christianity (in the *Contra Celsum*) and thereby establish Christianity on philosophical as well as theological grounds.[29]

By the fourth century Christians in the East began to associate the Christian life and Christian theological speculation with *philosophia*. Platonic or not, they felt that it was *their* tradition. Gregory of Nyssa made Neoplatonism the handmaiden of his mystical theology: in his mind the two were as one.[30] Probably John Chrysostom was the first Church Father to employ the term *philosophia* with a purely Christian connotation. For him the word tends to mean the Christian way of life. In a late letter he mentions a young theology student as practicing true *philosophia*.[31] Gregory of Nazianzus could accept a classical culture and literary education which was primarily rhetorical, but also included some philosophy. Yet his basic outlook closely associated true *philosophia* with Christian theology and the Christian life, especially the monastic life.

But the case of Synesius is quite different from those of his Christian predecessors and contemporaries such as St. Augustine and the Cappadocians. He did not identify classical culture with rhetoric and letters; neither did he tend to equate philosophy with Christianity. (Nor on the whole did Augustine in the West, but that was because of his idiosyncratic development: he had read Greek philosophy and the *libri platonici* before his complete conversion.)[32] Thus Synesius did not equate the *theoretikos bios* with Christian monasticism as Gregory of Nazianzen sometimes did. He neither used philosophy as a means of expressing Christian

29. Cherniss, 1.   30. *Ibid.*   31. Laistner, 53.
32. *Confessions* 7.9.13 (137.7–138.5), 8.2.3 (154.16–28).

truths from a Platonic angle, nor considered Christian revelation a superior authority needed to complement, correct, complete, and ultimately
transcend philosophical speculation. Religion *per se* (in *our* sense) was at
best an imaginative, symbolic, and allegorical expression of realities that
could only be fully understood by means of philosophy—albeit a philosophy with its own mystical and symbolic content: Neoplatonism. Indeed,
the distinction between philosophy and religion often becomes confused
and difficult because of the religious aims and nature of Neoplatonism itself. For Synesius, Neoplatonism was both the true way to salvation and
that to which revealed (or any) religion was subordinated if there was a
clash on doctrinal or ultimate questions. Late antique sages viewed Neoplatonism as the crowning achievement of classical culture, as its highest
and most characteristic expression. Contrary to the Church Fathers,
Synesius saw rhetoric and philosophy as two aspects of the same culture of
Hellenism. His position probably represents the best possible resolution
of the classical–Christian conflict from the point of view of the Neoplatonic philosopher. That it was not adopted by the Church is hardly surprising. He was not really a convert, but rather one who had accommodated himself to the new religion. Yet his stance is not without historical
importance, for it illuminates the motives that led to the Hellenization of
Christianity, and it is, moreover, closely related (as a mirror image) to that
form of Renaissance Neoplatonic syncretism which was in part responsible for the paganization and secularization of European thought.

Thus the religious development of Synesius is to be approached
from an entirely different direction than that appropriate to the study of
the relationship of Christianity and classical culture in the thought and
faith of the Church Fathers. The inclusion of his works in the Patristic
corpus should not mislead us. He did not come from a Christian family,
nor did he undergo an experience of conversion to become a convinced
Christian. Much less was he a Christian educated in the pagan schools,
who had to work out a new relationship to a classical culture not without
its attractions. On the contrary, Synesius, coming from the opposite
camp, tried to find a way to make Christianity fit the classical framework.
As we shall see, some of the results of his attempt were interesting and
perhaps unexpected.

Synesius, then, was never a Christian in the commonly accepted
sense of that term, even by fourth- and fifth-century standards. Nor did
he ever intend to be one. He accepted the Church as an institution, but
on his own terms. Christian doctrine interested him only insofar as it was
compatible with Neoplatonism and not vice versa. To the extent that it
was incompatible, it was bad philosophy, at best a *kalon pseudos* subject

to allegorical interpretation, as were the old Greek myths. Synesius states this openly in *Ep*. 105—a letter in which he reformulates Plato's old idea of the philosopher-king into the new idea of the "philosopher-bishop."[33] This position may also be seen in the *Hymns, On Providence, On Dreams* and other works. We may ask if there is any proof that he ever abandoned it. It seems that a careful reading of the evidence would indicate that he did not.

Synesius did not share the common attitudes towards Greek philosophy that the Church Fathers began to develop from the time of Justin Martyr in the second century A.D. For example, even at their most Platonic, Clement of Alexandria and Origen distinguished themselves from the pure Hellenes. The positions of Augustine and the Cappadocians vis-à-vis Greek philosophy and classical culture were more complex and somewhat ambivalent because of the heightened conflict of religions and the development of dogmatic theology from the mid-third century through the Constantinian-Theodosian age.

The position of Synesius the Hellene and philosopher-bishop differed completely. He did, however, accept Christianity *de facto*. Thus, he was forced to take a stand with respect to dogma and revealed religion. For this reason we cannot simply equate his religious position with that of Hellenes such as Porphyry or Julian, who interpreted religion philosophically without acknowledging any conflict between "reason" and "revelation." It is also difficult to compare Synesius to any Christian thinker of late antiquity. Although his ideas are similar to theirs on certain questions, his overall world view is different. Furthermore, when their ideas do coincide, it is usually because Christianity had become Hellenized.

Are there, then, any thinkers from the other great revealed religions with whom it is possible to compare him? A brief look at the philosophers of the Islamic world will be of help.[34] The basic attitude of many early Islamic thinkers toward Greek philosophy and religion was universalist: truth was not determined by any specific revelation or notion. Yet some Islamic thinkers modified the Neoplatonic-Aristotelian world-view to accommodate it to the basic tenets of Islam. Others either identified philosophy and religion, or maintained the primacy of reason. For example, the religious Al-Kindī affirmed the creation of the world out of nothing and the resurrection of the body on the day of judgment. But Ar-Rāzī rejected revelation and asserted that the supernatural powers of the prophets were suspect: they disagree with each other and contradict themselves. The three revealed traditions cause unhappiness and wars,

33. See below Ch. VII, 155ff.
34. For the following section I have consulted Walzer, *Greek into Arabic*.

whereas philosophy is the true path to salvation. Avicenna equated the
two. To quote Walzer:

> He also assesses the relation between Islam and philosophy in a way
> which reminds us of the Neoplatonic attitude to Greek religion: he
> neither subordinated philosophy to revelation—nor did he give in to
> Islam by upholding the primacy of revelation. Avicenna identified Is-
> lam and philosophy as it were and maintained that Islam could not be
> adequately understood except in terms of philosophy.[35]

After Avicenna, Averroës, in the spirit of a philosopher-king (or philosopher-bishop!), maintained the basic truths of philosophy: Islam and
the Law were popular presentations of these truths, meant to make them
understandable to the masses and maintain the social order. But it would
be rash to say that Averroës simply broke with the tenets of Islam. For
example, he was critical in his adoption of ideas from Plato's *Republic*.
There are indications that he makes use of it to better illuminate the
sharīʿa or Law,[36] yet he does speak of Plato in the following way: the multitude can know something of speculative truths, not through demonstration, but only through persuasive argument; e.g., what Plato calls "right
belief," (*orthe doxa*) as opposed to true knowledge[37] (*Summary of Plato's
Rep*. 24.14–23). This latter is the province of philosophers. Thus Islam,
as popularly understood, is analogous to truth as popularly understood by
the non-philosophers in Plato's *Republic*.

Before Averroës and Avicenna, Al-Fārābī insisted on the superiority
of philosophy and the primacy of reason. Islam was not to be discarded,
but interpreted philosophically and accorded a similar function in society
to that of the traditional religion in Plato's *Laws*. In addition, the Imām,
or successor of the prophet, was to rule as a philosopher-king.

Synesius shared certain attitudes with Avicenna, but his ultimate
position is closest to those of Al-Fārābī and Averroës. More Platonistic
than Aristotelian, he favored allegorical interpretation, reconciliation of
philosophy and religion, and a mystical approach to spiritual matters.
Thus much of the actual content of his thought is similar to that of Avicenna (as is Porphyry's). But unlike Porphyry he had to deal with Christianity and thus he clearly states that "dialectical demonstration" is the
final arbiter of religious truth. It might be added that this principle and
approach are even more important than what he actually believed (e.g., if
someone proved *philosophically* the Creation of the world in time, Synesius could accept it). For these reasons, the ideas of Synesius are, at bottom, in almost perfect agreement with those of Al-Fārābī: for him the

35. Walzer, "Early Islamic Philosophy" 668.
36. Averroës, *On Plato's Republic* xxiv.   37. *Ibid*. xxvf.

position of Christianity in society was indeed similar to that of the traditional religion in Plato's *Laws*: to be observed as an integral part of the
social order and provide a popular and palatable idea of divinity. The idea
of the Imām as philosopher-king fits well (in different ways) the conceptions of the Roman Emperor as philosopher-king and the Synesian philosopher-bishop. Finally, Synesius like Al-Fārābī resolved to maintain the
primacy of reason.

To sum up: it is possible to understand the religious position of
Synesius only if we discover the proper framework with which to approach the problems involved. Once this has been done, we can arrive at
a reasonably intelligible historical picture, one not completely without
ambiguities, but generally preferable to those which have been suggested
to date. Thus the *reversal* of the categories usually used for the study of
Christianity and classical culture, and even a suggestive and incomplete
comparison of Synesius with thinkers outside the Christian tradition are
sound procedures.

A brief look at the basic orientation of a representative sample of
some of the important recent literature on Christianity and classical culture will help to put this viewpoint into perspective.

Jaeger, in his *Early Christianity and Greek Paideia*, tried to show
that Christians absorbed classical learning, so that by the fourth century it
was possible to speak of a Christian humanism.[38] Cochrane and Marrou
have demonstrated that the Fathers and especially Augustine both absorbed and transformed classical culture and created a new synthesis.[39]
Pelikan, in his *Christian Tradition*, discusses these questions with great
learning as well as feeling for the subtlety of the issues. Ladner, in his
Idea of Reform, has made extensive comparisons between the two cultures. He has shown (among other things) the connections between pagan
and Christian imperial and reform ideologies. More recently, Peter
Brown has demonstrated the importance of the slow reorchestration of
themes which had their roots in the religious *koine* of the Hellenistic
world.[40] The new age began to emerge only after a long process of cultural
change which culminated in the crisis of the third century and the religious struggles of the fourth century.

More specifically related to our topic: Cherniss has argued per-
suasively that Gregory of Nyssa was basically a Neoplatonist rather thinly

38. *Passim*, esp. 3–12 and 100–102.
39. Cochrane, *Christianity and Classical Culture*, see esp. Pt. III; Marrou, *S. Augustin*.
40. *The Making of Late Antiquity* 7–11 *et passim*.

disguised as a Christian.[41] Daniélou has taken the opposite position: Gregory was a Christian who expressed himself in Platonic language, the intellectual *koine* of late antiquity.[42]

But Synesius has not found his Daniélou. This is not surprising, since he was unique in his world. For this reason, it is necessary to discover an approach that will enable us to put him in the correct historical perspective. Only in this way will we clear up the confusion that has surrounded this enigmatic personality.

41. *The Platonism of Gregory of Nyssa.*
42. *Platonisme et théologie mystique.*

I

The Early Years (A.D. 365?–395)

Early Life and Adolescence

Very little is known about Synesius' early life. Even the date of his birth is a matter of speculation.[1] Lacombrade, his most recent biographer, fixes the date at 370 A.D. strictly on grounds of probability,[2] and the question is of some significance in deciding at what age and at what point of mature development he took certain actions. A logical date for his birth seems to be 365 A.D.; in any case it was not later than 370. Thus there is general agreement that he was born sometime shortly after the death of Julian and lived under the emperors Valens, Theodosius the Great, Arcadius, and Theodosius II, until he disappeared from history about 413 or 414.

Synesius lived in a period of important religious developments in the Roman Empire. After the failure of Julian's revival, paganism was increasingly on the defensive. Julian's followers in the Senate, led by Symmachus, failed in their attempt in 382 to restore the Altar of Victory, which had been removed from the Curia; and they were defeated by Theodosius at the battle of the Frigidus in 394, which ended the last serious pagan attempt to regain power in the Roman Empire. In the East, the

1. Lacombrade, *Synésios* 13 reviews all theories on Synesius' birthdate. Because there is no epigraphical evidence from Cyrene, conjecture is necessary. Some of the main theories are: Krabinger, A.D. 379; Clausen, 365; Druon, 370; Kraus, 370–375; Volkmann, 365–370; Seeck and Grützmacher, ca. 370; Lacombrade, basing his choice on probability, 370. See also Fitzgerald, *Letters* 13. Much of the conjecture is based on different interpretations of Synesius' references to himself as young or old in *Hymn* 8, 12–14; *Epp.* 116 and 123. For an analysis of these passages, see Crawford, 8–9 and n. 9, who fixes the date at 360. Crawford's analysis is interesting but the actual fixing of a date based on relative concepts such as "young" and "old" must remain subjective; this rule is, of course, generally true when dealing with antiquity.

2. Lacombrade, *Synésios* 13: "En l'absence de tout indice positif, la vraisemblance, qui seule guide ici le biographe, incline à imposer la date moyenne de 370. . . . Le départ pour Constantinople, historiquement établi en 399, suppose, dans l'ambassadeur de Cyrène, non pas un adolescent, mais un citoyen rompu à la politique, et assez mûr pour donner des conseils de sagesse à Arcadios. . . ."

Serapeum at Alexandria was destroyed in 391, while Theodosius issued
legislation forbidding pagans to hold office in the imperial government
and severely limiting cult practices and the worship of the gods.[3] Indeed,
while Christianity was moving into the mainstream, paganism was fast becoming a forbidden minority religion in the Roman Empire. Hellenes of
Synesius' generation were acutely aware of this fact: they could quietly
and patiently wait and hope for the demise of Christianity; they could no
longer expect a dramatic reversal of the situation. It was now legitimate
for a reasonable pagan like Synesius, interested in the Empire's welfare,
to consider the consequences of conversion to Christianity.

Synesius seems to have spent his early years in the traditional manner of his Dorian ancestors.[4] Like Xenophon he was a gentleman farmer
and man of leisure.[5] Literature and the old-fashioned style of hunting remained major interests throughout his life,[6] and the possibility of having

---

3. Imperial anti-pagan legislation seems to have begun in the reign of Constantine,
when it moved from the traditional distrust of private magic, as a criminal matter, to the
banning of non-Christian cult acts *per se*. This type of legislation was implemented by the
subsequent emperors—with the exception of Julian—with increasing intensity. There is
some evidence that late in his reign Constantine prohibited sacrifice (Euseb. *VC* 2.45; *Cod.
Theod.* 16.10.2). But cf. Euseb. *VC* 2.48–60, which attributes a grudging tolerance of paganism to Constantine. For the probability that Constantine continued to maintain public support for the state cults in Rome, see Jones, *Later Roman Empire* 1.92. Constans prohibited
sacrifices in 341 by citing the law of the "late emperor our father" (*Cod. Theod.* 16.10.2).
Constantius declared nocturnal sacrifices illegal in 353 (*Cod. Theod.* 16.10.5); in 356 the
death penalty was invoked against those who worshipped or sacrificed to idols (*Cod. Theod.*
16.10.4 and 6). He also closed or demolished pagan temples (*Cod. Theod.* 16.10.3); and on a
visit to Rome in 357 he ordered the first removal of the Altar of Victory from the Curia (St.
Ambrose, *Epp.* 18 and 32). Edicts issued in 381 and 385 made sacrifices for the purpose of
divination illegal (*Cod. Theod.* 16.10 and 12). Petitions requesting destruction or conversion
of temples into churches were regularly granted, and many temples were destroyed amid
violence, bloodshed and rioting. See Zosimus 4.37; Theodoret, *HE* 5.21; Soz. *HE* 7.15; Lib.
Or. 30.8ff. For the destruction of the Serapeum see Ruf. *HE* 2.23–30; Soz. *HE* 5.16; Soz.
HE 5.15; Theodoret, *HE* 5.22; Eunapius, *Vit. Soph.* 471 (ed. Boissonade). See also Fowden,
JTS n.d. 29.53–78. This type of legislative "overkill" is characteristic of a system which had
difficulty enforcing legislation. In fact, pagans still held office well into the fifth century.
Nevertheless, the situation of paganism ought not to be minimized: the level of official per-
secution was higher than it had ever been.

4. See above, Intro. p. 3 and n. 4; *Epp.* 57 and 113; *Catastasis* 5.303A; Fitzgerald,
Letters 14.

5. For Synesius as "feudal lord" see Lacombrade, *Synésios* 15; *Ep.* 134, 1521B; *Ep.*
40. *Epp.* 41, 1365A; 132, 1516C–1517C; 125, 1505A–B indicate that he had a private army
in spite of a law issued by Valentinian I in 364: *Nulli prorsus, nobis inscius atque inconsultis,
quorum libet armorum movendorum copia tribuatur* (*Cod. Theod.* 90.15.1). See *Ep.* 15 for
a private expedition against desert pirates.

6. ἐμοὶ μὲν οὖν βίος βιβλία καὶ θήρα. Synesius, *De Ins.* 1308D. See introduction,
n. 5, for Synesius' acquaintance with early Greek poets. See also Lacombrade, *Synésios*
21–22. He also wrote a lost work on hunting, the *Cynegetica*. A sign of Synesius' old-fashioned life style may well be that he does not mention falconry as part of hunting: this was

to give up these pleasures is one of the things which made him hesitant to accept an episcopal appointment.[7] His familiarity with the Greek poets, philosophers, and rhetoricians reflects a thorough classical education. However, the details of that education are unknown to us and we must infer them from his remarks on education in general and the planned education of his oldest son and a nephew.[8] Reared as a Greek gentleman in a rural area, he had little early contact with the great social, cultural, and religious changes taking place in the centers of Greco-Roman civilization. Yet he was well aware of the isolated and archaic nature of the countryside surrounding his native Cyrene; in a very interesting letter he describes his escape from the cares of the world while living among people who believe that the king is still Agamemnon.[9] His classicism, which had a strong influence on his subsequent life and thought, remained evident after he had become a Christian bishop.

At some point in his adolescence, Synesius, like Julian, seems to have had the typically Hellenic religious experience of the divinity of the cosmos,[10] an experience and article of belief that was one of the main points of contention between pagans and Christians. Thus the youth who came to Alexandria to study in the school of Hypatia already possessed a religious sensibility in accord with the main tenets of Neoplatonism. Under the tutelage of Hypatia, his knowledge increased and his capacity for religious experience was deepened. His first *Hymn* exhibits a thorough familiarity with the mystical modes of thought and experience characteristic of Neoplatonism. In fact, Synesius seems to have experienced a genuine "conversion to philosophy"[11] while at the school of Hypatia. His *Hymns* reveal him as a metaphysical poet with considerable depth of religious insight. He was also, as his letters to Hypatia and others attest,[12] a lifelong member of a circle of Alexandrian initiates with whom he shared in the mysteries of philosophy.

---

only then coming into the Roman world from the barbarians: see Lindner, *Beiträge zu Vogelfang* 149–156.

7. *Ep.* 105, the famous letter in which he also brings up his objections to three important Christian dogmas.

8. Fitzgerald, *Letters* 14–15. For Synesius' conception of education (*paideia*) cf. his *Dion, passim.*

9. *Ep.* 148.

10. *Ep.* 101, 1469D: Δοκῶ δέ μοι καὶ τοὺς ἀστέρας εὐμενῶς ἐνατενίζειν ἑκάστοτε ὄν ἐν ἠπείρῳ πολλῇ μόνον ὁρῶσι θεωρὸν αὐτῶν σὺν ἐπιστήμῃ γινόμενον. Cf. also Julian, *Orat.* IV *ad init.*

11. The idea of conversion to philosophy is discussed by Nock in *Conversion* 164–186; this *Hymn* is ninth in the manuscript order but was certainly composed first.

12. *Epp.* 137–146; *Ep.* 54, 11, and 16.

Alexandria and Conversion to Philosophy

Synesius arrived in Alexandria about the year 393 and remained there until about 395.[13] This period of his life contains the key to the understanding of his later religious development, for not only did he become a Neoplatonist but, as we shall see, he studied a version of Neoplatonism under Hypatia which made it possible even for a devout Hellene to reconcile himself with Christianity. Despite her renown as a pagan martyr, there is no evidence that Hypatia was an avowed enemy of Christianity.[14] The head of the Neoplatonic "school" before her, her father Theon, had strong scientific and mathematical interests. Yet, in typical fourth-century style, he also studied occult subjects: the *Suda* credits him with a work on divination, while the Byzantine chronographer John Malalas says he was a commentator on the works of Hermes Trismegistus and Orpheus.[15] Hypatia's own works seem to have been strictly scientific and mathematical.[16] Nevertheless, there is no doubt that she had religious interests: she taught subjects such as astronomy and geometry in the context of a Neoplatonic view of the universe. It must be remembered that in Neoplatonism even the most rational concerns are rooted in a thoroughly mystical reality.

The fact that Hypatia's own works are lost makes the doctrine of her school difficult to reconstruct. However, certain things we know about her seem to correspond to elements of Synesius' work. Given her father's known interests, it would make sense to look for instances of Pythagorean number-mysticism in the work of her disciples.[17] On such evidence we could identify the influence of Hypatia at least tentatively. At any rate, Synesius spoke of her as "the genuine leader of the rites of philosophy" (*Ep.* 137, 1525A). In *Ep.* 143, Synesius, speaking of his friendship with Herculian and two others, says:

> For my part, nothing human is worth honoring, outside of the triad (*trittys*) you make up. And I myself, being added to the group, will

---

13. *Ep.* 145 partially establishes the date of Synesius' first stay in Alexandria because he mentions Heraclian, who was Comes of Egypt in 395; *Cod. Theod.* 11.24.3 (30 Sept. 395).

14. For more concerning the little we know about Hypatia see the article on her in the *Suda*; Socrates, *HE* 7.15 describes her famous martyrdom; cf. also Damascius, *Vita Isidori* and the *Suda* (on Isidorus).

15. The *Suda* (on Theon) credits him with a work περὶ σημείων καὶ σκοπῆς ὀρνέων καὶ τῆς κοράκων φωνῆς; Malalas, *Chron.* XII.34.3.10.

16. See n. 14. The *Suda s.v.* Hypatia.

17. At this time an aristocrat named Hesychius came to Alexandria to study the Pythagorean art: Synesius, *Ep.* 93.

straightaway complete our foursome (*tetractys*) of holy friendship. But let the nature of the like-named *tetractys* among the principles (*archai*) be passed over in silence (*euphemeistho*).[18]

It might be argued that the above example is a literary *topos* and merely represents erudite play between two persons sharing an aspect of a high culture.[19] But in the *Address to Paeonius*—an official of the court at Constantinople—Synesius speaks of astronomy in terms which make it difficult to deny that a real mystical element is present:

> I desire to inflame those astronomical sparks within your soul, and try to raise you to great heights by means of your innate powers. For astronomy is itself a divine form of knowledge, and might become a stepping stone to something more venerable. I consider it a science which opens up the way to ineffable theology. The blessed body of heaven has matter beneath it, and its motion has seemed to the chief philosophers to be an imitation of [universal] mind [*nous*]. And it [astronomy] proceeds to its demonstrations clearly and distinctly, making use of arithmetic and geometry as helpers; disciplines which one can properly call a fixed measure [*kanon*] of truth. Therefore, I am offering you a gift, most fitting for me to give and you to receive. A work of my own mind as my most revered teacher bestowed it on me. . . .[20]

---

18. *Ep.* 143, 1537A. In this series Migne's *PG* text runs one Epistle behind; 143, 1537A = PG 142, 1537A, etc. All translations are the author's own unless otherwise specified.

19. Festugière, in *Personal Religion*, has pointed out that even statements of cosmos-piety had become literary commonplaces in antiquity; but they were often sincere religious expressions. It is sometimes difficult to judge whether or not the author is serious. Subjective judgment along with an attempt to find more evidence outside the particular passage are often the only alternatives. After quoting a famous epigram of Ptolemy: "Mortal though I be, yea ephemeral, if but a moment I gaze up to the night's starry domain of heaven, then no longer on earth I stand; I touch the Creator, and my lively spirit drinketh immortality." (*Oxford Book of Greek Verse in Translation*, No. 621; tr. Robert Bridges), Festugière says (p. 118): "I could cite other texts . . . but they would add nothing to those I have just read, and we should not find in them the same personal note. For we must bear in mind that the praise of the heavens, of the planets, and of their regular movements, become a commonplace under the Empire. We soon tire of this sort of Cosmic dithyramb. Nor is it always easy to distinguish between what is no more than a literary cliché and what is the expression of true feeling."

20. On the occasion of the gift of an astrolabe to Paeonius, 1581D–1584A:

ἐρῶ τοὺς ἀστρονομικοὺς σπινθῆρας ἐνόντας σου τῇ ψυχῇ τούτους ἐξάψαι καὶ ἐπὶ μέγα ἆραι διὰ τῶν ἐνόντων ἐπιβαλλόμενος· ἀστρονομία γὰρ αὐτή τε ὑπέρσεμνός ἐστιν ἐπιστήμη, καὶ τάχ'ἀναβιβασμὸς ἐπί τι πρεσβύτερον γένοιτ'ἂν· ἣν ἐγὼ προσεχὲς ἡγοῦμαι πορθμεῖον τῆς ἀπορρήτου θεολογίας. ὕλην τε γὰρ ὑποβέβληται τὸ μακάριον οὐρανοῦ σῶμα, οὗ καὶ τὴν κίνησιν νοῦ μίμησιν εἶναι τοῖς κορυφαιοτάτοις ἐν φιλοσοφίᾳ δοκεῖ. καὶ ἐπὶ τὰς ἀποδείξεις οὐκ ἀμφισβητησίμως πορεύεται, ἀλλ' ὑπηρέτισι χρῆται γεωμετρίᾳ τε καὶ ἀριθμητικῇ, ἃς ἀστραβῆ τῆς ἀληθείας κανόνα τις εἰπὼν οὐκ

A playful aspect in these letters infuses their mystical matter: cosmic humor was not unknown to the Greeks.[21] Synesius demonstrates his ability at high parody in his early work, the *Praise of Baldness*: the bald head is superior to the hairy head because it is reminiscent of the sphere, which is the most perfect object in the cosmos; in fact, the cosmos itself is a sphere. In Platonism, the more perfect an object is, the closer it is to its immutable Form or Idea; therefore, the bald head is more real—in the Platonic sense of the word—than the hairy head because it enjoys a greater participation in Form.[22]

It is generally agreed—though the only evidence is indirect—that Hypatia preferred the Porphyrian to the Iamblichan version of Neoplatonism, and gave the doctrines of Porphyry a special place in her school.[23] Ironically, as we shall see, it was the teaching of Porphyry—that most scholarly enemy of Christianity—which opened up a relatively smooth path from paganism to the new religion. Those Platonists who moved to

---

ἂν ἁμάρτοι τοῦ πρέποντος. προσάγω δή σοι δῶρον, ἐμοί τε δοῦναι σοί τε λαβεῖν πρεπωδέστατον, διανοίας μὲν ἔργον ἐμῆς, ὅσα μοι συνευπόρησεν ἡ σεβασμιωτάτη διδάσκαλος, . . .

It is interesting to note that Ptolemy's epigram is included in this letter. (See n. 19).

Οἶδ' ὅτι θνατὸς ἐγὼ καὶ ἐφάμερος· ἀλλ' ὅταν ἄστρων
ἰχνεύω πυκινὰς ἀμφιδρόμους ἕλικας,
οὐκέτ' ἐπιψαύω γαίης ποσίν, ἀλλὰ παρ' αὐτῷ
Ζηνὶ θεοτρεφέος πίμπλαμαι ἀμβροσίης.
(*Anth. Pal.* 9.577. 1585C)

The standard study of this is Böll, *Kleine Schriften* 143ff. The poem inscribed upon the astrolabe with which the letter concludes is another paean to the cosmos.

Wisdom has found a path to the heavens—O mighty marvel! And intelligence has come from these heavenly beings. Behold! It has also ordered the curved form of the globe, and it has cut the equal circles with unequal spacings. See the constellations all the way to the rim whereon the Titan, holding his kingdom, metes out day and night. Accept thou the slantings of the Zodiac, nor let escape thee / Those famous centres of the noontide assemblages. (tr. Fitzgerald).

For a discussion of the differences between the pagan, Christian and Gnostic world-view with respect to the cosmos, its divinity, goodness, etc., see Jonas, 239–288.

21. E.g. Plato, *Laws* VII.796 where he equates the highest activities of life—including religion—with play; cf. Heraclitus, fr. 70 DK.

22. *Calvitii Encomium*, 1184B.

23. Bidez, *Vie de Porphyre* 134, believes that Porphyry was favored at Alexandria in the late fifth century. Lacombrade, *Synésios* 49, suggests that the teaching of Theon and Hypatia paved the way for a Porphyrian renaissance at Alexandria; cf. also Evrard, REG 90.69–74.

But there was certainly some exchange of students and ideas between the great centers of philosophy from the late fourth to the sixth century. See I. Hadot, *Le Problème du néoplatonisme alexandrien*, which revises all traditional views on the distinctiveness of the "Alexandrian" as opposed to the "Athenian" school.

Christianity, according to St. Augustine (*Ep.* 118), rather than down to theurgy and magic, did so by the Porphyrian route, for two main reasons. First, Porphyry's religious thought, unlike that of Iamblichus, is not dependent on pagan sacerdotalism but tends rather to play down its importance; thus cult and ritual have a peripheral rather than a central place in his theology. The believer need not involve himself in external and illegal ritual acts. Second, Porphyry's so-called monistic tendency enabled one to conceive of the Neoplatonic hypostases in a unique way, which was much closer than Iamblichan categories to an orthodox conception of the Trinity. Porphyry sometimes "telescopes" the hypostases by considering Soul to be in reality a part of the intelligible realm and by placing unified Soul and *nous* close to the unity of the One. He even goes so far as to push the noetic realm into the One. The later Neoplatonists not only postulated "vertical" emanation down from the One, but also "horizontal" emanation: thus if the first noetic triad, consisting of the existence of the Father (*hyparxis*), the power of the Father (*dynamis*), and the mind of the Father (*nous*), is identified with the One, the One may be said "to exist" (*to einai, esse, hyparxis,* but not *ousia*), while in the horizontal triad equal (not subordinate) powers can be identified with the Father (*hyparxis*), Son (Nous = Logos), and Holy Spirit (*dynamis*), thus opening a path from Porphyrian Neoplatonism to Christianity.[24]

24. On Porphyry's critical attitude toward pagan ritual and theurgy: theurgy was only a first step (for non-philosophers) that could help purify the soul but not, as Iamblichus, Julian and Proclus thought, return it to the noetic realm. See *De Regressu Animae*, fragments assembled from St. Augustine *Civ. Dei*, 10 and 27–28 in *Vie de Porphyre* 27*–44*. For the positions of Iamblichus and Proclus, see Iambl. *De Anima*, 370–375 and Proclus, *In Tim.* 3.234; Porphyry's *Letter to Anebo* is a general criticism of late pagan theology, demonology, divination and theurgy; Lacombrade, *Synésios* 49, see Synesius' criticism of magic (*On Dreams*, 1304C) based upon the hidden sympathies in nature to be a rejection of theurgy; but Iamblichus also criticized those who explained divination simply in terms of cosmic sympathy; this kind of magic might exist but it is of an inferior sort compared with theurgy, which is based on a union of our intellect with a divine intellect (*De Myst.* 3.26–27, 10.3). Lloyd (esp. p. 296) has helped greatly in bringing a new understanding to this problem. He points out that Iamblichus' attitude was consistent in this respect and "made the same kind of distinction (as in theurgy) in the case of prayer, sacrifice and astrology": *De Myst.* 2.11; 5.7–8, 10, and 15; 9.4–5. Cf. Wallis, *Neoplatonism* 100–110. For an up-to-date scholarly and positive account of theurgy see Trouillard, 171–189. The identifications can become more complex. This will be fully discussed below, Ch. IV, pp. 79–91. For a thorough analysis of Porphyry's "telescoping" of the hypostases see Lloyd, 283–301; for an outline of the main points see Wallis, *Neoplatonism*, 106, and for a brilliant demonstration that Marius Victorinus took this route, as did Synesius, see Hadot, *Porphyre et Victorinus*. The most helpful work for connecting the *Hymns* of Synesius to the Chaldaean Oracles—which were the basis of Porphyry's interpretation of the noetic triad—is Theiler, *Orakel*. Smith, *Porphyry's Place*, is an excellent study on Porphyry's religious and philosophical views compared with those of the other Neoplatonists; it carefully scrutinizes all ancient and modern scholarship on the above issues.

Moreover, the fact that science was an important element in Hypatia's teaching should make us wary of oversimplified associations of late
Neoplatonism with late Roman "failure of nerve" or the "decline of rationalism." These theories are regularly invoked to dismiss the religious
preoccupations of the late ancient world as symptoms of a loss of faith in
the efficacy of rational inquiry and practical human effort. There is no denying, as Dodds and others have demonstrated, that this was an "age of
anxiety" with more than its share of pathological phenomena; however,
we must be careful not to regard all the religious experiences of the period merely as pathological manifestations. It is true that certain extreme
groups gave up all concerns which were not related to their salvation. But
others—especially the late pagans—strove to keep their spiritual balance; Julian and Synesius were only two of the many political men who
tried to live according to the old Hellenistic cultural ideals. Hypatia herself, in contrast to the more ascetic Neoplatonists such as Porphyry, believed in practicing the civic virtues, an indication of her philosophical
independence if not originality.[25]

It seems then, that the Alexandrian "school" of Neoplatonism in the
late fourth century combined scientific research with a degree of social
concern unusual for the period. The religious doctrines were taught in a
confessionally neutral atmosphere which was neither particularly hostile
to Christianity nor dependent upon a sacerdotal paganism. In contrast,
Julian, Iamblichus, and Proclus gave the cults of Hellenism a special status and made their practice indispensable.

Hypatia's school was not involved in anti-Christian propaganda—
apparently it attracted Christian students, and was tolerated under the
cruel patriarchate of Theophilus.[26] Her martyrdom probably had more to
do with her charisma, popularity, influence, and reputation for piety and
purity than with any anti-Christian activity on her part: she could have
been considered dangerous by some in spite of her intentions. She, more
than any other contemporary figure, personified philosophy to Synesius.
Philosophy was a real way of life for her—a striving for perfection and a
reaching out for the divine which demanded a genuine love of wisdom.

25. The *Suda*, *s.v. Hypatia*, attributes a belief in civic virtues to Hypatia: ἐν τε τοῖς
ἐργοῖς ἔμφρονα τε καὶ πολιτικήν. Synesius' own form of Hellenism, which retained the
ideals of *paideia*, saw them in the perspective of a mystical religion—again, without Julian's
sacerdotalism. For the social concerns of later Hellenism in general see Julian, *Epp.* 84–89;
Themistius, *Orat.* 21, 23, and 29, which contrast speculative with practical concerns.

26. On students in Hypatia's school see Crawford, 415, who makes a case for the
presence there of Isidore of Pelusium, who supposedly became a friend of Synesius and possibly advised him on matters of dogma and heresy. Synesius refers to several of Hypatia's
pupils in *Epp.* 96, 99, 133, 148, 149, 144, 140, 4, 16, and 93.

She must have been instrumental in Synesius' conversion to philosophy. Some of Synesius' early works reflect the experience of this first conversion. The most important of these for reconstructing the philosophical religion which Synesius embraced in this period are his letters to Herculian (*Epp.* 137–146), probably written fairly soon after his departure from Alexandria, and his *Hymn* I, written between 395 and 397.[27] In *Ep.* 137, he calls Hypatia the hierophant of philosophy, and philosophy itself a mystery suited only to pure initiates; philosophy is the highest possible way to the divine:

> Life lived according to reason (*nous*) is the end of man. Let us pursue that life; let us ask for divine wisdom from God; let us ourselves—in whatever manner possible—gather wisdom from everywhere.[28]

Those destined to share in the philosophic life are an elect providentially brought together for the pursuit of wisdom:

> Whenever I recall our association in philosophy, and that philosophy over which we struggled so much, upon reflection, I attribute our meeting to God our guide. For nothing less than a divine cause could impel me . . . who holds philosophy among the most ineffable of ineffable things . . . to reveal myself, and all that I possess, to a man with whom I had only a brief conversation.[29]

The initiated are connected with one another, not only by common human interests, but also by a deeper noetic bond:

> And if human affairs join together in mutual sympathy those who share them in common, divine law demands that we who are united through the intellect, the best thing within us, should honor one another.[30]

In his letters to Herculian, Synesius not only takes delight in the mystique of initiation, but also discusses some of the specific elements that enable philosophy to lead its adepts to a more authentic and higher form of existence. Among his ideas he discusses the conception and practice of genuine virtue gained through philosophical reflection, the aid of

27. There is no absolute proof of this except that it seems to be purely pagan and the work of a recent "convert to philosophy."

28. *Ep.* 137, 1528A.

29. *Ibid.* 1525B–C: ὅταν δὲ πρὸς τὴν ἐν φιλοσοφίᾳ κοινωνίαν ἀπίδω, καὶ φιλοσοφίαν ἐκείνην περὶ ἧς πολλὰ συνκεκύφαμεν· ἐνταῦθα ἤδη τοῦ λογισμοῦ γινόμενος θεῷ βραβευτῇ τὴν συντυχίαν ἡμῶν ἀνατίθημι. οὐ γὰρ ἂν ἀπ' ἐλάττονος ἢ θείας αἰτίας Συνέσιος . . . φιλοσοφίαν δὲ, ἐν ἀρρήτων ἀρρητοτάτοις ἔχων . . . ἐμαυτόν τε, καὶ τὰ ἐμαυτοῦ κτήματα ἀνεκάλυψα ἀνδρὶ καταβραχὺ δόντι μοι καὶ λαβόντι τὸν λόγον.

30. *Ibid.*: εἰ δὲ καὶ ἀνθρωπικαὶ χρεῖαι τοὺς κοινωνήσαντας διαθέσει συνδέουσιν ἡμᾶς κατὰ νοῦν τῶν ἐν ἡμῖν τὸ ἄριστον συγγενομένους θεῖος ἀπαιτεῖ νόμος τ' ἀλλήλων τιμᾶν. (cf. *Ep.* 140 *ad init.*)

philosophy in improving our spiritual perception of the divinity within ourselves and all things, and the ascending hierarchy of virtues, corresponding to the ascending ontological order of things, which if mastered allows the philosopher to rise above his earthly condition. Before examining Synesius' variation on the traditional theme of philosophy as a mystery religion, let us glance at these ideas as they appear in his correspondence.

Following the Platonic tradition, Synesius contrasts natural or fideistic virtue unfavorably with philosophic virtue, in which the agent is fully conscious of the reasons for his actions:

> Self-control without reason and complete abstinence from meat-eating have been granted by nature to many unreasoning species. But we do not praise a raven or any other creature that has discovered a natural virtue, because it is without the power to think. Life lived according to reason is the end of man.[31]

Philosophy allows us to release the "eye of the soul," which is latent within us, and thereby enables us to look upon the divine:

> Goodbye, philosophize and continue to dig up the eye buried within us.[32]

This "eye of the soul" is in reality the divinity within us that corresponds and coincides with the divinity both within and beyond the cosmos. The final mystical goal is union of the internal divinity with the transcendent. Synesius, urging Herculian to keep striving to reach this ideal, alludes to Porphyry's quotation of the last words of Plotinus:

> Goodbye, philosophize, raise up the divine within you to the first-born divine.[33]

31. *Ibid.* 1528A: Σωφροσύνη γὰρ ἄλογος, καὶ ἀποχὴ κρειωδαισίας πολλὴ παρὰ πολλοῖς ἀλόγοις εἴδεσιν ἐνδέδοται παρὰ τῆς φύσεως. Ἀλλ' οὐκ ἐπαινοῦμεν οὔτε κορώνην, οὔτ' ἄλλο τι τῶν εὑρομένων φυσικὴν ἀρετήν, ὅτι φρονήσεως ἔρημα. Ἡ δὲ κατὰ νοῦν ζωὴ, τέλος ἀνθρώπου. ταύτην μετίωμεν· θεόθεν τε αἰτοῦντες θεῖα φρονεῖν, καὶ αὐτοὶ τὸν δυνατὸν τροπὸν τὸ φρονεῖν ἀπανταχόθεν συλλέγοντες.

32. *Ibid.* 1525D: "Ἔρρωσο, καὶ φιλοσόφει, καὶ διατέλει τὸ ἐν ἡμῖν ἀνακεχωσμένον ὄμμα ἀνορύττων. Synesius also refers to the "Intellectual eye" within us in *Hymns* I, 101–102; III, 577–579; the "eye of the soul" motif is found in many Platonic and Neoplatonic texts. For the eye of the soul in the Platonic tradition see Plato, *Rep.* 519b and 533d; *Oracles Chaldaïques* fr. 1, 8; fr. 112, 1; fr. 213, 2; Iamblichus, *Protrepticus* 21; Psellus, *Comm. in Or.* 113b; Lewy, 168ff, 169 n. 388.

33. *Ep.* 139, 1529C: "Ἔρρωσο καὶ φιλοσόφει, καὶ τὸ ἐν σαυτῷ θεῖον ἄναγε ἐπὶ τὸ πρωτόγονον θεῖον. Synesius refers to the last words of Plotinus, but in place of πρὸς τὸ ἕν ἐν τῷ πάντι θεῖον he has *protogonon* (firstborn); cf. *Hymn* IV.88; Lact. *Div. Inst.* (*Orph.* fr. 73): "Orpheus . . . deum verum et magnum apellat." *Protogonos* is essentially Nous–Logos but should be interpreted monistically as being "telescoped" with the One. Perhaps Nous thus understood should be thought of as all the potential specifications of the One's unity.

Synesius also demonstrates a complete awareness of the ascending hierarchy of philosophical virtues (*aretai*) through which the adept must pass if he is to purify himself for union with the divine:

> I had expected the pious Herculian to set his sights upon the things above and be entirely devoted to the contemplation of Reality; to look upon the first principle of mortal things, and, having long ago passed beyond the virtues which have been diverted and are connected with the ordering of things here below . . . exchange strength of body for manliness of soul. I do not mean that manliness pertaining to the first or earthly *tetractys* of virtues, but that which is conformable to the third and fourth levels of virtue. . . . Even if the division I have been making is still unclear to you—between those virtues closer to the principle of things and those of least importance and further away—still, let the following things be your standard and criterion for judging your attainment of first things: not to lament over everything and to justly despise things here below.[34]

In *Ep.* 143, which treats philosophy as a sacred mystery, Synesius rebukes Herculian for breaking his promise and divulging secrets to the uninitiated.[35] He claims that certain people, who spoke with Herculian, have now approached Synesius himself in order to demand that he reveal the meaning of certain expressions they had heard from Herculian. He then advises Herculian to read a letter of Lysis, the Pythagorean, which he quotes:

> To philosophize among the populace is to stir up among men a great contempt for the divine.[36]

The mysteries of philosophy are to be carefully guarded by the elect; this idea of philosophy as a mystery religion was widespread in late antiquity.[37]

34. *Ep.* 140, 1532B–C: Ἑρκουλιανὸν ἠξίουν ἄνω βλέπειν καὶ ὅλον εἶναι θεωρὸν τῶν ὄντων καὶ τῆς τῶν θνητῶν ἀρχῆς, τὰς ἀρετὰς διαβάντα καὶ πάλαι τὰς ἀπεστραμμένας καὶ κοσμούσας τὰ δεῦρο. . . . μεταθεῖναι τὴν τοῦ σώματος ἰσχὺν ἐπὶ τὴν τῆς ψυχῆς ἀνδρείαν, οὐ τὴν ἐκ τῆς πρώτης, καὶ περιγείου τετρακτύος τῶν ἀρετῶν, ἀλλ' ἐπὶ τὴν ἀνάλογον ἐν τρίταις καὶ τετάρταις. . . . κ'ἄν μήπω σοι σαφὴς ἡ διαίρεσις ἢ τοῦ λελεγμένου, τίνες ἀρχεγονώτεραι καὶ τίνες αἱ πολλοσταὶ τῶν ἀρετῶν· τὸ ἐπὶ μηδενὶ κλάειν ἀλλὰ πάντων τῶν τῇδε ἐν δίκῃ καταφρονεῖν ὅταν σοι παραγένηται, τοῦτο ἔστω σοι κανὼν, καὶ κριτήριον τῶν πρώτων τῆς τεύξεως, . . . On degrees of perfection in virtue cf. Porphyry, *Sententiae* 32; Plato himself is at the root of this tradition: μὴ καθαρῷ γὰρ καθαροῦ ἐφάπτεσθαι μὴ οὐ θέμιτον ᾖ (*Phaedo* 67B—this is Orphic in inspiration).

35. *Ep.* 143, 1536B: οὐκ ἐμπέδοις τὰ ὡμολογημένα πρὸς ἡμᾶς, ὦ φιλότης, μὴ ἔκπυστα ποιεῖν τὰ ἄξια κρύπτεσθαι.

36. *Ibid.*: τὸ γὰρ δαμοσίᾳ φιλοσοφὲν (οὕτω γάρ πως ὁ Λῦσις ὑποδωρίσας λέγει) μεγάλης εἰς ἀνθρώπους ἦρξε τῶν θείων καταφρονήσεως.

37. For a discussion of pagan secrecy and extensive references to works of the Pythagoreans, Plotinus, Porphyry, Iamblichus, Julian, Proclus, the Chaldaean Oracles and secondary studies, see Anastos, *DOP* 4.274–276. On the theme of secrecy among the phi-

Possibly Synesius was being "literary" in this letter, but his criticism of Herculian seems to be sincere and must be taken into account. Although his statements can be partially explained by reference to the literary mode of expression and standard practice of a long philosophical tradition, Synesius does seem really concerned to preserve the integrity of an esoteric teaching. He states clearly that, if the secret doctrines are taught openly, charlatans who think they understand the truth will set themselves up as teachers and wise men. These people, with their pretense of wisdom, seek to teach what they themselves have never learned. They are irresponsible and dangerous; for, unready themselves to receive the supreme doctrines of philosophy, they dare to teach them to others. Here Synesius reflects the Platonic view that only the elect are allowed to study philosophy; even these are carefully prepared so that "looking upon the Sun" does not endanger them.[38] It is clear from his correspondence with Herculian that Synesius considered philosophy to be a way of life, a constant, religious, and disciplined search for truth which continued throughout his life to have great appeal for him. Another of the concerns that made him hesitate to accept the episcopate was the fear that the office would force him to descend from the heights of philosophy to more mundane concerns.[39] The religious side of philosophy is again emphasized by Synesius in his insistence that the adept must guard the sacred mysteries of philosophy with the same care as an initiate into a mystery cult. Since Plato's Academy, schools of philosophy had shared an intimacy of membership and doctrine in common with religious associations (*thiasoi*)[40]—a tendency that became even more pronounced during the Hellenistic period. Finally, in the second and third centuries, philosophy came to be understood completely in religious terms.[41] Synesius' attitude to philosophy is only to be expected when we consider the fact that he lived during a period when religious issues were among those foremost in the minds of men. In fact, Christians and pagans shared many of the views and choices of how to live, at least among the more educated classes of society. The initiation to faith through an intimate congregation, such as Synesius experienced under Hypatia and defended on theoretical grounds, is a clear example.

---

losophers in the Roman Empire and a summary of much of the current literature on the subject see also MacMullen, *Enemies* 320 and n. 14.

38. Cf. Plato, *Rep.* 515A–E.   39. *Epp.* 96 and 105.

40. A most interesting study of schools of philosophy cult associations is Boyancé, *Cult des Muses.* For the change in attitude of philosophers toward religion see Merlan, *J. Hist. Phil.* 1.163–176.

41. On borrowing of the prestigious title of philosopher by religious figures, both pagan and Christian, see MacMullen, *Enemies* 320–321 and n. 16.

Of the several works of Synesius, the most important for the understanding of his religious development are the *Hymns*. *Hymn* I is of special
interest as an indication of his early conversion to philosophy. In *Hymn*
I—as in the others—he is less literary than in his letters, and his Platonism is not of the simplified belletristic variety we find so often in his
prose.[42] In the *Hymns*, Synesius appears to us as a metaphysical poet with
deep mystical insights and serious religious concerns. He employs the
imagery of Neoplatonism, traditional pagan mythology, and, in later
Hymns, Christianity, in order to express his innermost thoughts and
aspirations.

The first *Hymn* is clearly the most pagan of the collection. In it Synesius speaks of God in abstract terms as the "monad of monads" or as the
"unity of unities." He makes no specific mention of the Trinity, although
he does allude to the Chaldaean "monad at the head of the first intelligible triad," which he later identified with the Christian Trinity. Nor is the
figure of Christ mentioned. The whole emphasis of the poem bears on the
path of illumination that leads from the imperfect world of sense experience to the purely noetic realm. Considering the frequency of allusion to
purely philosophical doctrines in this *Hymn*, it is reasonable to suppose
that Synesius composed it in the 390s when he was studying with Hypatia
or shortly thereafter. A spirit of youthful enthusiasm for the esoteric
teachings of a venerable transcendental doctrine is apparent in this paean
to the Absolute—a spirit to be expected in a young man in close association with others of like age and temperament.

Hymn I and Synesius' Conversion to Philosophy

Hymn I opens with a classical introduction reminiscent of Doric
lyric. It is, in fact, an affirmation of the superiority of divine knowledge
and wisdom to earthly success—and the fervently expressed hope of at-
taining that knowledge (1.1–51). In this section, Synesius uses classical
imagery to contrast the worldly life with the new higher philosophical life
he has adopted: here he undoubtedly refers to his conversion to philosophy. Interesting is Synesius' joyful description of earthly things even
though he is rejecting them (1.1–10); his attitude is one of cosmic affirmation but ambivalence about, rather than total rejection of, things earthly.
This ambivalence never stopped him from leading an active life and playing a role in politics. Characteristically, he prays here and elsewhere for

---

42. Lloyd, 314, points out that the somewhat simplified Platonism of some of Synesius' prose works "was conventional in the 'belles lettres' he was writing."

adequate means of life, a journey here below sufficient "that want may not bend me down to dark forebodings."[43]

A description follows of the Neoplatonic chain of emanation, from the highest principle (the One), through the noetic and psychic realms, all the way down to the world of time, space, and matter; the final stage is presented as a description of the "fall of the soul" (1.52–99). The last section is devoted to the anagogic motif of the return of the soul to the One or the Father, its true home and origin. Many of these themes recur in the later *Hymns*; the main difference here is the complete absence of Christian imagery.[44] A brief analysis of certain passages in *Hymn I* may give us some insight into our author's mind:

He who is self-sprung first principle, guardian and father of the things that are, unengendered, established above the peaks of heaven, God, sits steadfast, rejoicing in his absolute glory; pure unity of unities and prime monad of monads. He unifies and gives birth to the simple natures of the highest principles, with super-essential engenderings, whence the monad itself, sprung forth through first-generated Form, ineffably poured out, holds the force of three summits. And the super-essential source is crowned by the beauty of chil-

43. Dodds, *Pagan and Christian* 1–37, discusses the problem of world negation and affirmation. His contention, that the later we find ourselves in antiquity the stronger is the tendency to reject the world, cannot be demonstrated; in fact, many fourth- and fifth-century figures, both pagan and Christian, have a more positive attitude to the world than many of their counterparts in the third and even second centuries, when Gnosticism flourished. Cf. Wallis, 157; Trouillard, 184: "Il était évidemment impossible à un théurge de tenir le pessimisme plotinien concernant la matière;" cf. also Julian, *Or.* IV, 135a and 137d; Proclus, *Hymn to Helios, In Alc.* I.204.14, *In Parm.* IV.155C and V.58C, *In Tim.* I.14.19, II.161.29, *In Remp.* II.220,11; Macr. *In Somn. Scip.* I.14.15; I.20.6; Iambl. *De Myst.* VII.3. Examples of pagan cosmos-affirmation could be multiplied.

44. Cf., e.g. Clement of Alexandria's *Exhortation to the Greeks*: Ἄδει δὲ γε ὁ Εὔνομος ὁ ἐμὸς οὐ τὸν Τερπάνδρου νόμον, οὐδὲ τὸν Καπίωνος, οὐδὲ μὴν Φρύγιον, ἢ Λύδιον, ἢ Δώριον, ἀλλὰ τῆς κοινῆς ἁρμονίας τὸν αἴδιον νόμον, τὸν φερώνυμον τοῦ θεοῦ, τὸ ᾆσμα τὸ καινόν, τὸ Λευιτικόν, . . . (*PG* 8.53C–56A).

Synesius uses classical imagery in a somewhat different spirit. But cf. *Hymn VII* and VIII *ad init.* written later (ca. 405–408), where he speaks of the Incarnation:

Hymn VII	Hymn VIII
Πρῶτος νόμον εὑρόμαν	Ὑπὸ δώριον ἁρμογὰν
ἐπὶ σοί, μάκαρ, ἄμβροτε,	ἐλεφαντοδέτων μίτων
γόνε κύδιμε παρθένου,	στάσω λιγυρὰν ὄπα
Ἰησοῦ Σολυμήϊε,	ἐπὶ σοί, μάκαρ, ἄμβροτε,
νεοπαγέσιν ἁρμογαῖς	γόνε κύδιμε παρθένου.
κρέξαι κιθάρας μίτους.	

See also Wilamowitz, 277 and 280. According to him Synesius had a classical heritage, wrote in Doric and compared himself with Sappho and Anacreon. He never abandoned his classicism but was able to use classic form in a Christian context without seeing any contradiction.

dren springing forth from the center and flowing back about the center.[45]

In the above passage, Synesius first (1.52–60) gives a poetic description of the source of all unity and Being in the universe. Then (1.61–70) he attempts to explain the ineffable and inexplicable: the mysterious way the completely transcendent and perfect One is able to become manifest through its own first-generated Form (*dia protosporon eidos*) and thereby act as the super-essential source and center (*hyperousios paga*) of the hypercosmic-cosmic process of procession out from (*proodos*) and back to (*epistrophe*) the One (*apo kentrou te thoronton, peri kentrou te kruenton*). These concepts are rooted in the tradition of Plotinus, Porphyry, and other Neoplatonists.[46] The process of descent and return takes on the aspect of a cosmic game, in which the "super-essential source is crowned by the beauty of children." Synesius beautifully captures the entire rhythm of the intelligible cosmos, its metaphysical expansion and contraction as it were, in these few short lines. Thus Synesius affirms the whole cosmos. The super-essential source pours forth and in turn is crowned by the dance of the cosmic process. Although the One is self-sufficient, It

---

45. Synesius, *Hymn* I, 1.52–70.

Ὁ μὲν᾿ αὐτόσσυτος ἀρχά,   ὑπερουσίοις λοχείαις,
ταμίας πατήρ τ᾿ ἐόντων,   ὅθεν αὐτὴ προθοροῦσα
ἀλόχευτος, ὑψιθώκων   διὰ πρωτόσπορον εἶδος,
ὑπὲρ οὐρανοῦ καρήνων   μονὰς ἄρρητα χυθεῖσα
ἀλύτῳ κύδεϊ γαίων   τρικόρυμνον ἔσχεν ἀλκάν,
θεὸς ἔμπεδος θαάσσει,   ὑπερούσιος δὲ παγὰ
ἑνοτήτων ἑνὰς ἁγνά,   στέφεται κάλλεϊ παίδων
μονάδων μονάς τε πρώτη,   ἀπὸ κέντρου τε θορόντων,
ἁπλότητας ἀκροτήτων   περὶ κέντρου τε ῥυέντων.
ἑνίσασα καὶ τεκοῦσα

46. Plot. V.1.11 speaks of the One in terms of a circle and its radii. This circle must be conceived abstractly as operating under conditions outside of time and space. The One (i.e., the first principle) becomes the second, just as a circle in course of development becomes a surface (i.e., develops out of a point into a circular area); a figure in which the circumference, the center, and the radii are distinct—but not really separate—things holding different "positions." All things, including our own nature, are connected with the One as the radii of a circle are connected with its center.

> This Highest cannot be divided and allotted, must remain intangible but not bound to space, it may be present at many points wheresoever there is anything capable of accepting one of its manifestations: thus a center is an independent unity; everything within the circle has its term at the center; and to the center the radii bring each their own. Within our nature is such a center by which we grasp and are linked and held; and those of us are firmly in the Supreme whose being is concentrated There. (tr. S. MacKenna)

See the rest of this tract, "On the Three Initial Hypostases," for a discussion of emanation and the relationship of all the hypostases. For the self-sufficiency and transcendence of the "needs" the rest of the universe because without it Reality would be far poorer; for when the metaphysical potentialities of things are actualized, the noetic realm takes on a deeper meaning.

In *Hymn* I, Synesius used poetic imagery and form to represent concepts which cannot be fully grasped save by a leap into pure abstraction.[47] The poem is a kind of guide for philosophical initiates, the images of which are meant to help lead one back anagogically to the noetic realm and the unity of the One. The description of the origin of all things culminates in a demonstration of our own soul's intimate connection with the divine; the poem concludes with a prayer and a description of the return of the soul to its rightful home above. Synesius himself declares that the *Hymn* is something which speaks only to those initiated into the mysteries of philosophy.

> Pause, my audacious Lyre
> Pause, and do not reveal to the multitude
> the mysteries without rites.
> Come, sing of the things here below
> but may silence cover those above.[48]

One, see Plotinus VI.8.7 and 9; Proclus calls it preexistent to all multiplicity (*In Tim.* I.52), self-identical and immobile (*Theol. Plat.* III.2), the cause of motion in all things (*Elem. Phys.* II, prop. 19). The idea of the incorporeality of the hypostases, which are not to be conceived of spatially, is explained by Porphyry, *Sententiae*, 27, 31, and 38. The idea of emanation is well summarized by Wallis, *Neoplatonism* 61:

> The generation of reality by the One is described by the Neoplatonists in terms of their well-known image of Emanation. The image's underlying principle is summarized in the scholastic maxim that 'good diffuses itself' (*bonum diffusivum sui*). In other words, entities that have achieved perfection of their own being . . . keep generating an external 'image' of their internal activity.

He goes on to point out that the examples Plotinus gives, like the radiation of heat from fire, cold from snow, or the outflow of light from the sun, must be dematerialized and despatialized (*Enn.* V.1.6.28–40; V.3.12.39–44; V.4.23–41).

47. But "pure abstractions" are living realities for Platonists and Neoplatonists. A good example of this is the emotional way absolute Beauty is spoken of in Plato's *Symposium* (201D–212A) as the object of desire (*eros*).

48. Synesius *Hymn* I (1.71–75):

> Μένε μοι, θρασεῖα φόρμιγξ,
> μένε, μηδὲ φαῖνε δήμοις
> τελετὰς ἀνοργιάστους.
> ἴθι, καὶ τὰ νέρθε φώνει,
> τὰ δ' ἄνω σιγὰ καλύπτοι.

Migne's text reads ἀνοργιάστοις which modifies δήμοις. Terzaghi's reading ἀνοργιάστους modifies τελετάς. There is something to be said for both readings but Terzaghi's reading seems more consistent with the meaning of the passage. The word is used in both senses by Greek authors, see *LSJ*, *s.v.* ἀνόργιαστος. For a different opinion see *Synesii Hymni* (ed. Terzaghi, 286).

Following the text of Terzaghi rather than Migne (see below, n. 50), the "mysteries without rites" seem to refer to the divine hidden sources of reality which the true philosopher can learn to perceive through his noetic or spiritual eye within. They are "mysteries without rites," strictly speaking, because they are part of the immutable noetic order. Rites on earth are a weaker reflection and imitation of these noetic mysteries in time and space.[49]

Synesius follows this brief mystical refrain with an account of the descent of *nous* and the engendering of the ambiguous lower realm with all of its inherent defects and difficulties: the noble principle of the human spirit, derived from the activity of *nous*, "has been divided indivisibly" (1.75–80).[50] This paradoxical statement is an example of a Neoplatonic "logic of mysticism"[51] based on the cardinal principle—accepted by all members of the school, although by some with certain qualifications—that "all things are in all things." Such paradoxical conceptions make it possible to think about emanation without falling into the trap of imagining it in physical terms. The spiritual realm is at once divisible and indivisible, but its division should not be thought about in the same terms as the separation and isolation caused by physical division. The divine never loses its power or character, yet it somehow seems to conceive of itself under a divided aspect and thus brings the world into being.

As we follow Synesius down the mystical chain of emanation, we reach the level of Soul, the third hypostasis. Here the idea of a succession from one specific event to another (i.e., time) is introduced.[52] The World

49. Iamblichus argues that rites such as sacrifice, theurgy, etc., are justified because, here below, man has a body as well as a soul; cf. especially *De Myst*. V.15–17.

50. Synesius, *Hymn* I, 1.76–80:

ὁ δὲ νοῦς οἵοισιν ἤδη
μέλεται νόοισι κόσμου·
ἀγαθὰ γὰρ ἔνθεν ἤδη
βροτέου πνεύματος ἀρχὰ
ἀμερίστως ἐμερίσθη.

51. John Findlay has suggested the outlines of a "logic of mysticism" to coincide with paradoxical statements made by mystics such as Plotinus and the Rhineland mystics: "I wish to see whether there are not peculiar rules and guiding principles governing these mystical notions and assertions, and whether it is not possible to raise questions of the well-formed and the ill-formed, of validity and invalidity, in regard to them, as we can in other fields of discourse" (*Rel. Stud*. 2.146; cf. Procl. *Elem. Theol*. prop. 103). In an unpublished lecture at Yale (Spring 1972), Findlay suggested that "Spinozistic" logical statements might bring us closer to understanding what the mystics are getting at, e.g., "The universe is tall and thin in its Johannine aspect and short and fat in its Jamesian." He considers this a perfectly valid, logical statement about realities that are distinct but not altogether separate. This is, of course, even more true about the noetic entities which are transcendent.

52. See Plot. III.7, "On Time and Eternity."

Soul begins to take on specialized cosmic functions: it turns the hollow of the heavens, while, at the same time, preserves the whole universe (*to holon*) because it is present in the division of forms allotted for specific tasks.[53] One part presides over the paths of the stars, another over the angels. But a third, by a "chain with a downward inclination" (*reponti desmoi*), finds an earthly form and is cut off from its generators: "wondering at the joyless earth, a god looking on mortal things."[54] Synesius' affirmation of the inherent divinity (and therefore immortality) of the human soul, which makes possible its return to the divine under its own power, is a clear indication of an essentially pagan faith.[55]

The finale (1.100–134) deals with the return of the soul, a theme maintained throughout the *Hymns*. There is here below a certain dimly perceived power of the soul that tends to lead it back to its true home. Synesius refers to it as a certain anagogic power (*anagogios tis alka*):

> Blessed is he who fleeing the devouring bark of matter and earth, rises up and with a leap of the spirit (*halmati kouphoi*) presses on his path to God. (1.108–109)[56]

The soul, purified by the philosophic virtues, can illuminate the divine spark buried within and reach the beatific vision, which is the end of life.

The profusion of anagogic imagery at the end of this poem has caused some scholars to suggest Gnostic—especially Valentinian—influ-

---

53. *Hymn* I, 1.88–90:

> τὸ δ' ὅλον τοῦτο φυλάσσων
> νενεμημέναισι μορφαῖς
> μεμερισμένος παρέστη.

54. On the fall of the soul see Plot. IV.8.6; IV.3.12 and 17.

55. The Neoplatonic thinkers did conceive of a kind of grace preceding union with the One, but it is not a special supernatural dispensation of God. Plot. VI.8.6 and 12–13; V.4.1 and 34–36. The One gives of itself freely because of its ungrudgingness (*apthonia*); however, this ungrudgingness is an impersonal result of the One's nature which, strictly speaking, has no needs. On the other hand, Proclus speaks of an *eros pronoetikos*, "providential love" in which the higher causes care for their lower effects (*In Alc*. I.54–56); cf. Wallis, 149 and 154. For Greek beliefs about the natural divinity and immortality of the soul see Jaeger in *Immortality and Resurrection* 97–114; for the differences between Greek and early Christian ideas on the subject, see also Wolfson, *ibid*. 54–96.

56.

> Μάκαρ ὅστις βορὸν ὕλας
> Προφυγὼν ὕλαγμα καὶ γᾶς,
> 'Αναδὺς ἅλματι κούφῳ
> Ἴχνος ἐς θεὸν τιταίνει.

Note the image of matter as a hungry dog and the wordplay on ὕλη and ὕλαγμα. But see *Synesii Hymni*, ed. Terzaghi, 293, who reads βάρος instead of βορόν in 1.108.

ences on the religious thought of Synesius.[57] Despite some notable differences in outlook, the Chaldaean Oracles and Gnostic writings share a certain amount of common terminology.[58] The Valentinians were at their zenith in second-century Alexandria, but by the late fourth century they probably no longer exerted a strong influence. On the other hand, the Chaldaean writings were familiar to Neoplatonists throughout the period. Porphyry knew them well and wrote a commentary on them; Iamblichus, and later the schoolmen of Athens, viewed them as scriptural, together with the works of Plato.[59] Moreover, Synesius' Hellenic reverence for the cosmos would certainly make him suspicious of the Gnostics' anti-cosmic theology, especially in the light of Plotinus' scathing series of attacks "Against the Gnostics" or "Against those that Affirm the Creator of the Cosmos and the Cosmos Itself to be Evil."[60] Thus, we need not speak of a "gnostic element" in *Hymn* I. Such ideas are to be understood within the framework of the esoteric doctrines regularly studied by the Neoplatonists.

With this in mind, let us briefly conclude our analysis. The blessed man leaves his earthly cares and sorrows and sets off on the pathway to *nous*, in which he beholds the "divine depth." Borne on the wings of "desire to be lifted up to the divine" (*anagogion eroton*), he moves toward the universal heart of things (1.117–119). In turn, the Father, revealing himself, holds out his hands to the adept (1.123).[61] The "noetic plain" (*noeton pedion*), the "origin of beauty" (*kalleos archan*), is opened to him (1.126–127).[62] Finally, Synesius entreats his soul to leave behind the things of earth and drink at the fount of the Good, in order that it may, itself a god, dance in God the Father (1.128–134).[63]

57. E.g., Fitzgerald, *Hymns* 482. But Chaldaean influence is more likely; cf. Theiler, *Orakel, passim.*

58. The term βυθός, for instance, was used to denote the "paternal depth" by both Gnostics and Chaldaeans. Synesius, *Hymn* I, 1.116: βυθὸν εἶδεν θεολαμπῆ; cf. e.g. *Oracles Chaldaïques*, frr. 18 and 163.

59. On the Chaldaean Oracles see Lewy and the review by Dodds, *HTS* 54.263–273. A new edition of the Oracles with translation, notes, and introduction, which takes all of the most recent scholarship into account, is E. Des Places, ed., *Oracles Chaldaïques* (Paris 1971).

60. *Enn.* II.9; other attacks against the Gnostics are in III.8; V.5 and 8; they were written because of a dispute with a group of (probably Christian) Gnostics who were members of the school of Plotinus; Porphyry, *Vit. Plot.* 16.

61. In this passage Synesius seems to be closer to the Procline than the Plotinian conception of "providential love"; see n. 55 above.

62. For Plotinus—although he is somewhat equivocal on the point—the Good is beyond Beauty and is its source; *Enn.* V.5.12. For a thorough discussion see Rist, 53–65.

63. *Hymn* I, 1.128–134:

The end of religious experience for Synesius is union with the divine. The soul, the divine spark within us, finds its true home with the divinity at the source of all being. *Epistrophe*, the tendency of all things to return to their source, is here beautifully depicted by Synesius, through the imagery of the soul's journey to the One. *Hymn* I is truly a Neoplatonic *itinerarium mentis ad Deum*.

Hymn I, then, contains a complete vision of reality. Lines 1–51 are an invocation for divine guidance and wisdom; 52–70 treat of God as the transcendent uncreated source of all reality without distinction or variation: a perfect unity at the root of all other unities. This unity mysteriously manifests itself as a trinity (1.67–69). *Nous*, the intelligible realm that emanates from the One as its self-specification and articulation, already contains the principles of things in "undivided division." In turn, *nous*, in a further plunge from unity into multiplicity, leads down to the realm of Soul, which holds sway over the visible world and gives birth to time and space (1.76–90). A depiction of the fall of the soul into matter (1.91–99) leads into the last section on the return of the soul to the divine realm (1.100–127). The final prayer is in reality a fixing of the soul (*intentio*)[64] upon the unity of the divine, an appeal for it to leave this earthly realm and become a suppliant of the Father (1.128–134). We have here, then, in a hymn of only 134 lines, a complete outline of the entire Neoplatonic system. It is also the fervent statement of a religious mind searching for wisdom and salvation: a mind, moreover, that believes mystical *experience* will bring about the fulfillment of all religious aspirations.

Both the letters to Herculian and *Hymn* I demonstrate that Synesius was a true convert to philosophy. Long before he became a Christian he saw a higher and better way of life culminating in *epistrophe*,[65] or conversion of the soul to God in the proper sense of the term.

Let us now look at his sojourn in the school of Hypatia in the light of the idea of conversion. Conversion is not merely a change from one externally defined set of religious beliefs to another; its essence is an inner spiritual transformation of the person. Nock, in distinguishing the idea of con-

---

Ἄγε μοι, ψυχά, ποῖσα
ἀγαθορρύτοιο παγᾶς,
ἱκετεύσασα τοκῆα,
ἀνάβαινε, μηδὲ μέλλε,
χθονὶ τὰ χθονὸς λιποῖσα·
τάχος ἂν μιγεῖσα πατρὶ
θεὸς ἐν θεῷ χορεύσαις.

64. Cf. St. Augustine, *Confessions*, Book 11 *passim*.

65. For a study of the use of the term *epistrophe-conversio* in both pagan and Christian thinkers, see Aubin, *Conversion, passim*.

version from that of adhesion—i.e., the acceptance of new worships which do not involve the taking of a new way of life in place of the old, as useful supplements to (but not substitutes for) the old—says: "By conversion we mean the reorientation of the soul of an individual, his deliberate turning from indifference or from an earlier form of piety to another, a turning which implies a consciousness that a great change is involved, that the old was wrong and the new is right." Whether it is a question of returning to the religion of one's childhood or embracing a new faith, the effect is much the same: "Psychologically the two have much in common, since the man who returns with enthusiasm will commonly feel that he has never before fully grasped the import of the faith of his childhood. The bottles are old, but the wine is new."[66]

Nock considers conversion in the above sense to be possible only for certain types of paganism; for instance, he calls Renan unhistorical for attempting to compare Christianity and Mithraism, and for considering Mithraism a real rival to Christianity: "It might and would have won many adherents, but it could not have founded a holy Mithraic church throughout the world. A man used Mithraism, but he did not belong to it body and soul; if he did that was a matter of special attachment and not an inevitable concomitant prescribed by authority."[67] In fact he goes so far as to say that in these rivals of Judaism and Christianity there was no possibility of anything which can be called conversion. He does, however, qualify this statement with two clear exceptions: conversion to philosophy "which held a clear concept of two types of life, a higher and a lower, and which exhorted men to turn from the one to the other. . . . Genuine conversion to paganism will appear in our inquiry only when Christianity had become so powerful that its rival was, so to speak, made an entity by opposition and contrast."[68] The latter of these two types of conversion is of great importance for understanding the conversion of Julian, as is the former for understanding the conversion of Synesius of Cyrene.

Synesius certainly meets the requirements for a convert to philosophy; his letters reveal him embracing it as a new and noble way of life,

---

66. Nock, *Conversion* 7. Nock echoes William James's definition of conversion as a motion from what is wrong, inferior and bad, to that which is right, superior and good (*Varieties of Religious Experience* 157). However, it must be kept in mind that conversion to paganism or to philosophy lacked some of the Christian nuances so familiar to James and others. For the pagan idea of the divided self becoming whole—an idea which is related to conversion—cf. Goodenough, *Psychology* 30–63.

67. Nock, 14.

68. Nock, 14–15. Philosophy held a dominant position according to Nock because: (1) it offered intelligible explanations of phenomena; (2) it offered a life with a scheme, a discipline, and a goal; (3) it produced the saints of antiquity; (4) it had the influence of the living teacher; (5) it made a literary appeal; (6) it evoked repentance and conversion (Intro. xi–xii).

into which he had been initiated; the observance of moral precepts and
the avoidance of "sin"—i.e., attachment to matter and the passions—
make up an important part of the philosophic life. He considered Hypatia
a saintly example of the way of philosophy, and remained devoted to her
throughout his life. He continued to appeal to her and ask her advice in
deep emotional and spiritual crises, even after he had become a Christian
bishop.

In addition to a knowledge of Neoplatonism, *Hymn* I reveals a desire for repentance and conversion, i.e., a desire for freedom from the
defilements of matter (*hyle*), which obscure the fallen soul's vision of the
divine, and for *epistrophe*, or return to the divine ground.[69] The way of
the soul in this world is purification through the virtues prescribed by
philosophy. This in turn leads to illumination or the revealing of the noetic path, and, finally, to union (*henosis*) with the divine. The process en-
tails a conversion which brings us up from the unhappy condition of mortals, deceived by appearances, to the happy condition of the sage, who
has overcome the "destiny of matter."[70] Thus the joyous affirmation in the
last lines of the *Hymn* may be to some degree equated with the joy of
the Christian convert who has "struggled away from sin" and found a
new self.

The idea of conversion to philosophy is particularly applicable in the
case of Neoplatonism, one branch of which formed the basis for a pagan
dogmatic theology, and a doctrine of salvation often in bitter opposition to
Christianity. The school of Hypatia, as we have seen earlier, was confessionally neutral, and not attached to any specific cult or mystery; it is
unlikely that she considered any religious belief superior to philosophy,
the true way to salvation. Her teaching made possible a less hostile attitude to Christianity (e.g., Christians, Jews, and pagans, perhaps devotees
of Isis or Sarapis, who might be students of Hypatia could each hold different religious beliefs containing some part of the truth, but could arrive
at the whole only through the discipline of philosophy). If, after discover-
ing the philosophic truth, they chose to interpret their various religious
traditions in its light, well and good, but philosophy was always to retain
its primacy as both the key to the riddles of the universe and the path to
the soul's salvation. In short, scripture—whatever scripture—was subordinate to philosophy. Even when considered revelatory—as in the Chal-

69. Cf. Nock, 296.
70. Cf. Wallis, 85 and 98 n. 1. "The four classes distinguished by Porphyry are the
civic (cf. *Enn.* I.2.1.16–21), purificatory (I.3.11–19), contemplative (I.6.22–27), and para-
digmatic virtues (I.7.1–6)."

daean Oracles—it was nevertheless interpreted through the doctrines of philosophy and rarely allowed to contradict or modify them. In this sense Neoplatonism proceeds in the opposite way to Patristic exegesis, which is theoretically obligated to deny the truth of philosophy if it cannot be made to harmonize with scripture.[71] This is especially true of Hypatia and the Alexandrians in general, because they never became active participants in the Julianic reaction, as did the schoolmen of Athens; for the Alexandrians followed the Plotinian-Porphyrian way of putting philosophy before theurgy.[72] Alexandrian Neoplatonism was therefore less subordinate to dogma than its more devoutly pagan counterparts. Acceptance of these views remained with Synesius all his life; he subordinated any particular cult or religion to the universal religion of philosophy. Christianity, it seems to me, was also a particular religion in his eyes, even though it was becoming the exclusive worship of the Empire: the true philosopher would still have the privilege of judging and interpreting Christian doctrine from the point of view of universal truth (see *Ep*. 96; cf. 105).

The Porphyrian teaching which Synesius seems to have first studied in Hypatia's school provided the best means available to a philosophic pagan for building intellectual bridges to Christianity. Synesius' conversion to philosophy is extremely important for the understanding of his later accommodation to Christianity. As we shall see, it provided him with some necessary bridges to Christianity, but it also prevented him from becoming an orthodox Christian: in the last analysis, he simply refused to deny philosophy's word on key issues. The religious neutrality of Hypatia's school prevented him from developing a hatred of Christianity; yet the doctrine to which he was so passionately converted in his youth prevented him from really accepting the new religion. This dual heritage of Neoplatonism has great implications for the history of religious thought. In the case of Synesius it caused perhaps the most unusual, if incomplete, synthesis of late antiquity. Synesius himself, as we shall see, was perfectly willing to reconcile philosophy with Christianity. But, as will also be demonstrated, he would only allow that reconciliation if it did not clash with what he thought to be the truth. This key to his thought, this essential hesitation or tolerance, grew naturally from the heterogeneous coterie that gathered around Hypatia. His successful reconciliation of the Neoplatonic-Chaldaean hypostases with the Trinity, and his apparent acceptance of other Christian ideas allegorically and symbolically,

71. Synesius' *Ep*. 105 of A.D. 410 clearly demonstrates this point.
72. For the list of philosophers who put philosophy before theurgy and vice versa, see Olympiodorus, *In Phaed*. 123.3–6.

may be understood as a type of Hellenistic syncretism—one that would be perfectly understandable to those of an earlier generation who were still willing to accept Christianity as one cult among many. But this was no longer a real option in the Theodosian age. Thus, in the last analysis, Synesius' seemingly "unorthodox" position was the result of his historical position and the hindsight provided by the victory of Christianity.

II

Transition (A.D. 395–402):
Return Home and Journey to Constantinople

We must now follow our convert as he leaves the comfort of his school and takes up an active role in a world where profound changes were taking place. Sooner or later the hard facts of life of the Theodosian age would force Synesius to see that paganism was no longer viable as an alternative to Christianity for the Roman Empire as a whole. In addition to his experiences at school, we shall see that his good relations with orthodox Christians at Constantinople caused him to choose the role of collaborator with the new religion, rather than that of member of a small aristocratic circle of devoted opponents to Christianity. Synesius was not sufficiently attached to the pagan cult *per se*, and too involved with the fate of the Roman world, to take the path followed by Iamblichus, Julian, Proclus, and the school of Athens.

After his schooling, Synesius returned home for about four years (395–399), a period in which he established his reputation as a leading local aristocrat; subsequently he got into political difficulties and found it expedient to take a brief holiday which included visits to Antioch and Athens. Synesius' visit to the latter resulted in his famous criticism of the school of Athens. Upon his return, his political prestige at home became so great that he became the political representative of Cyrene at the Court of Constantinople.[1]

When he first returned home (c. 395), Synesius was content to lead the life of a country gentleman whose principal interests were literature and hunting.[2] But soon he was pressed into service in the municipal council of Cyrene. He took his political responsibilities seriously and demonstrated a capacity for thought and action that impressed the population

---

1. For Synesius' activity as a *curialis* see Coster, 145–182 (= *Byzantion* 15 [1940–1941] 10–38); for Synesius as a member of the *boule* and his political program see *Ep*. 95; for his quick departure for Attica, *Ep*. 54; on his anti-Athenian sentiment, *Ep*. 136, 1524C; first barbarian war, *Epp*. 104, 113, and 124.
2. *Ep*. 103.

but involved him in political enmities.[3] Synesius also displayed considerable civic and military talent during the destructive barbarian raids through Cyrenaica in 395.[4] Because of his outstanding ability, the local citizens chose Synesius to appeal to the emperor at Constantinople personally for financial relief on behalf of Cyrene.

The emperor Constantine, sole Augustus by A.D. 324, had founded the city of Constantinople on the site of the ancient Megarian colony of Byzantium. Strategically located on the European shore of the Bosporus, the new Eastern imperial capital stood at the crossroads of Europe and Asia. It was near both the Danube frontier and the Sassanid Persian empire: the emperor could thus use the city as a headquarters and staging base against enemies of the Empire on two fronts.

The location of Constantine's city was also commercially advantageous. The Bosporus is a more accessible passage between the continents than the Hellespont, whether one is traveling from Asia or Europe. The large and protected harbor of the Golden Horn was a logical port for ships sailing the heavily traveled trade lanes between the Black Sea, the Aegean, and the western Mediterranean.[5] The city, set on the heights between the Golden Horn and the sea of Marmora, also could provide a safe harbor for a great fleet. The town itself was protected by sea on three sides and by land on one.

The balance of power in the Roman Empire had been shifting eastward for some time. Diocletian had realized that a new imperial center was necessary near the Danubian and Sassanian frontiers.[6] He chose the city of Nicomedia near the Asiatic shore of the Bosporus. But after his victory over Licinius, Constantine recognized the advantageous position of Byzantium.[7] His policy was a logical continuation of his predecessors'. The third- and fourth-century emperors, with their military backgrounds, their courts of new men, and their new strategic capitals, often found Roman senatorial tradition hostile and alien. Thus their ties with old Rome on the Tiber were not always strong. The need for a new center of administration had been felt by the emperor for some time. Constantine's con-

3. For departure to Athens see also Coster, 218–268 (*CJ* 55.290–312), esp. 235 and n. 34.

4. Concerning barbarian raids see n. 1 above; with the death of Theodosius in A.D. 395 the Eastern Empire entered a difficult period. In the following year Alaric sacked Eleusis; on the event and its connection with the prophesied end of the mysteries cf. Kerenyi, 32–34; cf. also Zosimus, V.6.

5. Runciman, 9–10.   6. *OCD*, art. "Constantine" 280.

7. For different perceptions of the strategic importance of Byzantium, from Periclean Athens to late Rome, see Runciman, 10–11.

version to Christianity, a religion that affronted the pagan senators at Rome, may have intensified this felt need but did not create it.[8]

Construction of the new city was inaugurated in the autumn of A.D. 324. The *consecratio* of the site was observed in 328, and the *dedicatio* on 11 May 330.[9] Traditional pagan rites and Christian ceremonies were performed. The city was officially named "New Rome," slightly lower in rank than the old. The citizens called it Constantinople.

The new urban center was to become a new synthesis of Greco-Roman and Christian civilization. Works of Greek art were imported from pagan temples to grace the streets of the new capital. Libraries were built that preserved the tradition of nearly a millennium of Greek thought and learning. Teachers of rhetoric and philosophy were attracted to the new capital, and by the fifth century several chairs had been endowed for these disciplines. The emperor recognized a *Tyche* of the city; he also erected a column of Apollo, with his own face replacing that of the god.[10] But according to Eusebius the new city never had pagan worship. Apparently, the old temples of Byzantium became "classical museums." Thus the city was a new center of Hellenism.[11]

But it was also a Roman city. New institutions were created on the model of Rome on the Tiber. A great palace was built, imperial *fora* were constructed, the Hippodrome, with its two obelisks, was inspired by the design of the Circus Maximus. The emperor Valens built an aqueduct and other imposing public works. The tradition of bread and circuses for the plebs was continued when a free grain dole for 80,000 persons was inaugurated on 18 May 332. Latin remained the official language of government and law; the citizens were called *Rhomaioi* ("Romans") until the end of the Byzantine empire. The administration was modelled on that of Rome with a *praefectus annonae, praefectus vigilum, magister census,* and other municipal offices of the old capital. In 340 Constantius II created a new Senate comprised largely of distinguished immigrant citizens of the East, including Latin speakers from the Balkans; imperial *adlectio* during a successful official career continued to be a frequent way into the Senate of Constantinople, as into that of Rome.

In addition to this continuity with the classical past, Constantinople

---

8. Runciman, 11.   9. *OCD*, art. "Constantinople," 281.

10. Constantine was a former solar worshipper; this face on the column brings to mind his vision of *himself* as Apollo in 310. On this see Brown, *Late Antiquity* 69. For a general discussion of the *genius* or "guardian angel" as one's spiritual double, see *ibid.* 68–72.

11. *OCD* 281.

was founded by a Christian emperor. It had no ancient pagan roots: the old cults and temples of Rome were conspicuously absent.[12] The state religion of Rome on the Tiber was paganism; the state religion of Constantinople would be Christianity. The city itself was dedicated to the Holy Trinity and the Mother of God. Constantine built the Church of the Holy Apostles where he and his successors were buried. The bishop acquired great prestige: in 381 the Council of Constantinople declared that he should "have the primacy of honor after the Bishop of Rome, because it was the 'New Rome.'"[13] Constantine himself had stated that he "bestowed upon it an eternal name by the commandment of God."[14]

All of this was to have important consequences for the Christianization of the aristocracies of the East. Without this upstart melting-pot Asia Minor might very well have remained pagan much longer. Living in ancient Greek towns that had long recognized the world power of Rome as a counterpoise to Hellenic cultural autonomy, urban philosophers and rhetoricians perceived themselves as still belonging to the old classical world. But Constantinople changed this. Classically educated Christians such as John Chrysostom and Gregory of Nazianzus could live in the city as serious Christians, but Christians who still maintained some of the bearing and outlook of Greek gentlemen. After all, they had studied rhetoric (and even philosophy) under the same teachers as Julian and his pagan friends.

Most of the classical teachers of the Greek East were pagans, although a few were Christians, e.g., Prohaeresius of Athens. The celebrated rhetorician Libanius of Antioch, a man of the old-time religion, numbered Christians as well as pagans among his pupils.[15] At Constantinople common background and social standing were often more important than religious differences. Pagans, such as Themistius, who advocated religious tolerance could support and be favored by Christian emperors. As long as the new imperial policies were accepted, a pagan could fit into the society of Constantinople. One could be "converted" to the new city which, in the fourth century, developed an imperial ideology different from that of old Romans and Hellenes. Thus a "new" pagan such as Themistius could fit in, and so also could classically educated Christians.

Themistius himself remained a pagan who was tolerant of Christianity. He justified his attitude intellectually by mental gymnastics: he seems to have associated Christianity with the ancient religion of the Syrians; thus, in Roman law, it could be considered an ancient *religio licita*,

12. *Ibid.* 280.   13. *Ibid.* 281.   14. *Ibid.* 281.
15. On Libanius as a teacher see Petit, *passim.*

and in philosophical terms one of those ancient cults ordained by the *summus deus*.[16] Gilbert Dagron, in a brilliant monograph on Themistius and Constantinople, has compared him to a tolerant *philosophe*, a religious skeptic like Montaigne.[17] Yet the events of the second half of the fourth century were such that a generation later, an old-fashioned pagan such as Synesius could not only follow in the footsteps of Themistius, but even go him one further by joining the Christian camp.

Important changes in the political climate during Synesius' youth and early manhood occurred for several reasons. These included the problems created by Jovian's disgraceful Persian peace, the disaster of Adrianople in 378, and the limited success of Theodosius' policy of peace and assimilation of the Arian Goths into the empire during the 380s. With the reestablishment of orthodoxy in 381 and the formation of a "nationalist" faction under the Praetorian Prefect Aurelian, the political conditions emerged for Synesius' pagan accommodation to orthodox Christianity. For the primarily orthodox leaders of the city had changed their position. By the 390s the pagan threat was on the decline, while the Goths were no longer seen as barbarians who could evolve and be assimilated as good Greco-Romans or Christians, as Themistius had hoped. They were now regarded as heretics—heretics, moreover, with powerful support in a city dreading an imminent coup d'état.

Thus, by the time of Synesius' mission to the court at Constantinople, the idea of a Christian empire with an ecumenical outlook was no longer feasible. Julian and the pagans had advocated the old policy: Rome on the Tiber in league with the old Hellenes would defend the Empire against barbarism from without and Christianity from within. For the pagans this was the only salvation possible for the Roman Empire; Constantinople and the innovations of "Constantinianism" had seemed to

16. See Themistius, *Or.* V.69C–70A: the different religions of the empire are like different legions. They are all necessary. God wills the plurality of religions. The "Syrians" (i.e. Christians) worship in one way; the Hellenes in another; the Egyptians in yet another, etc. (The name "Christians" was first used at Antioch: Acts 11:9.)

17. *L'empire romain* 189; for the agreement of important elements of Hellenic thought with Scripture, pp. 150–152; for legitimacy of Christianity see especially pp. 155 and 182; for Themistius' ideas on civilizing the barbarians and an ecumenical empire see pp. 112–114 and 117; also n. 197 on p. 118; Themistius appeals to a list of precedents which begins with the integration of the Gauls in the first century and includes many precedents from the days of Marcus Aurelius to the present: different cultures can be assimilated into the Roman world, p. 163; frontier wars negate universality, p. 93; thus Rome's civilizing mission might include peace with Persia and inclusion of the barbarians, p. 85–89.

This work is the best study of how members of the Greek elites adjusted to the fact of Constantinople; see also Dagron, *Revue historique* 241.23–56.

them dangerous anomalies.[18] Their cause lost. But by the 390s the orthodox Christians of Constantinople had perceived the threat to Christian
Greco-Roman civilization in a manner not altogether different from the
old pagan viewpoint: the barbarian heretics had to be stopped if the Roman world was to be saved. Synesius had similar ideas. He too had come
to realize that the pagan cause had lost; *Romanitas* would set him on the
only path possible for a man of his class and concerns. Rather than hope
against hope for the demise of Christianity, he would rally to the defense
of the Empire and support the new religion.

Synesius' career may be compared in this sense to that of Themistius. The latter was a "new" pagan who became a spokesman for the policies of the emperors and élites of the new Rome. Synesius, an old pagan,
arrived on the scene when the new policy had failed. Christians were now
proposing ideas somewhat akin to traditional policy. Synesius supported
them, even to the extent of accepting an episcopate.

Themistius was born about A.D. 317 of a family of pagan Paphlago-
nian landowners. He was educated in the East and began teaching at
Constantinople about 345. Imperial recognition soon followed: he was ap-
pointed to an official chair of philosophy and to the new Senate by *adlectio* (1 Sept. 355). He became an important proponent of the ideology of
monarchy and served under Christian emperors from Constantius II to
Theodosius I, crowning his public career as City Prefect in 384. He was
also given the responsibility of educating the future emperor Arcadius
and acted as protector for the young prince when Theodosius left the city
on an important mission.[19] His philosophical commentaries on Aristotle
were studied as a model for exegesis during the Middle Ages. Thus, in
the late antique tradition, he was both rhetor and philosopher.

Dagron, viewing the career of Themistius as an example of the new
Hellenism that developed at Constantinople, believes that by exaggerat-
ing the importance of the conflict between Hellenism and Christianity,
historians have distorted the reality of the fourth century. He regards the
infra-religious conflicts as more important: orthodox Christians against
heretics; old Hellenes against dissident Hellenes such as Themistius. The
social milieu of Constantinople allowed men to be Hellene and Christian
almost simultaneously. This is of great importance for the social historian:

18. Julian became the symbol of the old Hellenism, Constantine of the new. But the
policies of "Constantinianism" were actually practiced by Christian emperors from Constantius II to Theodosius I: Dagron, *L'Empire romain* 61–93 and 199.

19. For a good outline of the career of Themistius see Jones et al., *Prosopography*
1.893–894, from which the details of his career that follow are drawn.

a new Hellenism emerged completely secular in its pagan element. This novel synthesis was to become the essence of Byzantine culture.[20]

Dagron's view has some importance for the case of Synesius. It certainly is useful in describing social changes that took place in the fourth century: religious values were being adjusted to new cultural and political values.[21] The incubator of these changes was Constantinople. But in his enthusiasm for the "progressive" Hellene Themistius, Dagron fails to do justice to Julian and his followers. The reason is simple: his intellectual model for the old paganism is Libanius of Antioch. Undoubtedly, the great rhetorician believed in Julian's political policies of regeneration of the cities and cooperation between Roman and Hellene to save civilization. But, although Libanius had a sentimental attachment to the old cults and stood for the old cultural values, he failed to understand the theurgic Neoplatonism of Iamblichus and Julian. The same may be said of Dagron. Thus, the social historian will find Dagron's work most useful, but the historian of religion must beware of his reductionism. Theurgy implied a real religious commitment, which included a mystical notion that Greco-Roman civilization would collapse if the old gods, cults, and mysteries were abandoned. The fact that Synesius was not a theurgist had as much influence on his actions as the circumstances in which he found himself. As a serious Neoplatonist and late antique *homo religiosus*, he accorded to religious ideas the value of ultimate reality. Thus scholars should study them in the context of a given world of "transcendent meanings" as they are meant. The historian accordingly must focus his attention on the noetic reality as well as the social reality of the fourth century. For this reason Dagron himself distorts fourth-century reality when he simply states that "Synésios, chrétien, reste un hellène un peu démodé; Thémistios, païen, préfigure aussi bien qu'Eusèbe de Césarée l'hellénisme byzantin."[22] It might be added that the above also ignores the important effect the politics of the 390s had on the decisions of Synesius.

However, there can be little doubt that Dagron is right to consider Themistius the champion of a new Hellenism. Traditionally, a Greek philosopher could be influential in his home town, on special missions to Rome, and on embassies to governors or to the imperial court. But he was not to be a courtier in the permanent retinue of the emperor: Constantinople had changed things drastically. The old order had been upset. A new Greek Rome had appeared in the East. Now imperial power was close to home—too close. And it was the power of Christian emperors.

20. Dagron, *L'Empire romain* 2.   21. *Ibid.* 3.   22. *Ibid.*

Conservative Hellenes were disturbed by their innovations. The position
of Themistius was sensitive. He was a pagan philosopher who advocated
imperial policy and a Senator with real influence: he might well appear to
be the "house pagan" of the Christian emperors of Constantinople. It is
not surprising that Julian avoided giving him honors. Nor is it surprising
that Christians of the period praised him: his tolerance extended to pro-
testing Arian persecution of the orthodox.[23]

Yet in fairness to Themistius, it must be said that he did his best to
preserve Hellenic letters and thought in the new environment of imperial
Christianity and, though a propagandist for the Constantinopolitan re-
gime, he continued to enjoy the friendship of Libanius.[24] Indeed, Peter
Brown has suggested that his role was to "rally the educated classes of
Asia Minor and the Near East to the upstart capital." Although his position was sensitive, he was seriously challenged only when he accepted the
office of City Prefect. At that point he appeared to be living in unphilosophical luxury.[25]

Themistius received many honors in his lifetime. In 357 he was en-
voy to Rome for the Senate of Constantinople; there he presented Constantine with a golden crown on his *vicennalia*. He was Proconsul of Constantinople (358–359), in charge of the enrollment of new senators and
the grain supply. A law of 361 gives him special status as a member of the
quorum necessary for the election of praetors; it recognized him as a philosopher who increases his *dignitas* through knowledge: *Themistius quo-
que philosophus, cuius auget scientia dignitatem (Cod. Theod.* VI.4.12).
In 376 he traveled again to Rome with the emperor Gratian. During his
career he went on ten embassies for the Senate and was twice honored by
emperors who presented him with bronze statues. He made many court
speeches celebrating important occasions, in which he represented the
position of the new order as a tolerant and moderate "progressive."

The scandal caused when this pagan confidant of Christian emperors accepted the office of City Prefect under Theodosius (384) symbol-
izes the clash between old and newly emerging cultural values. He rode
in a newly designed silver-rimmed carriage that went with the office. The
philosopher, upholder of the values of simplicity, contemplation, and
avoidance (when possible) of the limelight could now be caricatured as
the corrupt courtier. The poet Palladas mocked him (*Anth. Gr.* XI.292)
and accused him of shameful behavior: having ascended the heights, he

23. Brown, "The Philosopher and Society" 7–8; Socrates, *HE* 4.32.
24. See Downey, *HTS* 50.259–274. [Libanius considered Themistius a great professor and a gentleman: e.g. *Ep.* 793 (A.D. 362)].
25. Brown, "The Philosopher and Society" 8.

had in reality descended to the depths.[26] Philosophy had been given a bad name. The Greek sage had become a wealthy high official, a functionary of East Roman imperial power.

Themistius was not unaware that he was in danger of seriously alienating conservative Hellenes. After he left office he defended himself in an oration (Or. 34) in which he maintained that philosophers must not denigrate the art of government: Plato prefers to contemplate the things above (anō); Epicurus indulges in pleasures. He asserts that he himself follows the mean between these extremes: when "above" he contemplates, when involved in worldly affairs he participates in them, always cognizant of the philosophical virtues that guide his conduct.

In his rhetoric on monarchy Themistius often claims that the emperor should display the qualities of a philosopher-king: he must be both a perpetually conquering Alexander and a wise Socrates or Cato.[27] These were by now traditional Greco-Roman ideas on kingship, but the context was new: the pagan philosopher was now an official in the new Rome. There, Christians in religion were Greeks in culture and Rhomaioi.[28] For better or for worse Constantinople had Romanized the East: the Christian Roman Empire was a reality.[29] Themistius had established a new role for the philosopher, one of central importance at the imperial court.[30] In this sense he paved the way for Synesius. Emperors and the educated had become used to an important public figure who was a philosopher. The city that was still Hellenic but no longer pagan was prepared for the embassy of an old Hellene and philosopher. Themistius had done his best to preserve the old culture in a new setting. Thus, paradoxically, Synesius received a welcome that must have surprised him. Moreover, the political changes of the 390s allowed him to advocate a policy more conservative than that of Themistius. As we shall see, he too would preserve the old culture in a new setting, but not in the same way as Themistius. He would have to forge an individual path in a world that respected Hellenism, but was no longer pagan. His continued commitment to Neoplatonic philosophy would make that path unique and significant.

Synesius' sojourn at Constantinople lasted three years (399–402).[31] They were difficult years of absence from his native land, but of consider-

---

26. For a good discussion of Palladas' poem and Themistius see Cameron, *CQ* 15.215–229, esp. 221–223. See also Dagron, *L'Empire romain* 46–53.

27. Dagron, *L'Empire romain* 35.   28. *Ibid.*

29. *Ibid.* 202.   30. *Ibid.* 199.

31. Seeck, *Philologus* 52.442–460, settled the chronology for the voyage (A.D. 399–402); see also Gibbon, ed. Bury 3.506; A.D. 399: Synesius arrives at Constantinople with Aurelian as Praetorian Prefect in A.D. 400; Stilicho, manipulating from the West, brings

able importance in determining his future development.[32] At court he became acquainted with some of the most powerful and important figures of
the period: Aurelian, Praetorian Prefect of the East; his brother, Caesarius; Gaïnas, the leader of the Goths, who was being instigated and ma-
nipulated from the West by Stilicho; and the emperor Arcadius, who was
sweet, pious, dull, and at a loss over what to do about the barbarians. The
evidence for Synesius' connection with events and personages at court is
tenuous. None of the histories of the period mention him in this regard,
and the only clues we have come from his own writings. His three letters
to Aurelian demonstrate that Synesius considered him an excellent ad-
ministrator whose actions imitated the divine.[33] Moreover, he did not hesitate to recommend to Aurelian one of his own relatives who was an official in the government with a legal problem. In *Ep.* 61 he alludes to
Aurelian as "dear friend and consul." Synesius' other friendships, including his friendships with the soldier-scholar Paeonius and some local men
of letters, were of the sort that a man in his position would ordinarily
make. They do not throw much light on his specifically Christian connections, although it is safe to assume that most of these men were supporters of Aurelian for the same reasons as Synesius.

In *On Kingship* he outlines a policy of reform attractive to the
anti-Gothic faction at court. In *On Providence* he allegorizes the political events of the turn of the fifth century—events in which the author himself seems to have participated.[34] Although there is little solid evidence
of the details of this period in Synesius' life, we can at least conclude
that he established friendly ties with important orthodox Christians at
Constantinople.

When Synesius arrived at the capital, the political situation was volatile. Many Arian barbarians were prominent at court and held influential
positions. The violent events and reversals of fortune of the next few years
provide evidence of serious infighting among the different cliques at

---

pressure to bear on Arcadius to bring in Caesarius, Gaïnas, and the Goths in place of Aurelian in the same year; Aurelian returns in 401; Synesius' description of earthquake follows
in 402.

Arcadius was weak and did not know how to handle the barbarian problem. Cf.
Zosimus, V.12.

32. For Synesius' ambivalence over these "three unspeakable years" see *De Ins.*
1308D and *Hymn* III 1.431.

33. *Epp.* 31, 34, and 38.

34. *De Prov.*, 1253A–1256B. In this passage the philosophical opponent of Typho
(Caesarius) and friend of Osiris (Aurelian), who grants him exception from curial burdens, is
surely Synesius himself.

court.[35] For the moment (399) Aurelian and his orthodox Christian friends were in power. The Goth Gaïnas, who had risen from the ranks to a position of command in the army, was in Asia Minor ostensibly putting down the revolt of Tribigild.[36] In reality, he himself had instigated Tribigild in order to find a pretext to put an army into the field and thereby gain control over the Eastern Empire and the throne at Constantinople. As commander of the army he had already sent for many of his Gothic compatriots and had placed them in positions of power in the military. In this tense atmosphere it is likely that Synesius presented his speech *On Kingship* to Arcadius with some urgency. The emperor had to be warned of the impending danger and decisively won over to the right side.

The purposes of Gaïnas soon became apparent. In hope of appeasing the barbarian, Arcadius sent an embassy to him. Gaïnas demanded that his enemies, Saturninus and the consul Aurelian,[37] must be turned over to him. Having little choice in the matter, Arcadius complied with the request. Saturninus and Aurelian went to a place near Chalcedon, willing to accept whatever fate had in store for them. Traveling with them was one Joannes, a favorite of the emperor whom the Goth had also demanded. Gaïnas, however, after behaving in a threatening manner, decided to send them into exile unharmed.

Not satisfied with this concession, the barbarian moved into Constantinople itself. His ally Caesarius, who in 399 had been deposed as Praetorian Prefect in favor of his brother Aurelian, was in power again and ready to receive and encourage Gaïnas and his troops.[38] The success of the

35. For a necessarily tentative discussion of politics and political figures at the court of Arcadius *vis-à-vis* Synesius' mission and speech see Lacombrade, *Discours* 5–30.

36. The account that follows is based on the original sources. With some variations all the histories of the period, pagan and Christian, tell the same basic story. Socrates, *HE* 6.6; Sozomen, *HE* 8.4; Philostr. *HE* 9.8; Eunap. frr. 75.6–82 (Dindorf); Zosimus, V.7–22. It is interesting to note that Christian historians attribute the exit of Gaïnas from the city to miracles: the auspicious appearance of a comet in the sky and the appearance of angels in the guise of Roman soldiers. Zosimus, a more than nominal pagan, does not report these occurrences, but says that Gaïnas feigned war-weariness so that he could retire from the city and direct the coup from a position of safety outside of the gates. But in another place (V.6) Zosimus says that Attica was spared when Alaric invaded Greece because the barbarian was frightened off when he saw an apparition of Athena Promachos patrolling the wall. Synesius' allegorical version of the events found in the *De Prov.* differs in certain details from contemporary histories. His role in the affair must be worked out through a comparison of his writings with sources that do not mention him. On Gaïnas' campaign against Tribigild, see Coster, 159.

37. A.D. 400 was the year of Aurelian's consulship.

38. The role of Caesarius, also ignored by historians of the period, has been reconstructed here from the account of Synesius in the *De Prov.*; Philostratus, *HE* 11.5, mentions Caesarius as the successor to Rufinus in the office of Praetorian Prefect.

coup seemed imminent. Gaïnas discharged many of the troops who had served under him, thereby greatly weakening the defenses of the city. At this point, either because of reports of armed resistance and the unsettled character of the situation in the city, or simply to direct the fighting from outside the walls and enter the city during the ensuing chaos, Gaïnas began to retreat to a suburb a few miles outside of town.[39] Soon afterward, the over-anxious Gaïnas got into a skirmish with the guards at the gates before his men inside the city were ready to initiate the coup. The alarm was raised and everybody in the city began to attack the Goths and repel Gaïnas at the walls. The usually indecisive Arcadius finally declared Gaïnas a public enemy and ordered the Goths who had remained within the walls killed. The imperial decree was carried out with the aid of an outraged populace.[40] Gaïnas himself did not attempt to return to Constantinople, but made his way to the Thracian Chersonese, where he was soon pursued and defeated by a Roman officer named Fravitta. He managed to elude the Roman troops, but was eventually killed by Uldes the Hun, who subsequently brought his head to Arcadius. A great threat to the East Roman Empire had finally been destroyed. Aurelian, who had gone into exile, was able to return in triumph several months after the Goths had been driven out of Constantinople. Orthodoxy triumphed over heresy, Greco-Roman civilization over barbarism.

These events formed the backdrop against which Synesius composed both *On Kingship* and *On Providence*. In them, Synesius gave voice to his conviction that the Goths represented a form of barbarism that threatened to destroy the ancient way of life. Aurelian, who stands for goodness and civilized values, is allegorically represented in *On Providence* by Osiris; his brother and ally of the Goths Caesarius, who stands for evil and barbarous values, is represented by Typho. The Arian Goths represented to Synesius what the Christians represented to Julian—outsiders hostile to the Greco-Roman way, and a threat to the good order of the world. Hence Synesius' reference to the religion of the barbarians as a distorted and false caricature of religion. As Christianity had been a kind of anti-cult to Julian, so was the barbarized heresy of the Goths to Synesius.

On the cosmic level, Osiris in *On Providence* represents the good, orderly, and unifying element in things. Typho represents the bad, chaotic, and disorderly element. In typical Neoplatonic fashion, Synesius

---

39. See above, n. 36.

40. Caesarius, an instigator of the coup, managed to remain in office for a few more months, although his power and popularity rapidly declined. Aurelian returned late in 401 or early in 402; cf. Lacombrade, *Synésios* 104; Fitzgerald, *Letters* 19 n. 1.

connects the cosmic with the mundane by means of the principle of correspondence: events on earth reflect and imitate different aspects of the principles that underlie reality. Everything in the cosmos in some sense reflects everything else.

For Synesius, then, not the orthodox Christians, but rather the barbarian heretics, threatened the stability of the world. Julian had perceived Christianity as a new kind of spiritual barbarism—one that could neither be rationalized nor absorbed into the Greco-Roman order. Synesius did not perceive Christianity in this way, at least not as practiced by the orthodox Christians with whom he had come into contact; hence the importance of his experience at Constantinople for helping to make possible his accommodation with Christianity.

Given Synesius' views as expressed in his writings, and given the background of contemporary events at court, it is distinctly possible that Synesius' speech *On Kingship* became a rallying point for the anti-Gothic forces at court. Moreover, it is likely that it became "the anti-German manifesto of the party of Aurelian,"[41] at a time when, both from within and without, the Goths threatened to overwhelm the Eastern Empire. Thus we might think of the speech as the appeal of a "lobbyist" for the cause of Mediterranean ideals and civilization against the threat of northern barbarism.

We have seen that Synesius believed the philosopher should be an active citizen involved in the issues of his day. Consequently, in *On Kingship*, he applied his philosophical vision to political analysis in an effort to save the state from immediate danger, and to suggest a policy of general reform that might help to avoid a recurrence of similar dangers. He cleverly used Platonic themes to reinforce the arguments employed in his discussion of army reforms. He recommends that the army be made up of loyal citizens rather than hired foreign mercenaries: like Plato's class of "auxiliaries" in the *Republic*, they will be fierce to external enemies, but kind and well disposed toward their fellow citizens. The foreigners, who have no reason to be loyal, are like a pack of wild animals who will turn on the citizens at the first opportunity.[42] Following this line of argument,

---

41. Lacombrade, *Discours* 5.

42. *De Regno* 23C–25A (pp. 46–49, Terzaghi ed.); Plato, *Rep.* 416A–D; cf. also *De Regno*, 1089C–D, where this image is applied to the contemporary situation. For a possible (partial) explanation of why Synesius would be willing to accept orthodoxy, and even allude unfavorably to the Arians, see Brown, *Religion and Society* 90f and 148. Orthodoxy was becoming the new way to romanization: "for a bishop, Orthodoxy was the only bridge over which a barbarian could enter civilization; and in the eyes of John Chrysostom, a Goth who was fully identified with the Roman Order by pagan standards but who had remained an Arian, might just as well have stayed in his skins across the Danube" (see Theodoret *HE*

Synesius adds that the barbarian should be excluded not only from the armies, but from both the high magistracies and the imperial council.

Couched within this appeal for his town, then, is a discourse on ideal kingship and imperial reform.[43] This medley is clearly in the tradition of local patriotism, which became very important to Greek cities under the Roman Empire. To compensate for lack of political autonomy these cities would compete with each other for imperial favor and generally try to outdo each other in architecture and other cultural endeavors. The local nobles competed in public benefaction. The prize was *time* ("honor," or better yet, "social recognition and standing").

Orations on kingship were common in the Roman Empire. Delivery of such orations before the emperor became a solid tradition at court between the second and fourth centuries. In the baroque atmosphere of the Late Empire they were often merely dazzling showpieces aimed only at enhancing the aura surrounding the throne. However, some of them, like Synesius' *On Kingship*, were persuasive pieces meant as serious appeals to the emperor. This seems to be true of the speech of Synesius. One indication that *On Kingship* went beyond being a tissue of *topoi* presented to a Christian emperor showing traditional tolerance to a pagan orator is the fact that Synesius addresses specific recommendations to Arcadius himself, rather than to some hypothetical philosopher-king; these nearly always present the perfect ruler as one who rules wisely and justly because he imitates and tries as far as possible to assimilate himself to some metaphysical entity such as the Platonic Good or Stoic Logos.

Without involving ourselves in an extraneous analysis of the speech in its historical setting, let us briefly review some of its main themes.

5.32 and Brown, *ibid.* 53f). Brown, *ibid.* 148, believes that whereas in the West the new Christians showed themselves only too ready to collaborate with other new rulers untainted by the classical-pagan past (i.e., the barbarians), in the East, orthodox Christians absorbed many old pagan ideals. In the West new Christians were less Roman about orthodoxy. Needless to say the pagan-influenced Senate at Rome was an exception.

43. *De Regno* 2D (ed. Terzaghi, p. 7): Ἐμὲ σοὶ πέμπει Κυρήνη, στεφανώσοντα χρυσῷ μὲν τὴν κεφαλήν, φιλοσοφία δὲ τὴν ψυχήν, πόλις Ἑλληνίς, παλαιὸν ὄνομα καὶ σεμνόν, καὶ ἐν ᾠδῇ μυρία, τῶν πάλαι σοφῶν νῦν πένης καὶ κατηφὴς καὶ μέγα ἐρείπιον καὶ βασιλέως δεόμενον, εἰ μέλλοι τι πράξειν τῆς περὶ αὐτὴν ἀρχαιολογίας ἐπάξιον. Cf. Lacombrade, *Discours* 7.

For the tradition of Platonic-Pythagorean theories of ideal kingship see Goodenough, *YCS* 1.55–102; Délatte, *passim*; cf. also Ladner, 113–132 and notes. If we confine ourselves to the Roman Empire, Synesius' predecessors in this genre include among others Musonius Rufus, Plutarch, Dio of Prusa, perhaps the Neopythagorean writings on kingship, *Corpus Hermeticum* 18, Libanius, Themistius, and the many speeches collected in the *Panegyrici Veteres*. For the ancient rhetorical rules pertaining to court panegyric (*egkomion Basileos*) see Menandros Rhetor, *peri epideiktikon*, in Spengel, *Rhetores Graeci* 3.368ff.

We must, says Synesius, return to the Platonic ideal of the philosopher-king: the emperor is the *imitatio dei*; as such he must attempt to organize his kingdom in the way God orders the universe, providentially.[44] The political plan is a critique of what the Roman Empire had become from what it had been and could be once again. Synesius adverts to the pomposity of the court, with its elaborate ceremonial and oriental luxury, its corruption and abuses, which is detrimental to the health of the Empire. The monarch must be as bright as his model, the Sun (here, of course, thought of as the epiphany of the Good in the visible cosmos). Living as simply as Agesilaus or Epaminondas, he is to come out of seclusion and be both a soldier among his troops and the leading citizen among his fellow citizens.[45] If the Empire is to survive, expensive court costs must be reduced, taxes reformed, the leading classes in the cities rehabilitated, so that urban life can be restored to its old vitality.[46] The monarch must choose able administrators to run the provinces; acting in the state as the deity does in the cosmos, he is to delegate powers for all needs without attending to every detail.[47]

Thus Synesius outlined a policy of reform that was conceptually Platonic and "nationalistic" in its main outlines, a policy, moreover, that could be applied to the immediate situation as well as to the general and abiding problems of the Empire. If Hellenism was to be saved, barbarous practices had to be curbed both internally (i.e., the luxury of the court) and externally (i.e., the use of Gothic armies). Such reductions in imperial expenditure were a normal remedy urged by conservatives in the fourth century. It is likely that some important members of Synesius' audience agreed with him, for the policy was implemented and seems to

44. *De Regno* 1064B–1068C (pp. 11–13, Terzaghi ed.); cf. also Lacombrade, *Synésios* 84–87, who says that for Synesius in *De Regno* prayers, mysteries, etc. do not glorify power but adore the providence of the divine prince as the image of God.

45. *De Regno* 1077D–1081A, 1085B–1088C; see also Bidez, *Julien* 40–50, 213–219, and 236–241. But cf. Ladner, 118 no. 34: "The 'imperial' ideology of Christian reform continued to a large extent pagan ideas about the ruler as savior, liberator, benefactor, reformer of mankind." Synesius' extensive quotes from the classics, however, his deference to Plato and Aristotle, and his concept of deity derived from the school of Hypatia, all indicate that his program had its roots in Greek philosophical ideas of reform, which were compatible with many Christian ideas of the same kind. Many of his statements on political reform can also be traced back to the political writings of earlier Greek philosophers, e.g., Aristotle, *Politics* 1273a23, Ἀριστίνδην οὖν, ἀλλὰ μὴ πλουτίνδην, ὥσπερ νῦν τῶν ἀρξόντων αἵρεσις γινέσθω; see *PG* 66.1104D.

46. *De Regno* 1100B.

47. Synesius seems quite pagan here if we think of the delegated powers as the different orders of gods who create, animate, harmonize and guard the cosmos; cf. Sallustius, *De Diis et Mundo* 6.

have lasted through the praetorian prefectures of Aurelian and Anthemius.[48] Orthodox Christians in the audience applauded and supported
Synesius at the court in a policy that was—with the obvious exception of
the idea of a sacerdotal pagan church—virtually identical with that of
Julian and many other traditional Greco-Roman aristocrats throughout
the Empire. Indeed, at this time they were much more frightened by the
threat of an Arian empire than that of a revived pagan Rome. They saw his
interests as their interests, probably approached him when he arrived at
court, and formed a political alliance with him—both because of the immediate political situation, his social position and the nature of his conversion to philosophy.[49] Synesius was forced to play the role of the activist
philosopher. Thus he adopted a role that unexpectedly brought him into
the Christian camp.

Synesius, who had been educated in a school of Greek philosophy
not actively hostile to Christianity, which had even attracted Christian
students, now began to find positive reasons to favor Christianity: he
could claim that, far from undermining the safety and health of the state
(a perennial pagan criticism), orthodox Christians were perfectly in accord with the traditional ideology of the Greco-Roman world and would
defend the traditional state. Not only would they fight the barbarians, but
they would also adopt a program in accord with the highest principles of
ancient wisdom. Julian, if he had been alive, might have considered Synesius a collaborator yet he could not have claimed with full justice that
he was collaborating with those who would destroy the ancient way of life.
Moreover, Synesius was not attached to cults in the mystical-ontological
way of Julian's followers;[50] that is, he did not believe that the order of society or the cosmos was endangered if certain mysteries were not celebrated, or if certain rites were neglected: if the survival of civilized mankind now required a single religion or cult, Christianity—which Synesius
was beginning to think of as the wave of the future—could be accommo-

48. Coster, 161, points out that with the exception of a few Armenian or Persian
names, we know of no military officers in the Empire of the East during this period with
barbarian names; cf. RE 11.1151; Stein, Histoire du Bas-Empire, 1.362ff.

On reductions in expenditure: Julian thought that sophrosyne (meaning austerity)
rather than increased taxes (phoroi) would reverse the decline; see the edict ascribed to
him, P. Fayum 20 col. II in Juliani epistulae et leges 86 and 57; and Mazzarino, n. 63 on
pp. 379–380. Fiscal discipline was a normal remedy urged by conservatives in the fourth
century. It was about as far as their economic sense could reach.

49. Cf. De Regno 2B (ed. Terzaghi, p. 6); cf. also 26C–D (ed. Terzaghi, p. 52), where
Synesius gives praise to philosophy—which he almost personifies in the manner of Boethius—as a religion to which conversion is possible.

50. For cosmic anxiety connected with the downfall of the mysteries, cf. Eunap. Vit.
Soph. 471 (ed. Boissonade).

dated to the Hellenic spirit. Thus, differing from exclusivists on both sides, Synesius embarked upon his unique synthesis.

In addition to his perception of common interests with Aurelian and the anti-Gothic party, Synesius was beginning to find common ideological ground with Christianity. Ladner has demonstrated that the "renovation of the empire, accompanied by age-old traditions of ruler worship and of the eternal rejuvenation of Rome, became one aspect of Christian reform ideology" in the Constantinian-Theodosian age.[51] The king as the living image of God imitating the hypercosmic-noetic realm also has parallels in Christian thought.[52] Besides Eusebius' imperial ideology beginning in the second century, the school of Alexandria had made possible a type of Platonic Christianity potentially having much in common with the thought of Synesius. His Christian friends, both in the school of Hypatia and at court, could have made him cognizant of this fact—whether or not he was familiar with Patristic authors. Moreover, the issue was not only religious and philosophical, but also involved the concrete social concerns of a politically responsible gentleman.

Thus, whereas Julian outlined his policy as opposition to Christianity, Synesius was able to outline a similar policy with enthusiastic Christian support. Whereas Julian saw no possibility of reconciliation with Christianity, Synesius not only saw the possibility, but helped to make it a reality. Paganism was dying as the way of life of the Empire:

51. Ladner, 118. "The return to the ancient state of affairs brought about through renewal of the kingship ἐς τὸ ἀρχαῖον πρᾶγμα is the political application of that ἀποκατάστασις εἰς τὸ ἀρχαῖον which one meets in a mystical and eschatological sense, for instance in Gregory of Nyssa" (see also 123 n. 42 for further references).

52. *Ibid.* 122 n. 42; see also 144 n. 25: "Why was the earthly Basileia of Constantine an imitation of the heavenly one? The divine Logos, who had fashioned man according to the image and likeness of God and had made him, alone among all earthly creatures, capable of ruling and of being ruled, had renewed (ἀνανεούμενος) this seed laid in creation through his Gospel of the heavenly Kingdom. Now Constantine has become a participant [it seems to me that the Platonic idea of 'participation in Form' is operative here] in the Kingdom of God already on earth, shaping through truly royal virtues a copy (μίμημα) of the Kingdom beyond in his soul. The βασιλεύς friend of God, who bears the image of the supernal βασιλεία can be said to govern the affairs of the world with and through the word of God in imitation of the Almighty. The emperor's relationship to God is seen as an imitation of the relation between the divine Logos and the Father: just as the Logos rules together (συμβασιλεύων) with the Father from and in infinity, so Constantine rules over the earth for many years; just as the Saviour orders the supernal Kingdom for His Father, so the emperor makes his subjects on earth fit for it; just as the one opens the doors of the Father's Kingdom to those who leave this world, so the other, after having purged his terrestrial kingdom of godless error, calls all pious men into the mansions of the empire (εἴσω βασιλικῶν οἴκων). It would indeed be hard to imagine a closer representation of the heavenly in the terrestrial Basilica, of the Kingdom of God in the Roman Empire renewed by Christ and Constantine"; see also *ibid.* 121f and nn. 39, 40, and 41.

Synesius had seen in his youth the destruction of the Serapeum, the severe anti-pagan legislation of Theodosius, and the final defeat of pagan political hopes in the battle of the Frigidus. Is it surprising that he was willing to ally himself with Christians who seemed interested in and responsive to his beloved Hellenism? Nor was this simply a matter of compromise on the part of Synesius. He criticized those aspects of Christianity that conflicted with his ideals, for instance, the desert ascetics whose ideal was in many ways opposed to that of the classic city-bourgeoisie: Synesius considered their way of life uncivil and uncivilized, too un-Hellenic to be acceptable. Rather than join the now rapidly forming pagan underground and involving himself in a movement like the Athenian, Synesius chose to stay with the mainstream and to attempt to influence the society of his time. The alternative was to nurture pagan hopes that Christianity was a passing phase and that the old religion would return in all its glory. This became a received principle among Neoplatonists at Athens from the late fourth to the early sixth century.

In dealing with pagan-Christian theological issues, Synesius was to continue in the spirit and pattern of the ideological and political entente he made with the Christians at Constantinople. The battle to save Hellenism from barbarism, to save *Romania* and its civilized institutions from the barbarization of its population, was more important to him than the battle between paganism and Christianity. If Christians were ready to take up this battle, in an era when paganism was on the wane, it could no longer legitimately be called collaboration for a true Hellene to ally himself with them. Moreover, in certain respects, the religious and philosophical distance between the two was not as wide as many had thought. Such must have been Synesius' thoughts during his stay at court. If he left Constantinople not yet a baptized Christian, or even officially a catechumen, he certainly left as a strange kind of fellow-traveler: one who would adapt Christianity to Hellenism while, at the same time, moving close enough to Christianity to eventually accept the new religion on his own terms.[53]

Late Roman aristocrats such as Symmachus have often been characterized as noble but myopic conservatives in a dynamic age, who could not understand the significance of the changes taking place in their midst. If so, this judgment cannot be applied to Synesius. He was a traditional

---

53. Momigliano, *Conflict* 14, speaking of the differences of East and West on the issue of Paganism v. Christianity, says: "The Greek Fathers never produced searching criticisms of the Roman State comparable with those of St. Augustine and Salvian. On the contrary, St. John Chrysostom supported the anti-German party in Constantinople, and Synesius became a convert and a bishop after having outlined the programme of that party"; cf. above n. 42.

aristocrat who was flexible enough to try to adapt what he considered to
be perennial values to the new age. He never attempted to make the type
of transformation and new cultural synthesis that an Augustine or Gregory of Nyssa made. This was not his intention. Nor was such a viewpoint
available to him, for Synesius identified with the values of the old nobility. After all, someone like Augustine was not rooted in the old Greco-
Roman way of life as Synesius was: he was half a product of it and half
something new. Synesius' purpose was the opposite of that of Augustine
or the Cappadocians: he wanted Christianity to be a new form of expression for Hellenism.

III

The Middle Years (A.D. 402–409): From Constantinople to the Bishopric

Having successfully completed his mission,[1] Synesius departed from Constantinople in 402, apparently during an earthquake (*Ep*. 61), and returned home via Alexandria, where he married a Christian in 403. Theophilus, Patriarch of Alexandria, presided at the wedding (*Ep*. 105, 1485A). The name and family of Synesius' wife are unknown to us. She is thought to have belonged to a prominent Christian family because of Theophilus' presence at the ceremony.[2] Synesius' Christian marriage suggests the likely conjecture that he was or was about to become a catechumen, although the evidence is scanty and inconclusive.[3] But there is no evidence for the baptism of his children, and the Church historians indicate that his own baptism took place only upon his entry to the priesthood in A.D. 410.[4] The evidence is lacking on which to base a conclusion on Synesius' confessional stance vis-à-vis the Church at this time; but we may note that he was now in close contact with prominent Christians close to home.

The alliance, which began when orthodox Christians turned to support the interests of Hellenism and Roman patriotism, was to be a lasting

1. *De Prov.* 1253C and 1256B, indicate that Synesius won fiscal benefits for the cities of his province; he was exempted from curial responsibilities by Aurelian as a result of his service (*Ep*. 100, 1468D).

2. This statement is based on *Ep*. 105, 1485A: Ἐμοὶ τοιγαροῦν ὅ τε θεὸς, ὅ τε νόμος, ἥ τε ἱερὰ θεοφίλου χεὶρ γυναίκα ἐπιδέδωκε.

3. Lacombrade, *Synésios* 218 n. 16. "Est-il besoin, après cela, d'insinuer davantage que, en ce qui concerne Synésios encore non baptisé, cette 'raison d'État' de la cité de Dieu dut peser davantage que la rectitude éprouvée de son sens moral et que ses sympathies manifestes à l'endroit de la cause chrétienne? Les témoignages des auteurs ecclésiastiques sont formels, cf. Evagr., *H.E.*, I, 15; Nicéphor Call., *H.E.*, XIV, 55; Phot., *Bibl. can.*, 26. Synésios, du moins, devait être, depuis son mariage chrétien, catéchumène. Le concile de Chalcédoine n'autorisera par la suite (451) le mariage mixte que sous promesse de conversion du conjoint non chrétien." But could not the political Theophilus have blessed a mixed marriage in this case because he felt the alliance was important enough to warrant such an act? We would do well not to be overly legalistic in our approach to this question.

4. Cf. Evagrius *HE* 1.15: πείθουσι (the Christians) δ' οὖν αὐτὸν τῆς σωτηριώδους παλλιγγενεσίας ἀξιωθῆναι καὶ τὸν ζυγὸν τῆς ἱερωσύνης ὑπελθεῖν, οὔπω τὸν λόγον τῆς ἀναστάσεως παραδεχόμενον οὐδὲ δοξάζειν ἐθέλοντα, κτλ.

one. Paganism, as a movement, was completely dependent upon its hold on the old aristocracy: if the nobility of the Empire joined the Church, paganism would be doomed and the Church strengthened as an institution. Although it had been officially legitimized through its association with all the emperors since Constantine except Julian, the Church still had something to gain from the unofficial but still enormous social prestige that aristocratic converts could bring to it. The Church's best answer to those pagans who still looked back to Julian was the accession of Synesius and others like him.

After about two more years (404–405/6) in Alexandria, in which he completed *Hymn IV*, *Dion*, and *On Dreams*, Synesius was called to the defense of the Pentapolis and Cyrene against an Ausurian barbarian invasion.[5] The evidence for this next period in Synesius' life is extremely meager, but he seems to have been able to continue working on his *Hymns*, and probably completed the whole series by the year 409 or 410. Some of his letters reveal that the increasing pressure of the invasions forced him to give up much of his intellectual activity. Again he became a prominent political figure, incurred enmities, and by 409 was once more in exile— this time apparently moving to Ptolemaïs.[6] In addition to all of this, Synesius' own villa was ravaged by the barbarians.

During the next year (410) another turning point in the life of Synesius arose when Theophilus decided to appoint him Bishop of Ptolemaïs. Bishops played an important political role in the Late Empire; undoubtedly one of Theophilus' main aims in appointing Synesius bishop was the preservation of the Pentapolis and Libya as part of the Roman Empire. Indeed, one wonders whether the fact that Synesius was a Cyrenaican and an Egyptian by province did not help in his conversion quite as much as the distant fear of the Goths. There is evidence that pagans were accused of being in league with the barbarian pagan Blemmyes (who remained pagan into the sixth century) and that there was a growing sense of the need for solidarity against these local nomads and raiders.[7] Peter Brown has aptly described this mood: "Compared with the vast and menacing stretches of their own countryside and the new horizons of the bar-

---

Phot. *Bibl.* 1.26: . . . τὸν δὲ περὶ ἀναστάσεως οὐκ ἐθέλειν προσίεσθαι λόγον. ᾿Αλλ᾿ οὖν καὶ οὕτω διακείμενον ἐμύησάν τε τὰ ἡμέτερα καὶ ἔτι καὶ ἀρχιερωσύνης ἠξίωσαν, κτλ.

5. *Epp.* 130, 132, and 133 (which mentions the recent consulship of Aristaenetus in 405 or 406); see *Ep.* 53 for the birth of twins, summer 405 (?); for political affairs see *Epp.* 22, 30, 109, 110, and 120.

6. For political enmities see *Epp.* 50, 95, and 137; also *Epp.* 44 and 147.

7. Barns, "Shenute" 151–159. For the relations of settled and nomads in Cyrenaica see Johnson, *Jabal al-Akhdar*; and Evans-Pritchard, *The Sanussi*.

barian world, a hair's breadth separated pagan and Christian members of
the intelligentsia."[8] Furthermore, the Patriarch needed a strong political
bishop in Libya who would follow the orthodox line: since the Council of
Nicaea the province had nurtured a strong Arian faction, which was now
becoming yet another politically divisive force.[9]

Most bishops in this period came from upper- and middle-class families, were often well educated, and were either of curial rank or members
of the professions at the time of their ordination.[10] Many of the nobly born
were of families that had been converted to Christianity in a previous
generation. Notable among these were St. Ambrose and St. Basil of Caesarea. Very few were originally pagans.[11]

By the fourth century, the Church needed men of education and
ability to perform the increasingly complex social functions demanded of
bishops.[12] Constantine had increased their legal responsibilities,[13] and under subsequent emperors bishops often played an important role in diplomatic, political, and economic affairs.[14] But in the East the precise criteria
for the status of a Greek *curialis* differed from those for a Western senator. The Greek Curia was a far more diffused peer group of men who were
roughly equal. Gregory of Nazianzus was well aware of this:

> If certain men could look upon us naked and consider our suitability
> for priestly office among themselves, what would one of us have that
> was superior to what the other has? Birth? Education? Freedom of
> intercourse with the great and illustrious? Theological knowledge?

8. *Religion and Society* 89.

9. Chadwick, *HTS* 53.171–195, esp. 190–195; cf. below pp. 171–176.

10. Gilliard, 9–40, lists fourth century bishops according to social rank, background
and education. Many in the East studied with leading rhetoricians such as Libanius, or were
trained in law, medicine or philosophy. A few, such as Martin of Tours (p. 33), came from the
military. Only a handful had their origin in the lower artisan or peasant classes. See also List
II, pp. 59–62; List III, pp. 63–66, 78–79, and 81. The talented often became bishops *per
saltum*.

11. But see Gilliard, 33: Hilary of Poitiers, who came from a noble Gallic family, was
converted c. 350. Simplicius of Autun (mid-fourth century) studied with Julian under the
wonder-working pagan Maximus of Ephesus (p. 37); Libanius' statement indicating that St.
John Chrysostom would have been the worthiest to succeed him if the Christians had not
"stolen" him (p. 19). Cf. Sozomen, *HE* 8.2.

12. On the duties and social functions of bishops, see Gilliard, 90–98.

13. Gilliard, 90: ". . . in 318 Constantine declares that in any case of civil law a Christian litigant might substitute an episcopal court for the civil court. *Cod. Th.* 1.27.1, 318."

14. *Ibid.* 93: ". . . in 360 a bishop undertook on behalf of his city to dissuade the
Persian king Sapor from an attack; about 388 Flavian, bishop of Antioch, was sent before
Theodosius on a matter of great municipal concern; Athanasius was powerful enough to im-
pede the transport of grain from Egypt to Rome."

All of these qualities are found among us in a more or less equal measure. (*Ep.* 249.32)[15]

Synesius certainly possessed all of these qualifications. His Hellenic beliefs and heterodoxy were less important than his social rank and proven abilities. His noble lineage must have also been impressive. Synesius might have been a local aristocrat, but his pedigree—which he traced back to the Dorians who founded Sparta—could not be ignored. Surely the adhesion to the Church of such a personage as Synesius would be a very special victory for Theophilus.

Having by this time moved as close as he could to Christianity without compromising his principles, Synesius finally accepted the bishopric without all of his doubts resolved. His stay at Constantinople had opened the possibility of a reconciliation with Christianity. In the period after his return, between about 402 and 409, the impact of his initial contact with important Christians at court was strengthened and amplified by his alliances with important Christians at home. Although this study emphasizes the intellectual aspects of Synesius' accommodation, these can never really be separated from his existence as a man with serious social commitments. His attempts at philosophical reconciliation represent only one side of his efforts to find a place for himself in the emerging Christian world. As we shall see, his conception of the bishopric also had much in common with his ancient philosophical aristocrat's idea of political office and the social responsibilities that office entailed.

During these years, he also meditated on, and was able to accept in varying degrees, such dogmas as the Trinity and the Incarnation. His basic method was to attempt to harmonize the doctrines of the Chaldaean Oracles with those of Christianity; e.g., he equated the Seal of Baptism, identified with the Logos-Son or Spirit in Christianity, with the Chaldaean Seal of the Father as a symbol of the Neoplatonic Nous. After following this method as far as he could, he openly expressed his remaining doubts in *Ep.* 105, on the eve of his episcopal appointment.

Before studying the implications of this letter and his election to the episcopate, however, let us analyze some of the works he wrote during this transition period in order to see, in specific cases, precisely how he employed this method in his attempts to reconcile pagan Neoplatonism with orthodox Christianity. There is some evidence that Synesius began

15. *Ep.* 249.32: εἰ δέ τινες ἡμᾶς γυμνοὺς τοῦ κατὰ τὴν ἱερωσύνην ἀξιώματος ἐφ'ἑαυτῶν βλέποιεν, τί τοῦ ἑτέρου πλέον ἔχει ὁ ἕτερος; Γένος; Παίδευσιν; Ἐλευθερίαν πρὸς τοὺς ἀρίστους τὰ καὶ εὐδοκιμωτάτους; Γνῶσιν; ταῦτα ἢ ἐν τῷ ἴσῳ καὶ παρ' ἡμῖν ἔστιν εὑρεῖν ἢ πάντως οὐκ ἐν ἐλάσσονι, κτλ.

to harmonize the conflicting traditions of paganism and Christianity while he was still at Constantinople. In *Hymn* III he refers to the visits he made to all of the temples around Thrace and Chalcedon:

> Night after night, as many temples as have been built for your sacred mysteries, Lord, to all these I came, prostrate, a suppliant, drenching the ground with tears, that my pilgrimage should not have been fruitless. I supplicated the divine ministers, as many as occupy the fertile plain of Thrace, and those on the opposite shore, who oversee the Chalcedonian lands; your sacred ministers whom you have crowned with angelic rays, Lord. . . .[16]

Although in many cases these words, scenes, and acts could be legitimately interpreted as purely Christian, expressed in the traditional vocabulary of a classicizing poet, this is not a likely possibility in the case of Synesius. His references to emanation imply a divine cosmos in which "angels" must be thought of as divinities according to a common pagan usage. His subsequent religious thought and activity, as well as his openly stated position in *Ep.* 105, suggest rather that we have here an early example of what was to become his basic methodology: to attempt to build hermeneutic bridges between the old and the new religion. The way he approaches the Trinity in this *Hymn* is a more complex instance of the same thing.

But before passing final judgment, let us further analyze his poetry.

16.

νύκτ' ἐπὶ νύκτα.
νηοὶ δ' ὁπόσοι
δώμηθεν, ἄναξ,
ἐπὶ σαῖς ἁγίαις
τελετηφορίαις,
ἐπὶ πάντας ἔβαν
πρηνὴς ἱκέτας,
δάπεδον βλεφάρων
δεύων νοτίσι,
μή μοι κενεὰν
ὁδὸν ἀντᾶσαι.
ἱκέτευσα θεοῦ
δρηστῆρας, ὅσοι
γόνιμον Θρήκης
κατέχουσι πέδον,
οἵ τ' ἀντιπέρην
Χαλκηδονίας
ἐφέπουσι γύας,
οὓς ἀγγελικαῖς
ἔστεψας, ἄναξ,
αὐγαῖσι, τεοὺς
ἱεροὺς προπόλους.
(*Hymn* III,
1.449–470)

οἱ περὶ κόσμον,
οἱ κατὰ κόσμον,
οἱ ζωναῖοι,
οἵ τ' ἄζωνοι
κόσμου μοίρας
ἐφέπουσι σοφοὶ
ἀμφιβατῆρες.
οἱ περὶ κλεινοὺς
οἰηκοφόρους,
οὓς ἀγγελικὰ
προχέει σειρά.
(*ibid.*, 280–290, on
the "Angelic Chain")

Considering the language and imagery of this passage, there seem to be three possible ways to understand Synesius' religious activities in this context: he was celebrating pagan rites in secret (i.e., hidden) pagan temples; he was celebrating pagan rites in Christian churches, which might have once been pagan temples, by ignoring the fact that they had become Christian; he decided in a syncretistic spirit to accept churches along with temples as symbolic dwelling places of divinity. The mention of mysteries, the references to divine ministers (i.e., pagan gods), and the use of terms such as *neoi* all strongly suggest pagan religiosity. In addition, other parts of the poem allude to different orders of divine beings with different cosmic functions, suspended from the "angelic chain" of emanation (e.g., 1.280–290). But though this prayer is couched in pagan terms, might it not still be given a Christian interpretation? The "sacred mysteries" might be applied to Christian as well as to pagan rites; the local Thracian and Chalcedonian gods might be understood as Christian angels. As has been seen, angels had a definite place in the scheme of Neoplatonic-Chaldaean emanation. These angels were thought of as divinities in paganism,[17] but the Hellenes considered almost everything immortal *theos*, even the purified human soul. Then again, it is not likely that he understood the angels as creatures rather than as limited aspects of the Absolute. Synesius, it seems to me, had a universalist attitude in religion not unlike that of Proclus "from whom shone in no irregular or uncertain rays, Orpheus, Pythagoras, Plato, Aristotle, Zeno, Plotinus, Porphyry and Iamblichus, who so comprehended all religions in his mind and paid them such equal reverence, that he was, as it were, the priest of the whole universe."[18] Synesius was also able to accept Christianity in this spirit, whereas most of his pagan counterparts viewed Christianity as one of the very few unacceptable religions. Even Judaism had a place in the scheme of things because it was the eternally ordained national religion of the Jews. It was the (specifically limited) form of Jewish worship and national character, i.e., that mixture of specific qualities which sets Judaism apart from other traditions. Strictly speaking, the Jewish religion partook of a lower and limited aspect of *nous*.

Christianity, on the other hand, was viewed as a kind of anti-religion, the negation of all true religion and a threat to the established world order, in which all religions and peoples received their special character by means of a Platonic "preestablished harmony."[19] Synesius was al-

17. For a collection of many passages from Patristic authors on the pagan divinities, which they considered to be evil demons, see MacMullen, *GRBS* 9.93 n. 42.

18. Fitzgerald, *Letters* 1.33 (quoting Victor Cousin).

19. See *Against the Galileans, passim,* for Julian's views on Judaism and Christianity.

ready beginning to realize that the world was becoming Christian: all that
was good in paganism must now be absorbed into the Church. Christianity might indeed be the negation of all religion, but only in the sense
that it would incorporate in its own way all religion. It must be remembered, however, that Synesius did not alter or transform his basic world
view. Christianity provided a new type of religious society and organiza-
tion along with new religious symbols; but these symbols were not, so far
as Synesius was concerned, an expression of a metaphysical-theological
reality different from that perceived by philosophical pagans of the period. Therefore, it seems most likely that Synesius had decided, in a syncretistic spirit, to accept churches, along with temples, as symbolic dwelling places of divinity.

   On Providence or the *Egyptian Tale* was completed either during
his stay in Constantinople or in 402 soon after he left the city. It is widely
believed to be a thinly disguised allegory of political events that took
place during his stay in the capital.[20] Among the more important events
alluded to are the responsibility of the new Praetorian Prefect (Aurelian's
brother Caesarius) for the repeal of the laws against the Arians, the giving
of a temple to the Arians for their worship (1257A–B), Synesius' exemp-
tion from curial responsibility as a result of his service (1468D; *Ep.* 100),
and the ultimate success of the orthodox Christian clique.[21] On another
level *On Providence* is a work in which Synesius puts forth his theory of
the working of divine providence in history. Man lives in a world peopled
by demons who are associated with dark matter. Their sole purpose is to
drag him down with them or destroy him if he resists. Thus the plots and
counterplots of history are often merely manipulations of these demons.
The highest gods are immersed in contemplation of the most sublime realities and have no (direct) regard for the affairs of men. Only to the lower
deities is allotted the task of coming down to earth and aiding mankind,
but these deities desire contemplation also, and take up the burden of
their task with reluctance. The gods give man a certain impetus when
placing him in this world; this force, however, runs down and has to be
renewed by periodic divine intervention.[22] Meanwhile, man is constantly

   20. For a review of the evidence cf. Fitzgerald, *Essays and Hymns* 25ff and Lacombrade, *Synésios*, 102ff and 104 n. 15.
   21. For the demand of the temple for the Arians and its final rejection by St. John
Chrysostom (whom Synesius might have admired), see *Epp.* 66 and 67, 1432B; cf. Socrates, *HE* 5.1 and 6. For the daily life, friendships, and court intrigues of Synesius, see *Ad
Paeonium*; *Epp.* 61, 124, 142 (1536A–D), 31, 34, 38, 130, 75, 47, 49, 99, 26, 73, 91, 112,
118, 123, 22, 43, 46, 79, 101, 74, 152, 61, 129, 100, 131, 102, 150, 153, 108, and 134. Theophilus observed Synesius' success during this period: *Epp.* 71, 151, and 48.
   22. *De Prov.* 1229A.

threatened by the demons of the lower world and must do everything in his power to fight them.

The doctrine on souls that Synesius outlines in *On Providence* also contains a strongly dualistic note:

> The kinships of souls and of bodies are not the same; for it is not fitting for souls to be born on earth from the same two parents, but to flow from a single source. And the natural process of the cosmos furnishes two types: the luminous and the indistinct. The latter gushes up from the ground, since it has its roots somewhere below, and leaps out of the earth's cavities, if somehow it compels the divine law by force. But the former is suspended from the back of the heavens.[23]

This conception of souls having their ultimate sources in different places, both higher and lower, seems to imply an absolute dualism of good and evil, which is not typical of Neoplatonism. Are we then dealing with gnostic elements in the thought of Synesius? If we take the doctrine at its face value, Synesius seems to admit a rationally irreconcilable dualism as an integral part of his thought. This dualism seems to be based on a feeling of cosmic alienation found among some philosophers and religious thinkers of the later Roman period. However, it must be remembered that those who called themselves Hellenes in this period were less susceptible to the temptations of devaluation of the material cosmos and flight from the world than many other religious groups: for instance, Plotinus is now generally believed to be the champion of Hellenic "rationalism" against the rising tide of gnostic anti-cosmic speculation. Nor can gnostic attitudes to the world be postulated of the population of the Empire at large, who never gave up their worldly concerns. Has Synesius, then, wandered from the ideals of Hellenism? We shall be better prepared to answer this after we complete our analysis of *On Providence*.

In reminding Osiris that the gods are too busy with their own contemplation to spend much time on earth, and only come periodically to renew its energy supply, his father tells him:

> Try to ascend yourself, but do not cause the gods to descend, employ every form of prudence on your own behalf, as if you lived in an army camp in enemy territory, a divine soul among demons, who, being

23. *De Prov.* 1212B–C (89B–C, Terzaghi ed.): ἔστι δὲ οὐ μία ψυχῶν καὶ σωμάτων συγγένεια· οὐ γὰρ τὸ τοῖν αὐτοῖν ἐπὶ γῆς ἐκφῦναι γονέοιν τοῦτο προσήκει ψυχαῖς, ἀλλὰ τὸ ἐκ μιᾶς ῥυῆναι πηγῆς. δύο δὲ ἡ τοῦ κόσμου φύσις παρέχεται, τὴν μὲν φωτοειδῆ, τὴν δὲ ἀειδῆ· καὶ τὴν μὲν χαμόθεν ἀναβλύζουσαν, ἅτε ἐρριζωμένην κάτω ποι, καὶ τῶν [τῆς] γῆς χηραμῶν ἐξαλλομένην, εἴ πῃ τὸν θεῖον νόμον βιάσαιτο· ἡ δὲ τῶν οὐρανοῦ νώτων ἐξῆπται· The idea here is that although the natural brothers Osiris and Typho have bodies from the same earthly parents, their souls have entirely different cosmic origins; cf. Plato, *Phaedrus* 247C.

earth-born, it is reasonable to suppose will attack you, since they become angry if anyone maintains foreign laws and customs within their borders.[24]

But it is precisely the Gnostics who are always stressing the fact that man is not at home in this world, that he is in alien territory and must always be on guard.[25] They adhered to a cosmic-plot theory of the universe, in which all creation is a vast conspiracy to enchain the human spirit and keep man from escaping to his true home beyond the stars. Similarities can be found between the thought of Synesius and the Gnostics, but there are also differences. Synesius does not condemn, but rather affirms, the cosmos in a spirit which ultimately—at least ideally—overrides the problems arising out of moral, spiritual, and cosmic dualism.[26] The warning of Osiris' father is not a condemnation of the entire cosmos, but a warning to be on guard in a world in which it is easy to fall away from the good. The world is not to be literally thought of as an enemy country: yet one must be morally prepared to live as if in hostile territory in order to maintain the soul's purity and connection with the higher realities, rather than allow it to sink to the level of the lower elements.

In addition, a doctrine of two world souls can be traced to Middle Platonism. It is prominent in Plutarch's work *On Isis and Osiris*, one of the sources of *On Providence*. Numenius thought that evil was present in the celestial spheres. The Chaldaean Oracles, first formulated in the Middle Platonic period (A.D. 170–180), seem to contain Zoroastrian influences, as Lewy and others have maintained. This particular doctrine

---

24. *De Prov.*, 1229B (Ch. X, 99C Terzaghi ed.): πειρᾶσθαι δὲ σαυτὸν ἀνάγειν, ἀλλὰ μὴ τοὺς θεοὺς κατάγειν ἔχειν τε προμήθειαν ἑαυτοῦ τὴν πᾶσαν, ὥσπερ ἐν στρατοπέδῳ ζῶντα ἐπ'ἀλλοτρίας, ψυχὴν θείαν ἐν δαίμοσιν, οὓς εὔλογον γηγενεῖς ὄντας ἐπιτίθεσθαι καὶ ἀγανακτεῖν, ἤν τις ἐν τοῖς αὐτῶν ὅροις νόμους ἀλλοφύλους τηρῇ. See Smith, *Porphyry's Place* 132, comparing Porphyry's higher man who escapes rebirth but becomes a special emissary of the gods to Synesius' Osiris in *De Prov*. This proficient is sent down to the world—others fall; cf. also pp. 32, 36, and 63 for comparisons of Porphyry and Synesius' ideas of ascent and descent in the *De Ins.*, the *De Prov.*, and *Hymn* I, 573ff, where soul is sent down by a god as a servant; for Porphyry as a source for such ideas in the *De Ins.*, cf. Lang, *Traumbuch* 65–66.

25. See Jonas, 42–46.

26. Nicolosi, 127, says: "Ma offrioro tuttavia, in Sinesio una visione otti mistica del 'cosmos', in cui il dualismo morale dell'uomo, il dualismo politico dello State, il dualismo dell'universo tendono a comporsi in un' armonia nella quale i contrastanti elementi cooperano l'uno con l'altro, in attesa del trionfo definitivo del bene."

A tension between the dualism and "otherworldliness" of the *Phaedo* and *Phaedrus* and the optimism and cosmic affirmation of the *Timaeus* is common in Platonism. Many believe that Plotinus moved from a doctrine that was dangerously close to a Manichaean dualism in his early years to a position of cosmic affirmation later in his life. Thus the enthusiastic style of *Enn.* II.9. This tension is not easy to resolve and is always possible in Platonism.

seems to have been extracted from Plato, *Laws* 10, 896E, which was interpreted in terms of a conflict between a good world soul and an evil one. Indeed, many scholars believe that Plato himself was influenced by Zoroastrianism and even had Zoroastrian students.[27] At any rate, much of what Synesius says can be found within the traditions of later Greek philosophy. We need not look for direct influences of doctrines such as Valentinian Gnosis on the thought of Synesius. It is interesting to note that Synesius, shortly after introducing the idea of a dual origin for souls, quotes not from a gnostic source but from a poem of Empedocles which is "Orphic" in inspiration,[28] further evidence that, as usual, we need not depart from the Greek tradition in our search for the sources of his thought.[29] But this doctrine does represent a gnosticizing tendency in the Platonic tradition itself. That tradition certainly had a dualistic element, which was at times more and at others less pronounced. The point is that in the context of Platonism, this dualism can become transformed and relativized: the language of such passages must be read with an understanding of its context and interpreted accordingly. Even if Synesius does display a strong dualistic tendency here, which he has not attempted to completely resolve according to Plotinian-Porphyrian Neoplatonism—that is by viewing evil as a *privatio boni* rather than as a separate and autonomous principle, as did Augustine when he read the books of the Platonists and

27. For doctrine of two world souls see Dillon, 202–204; cf. Anastos, *DOP* 4.283: "Even many modern authorities are convinced that there was contact between Zoroastrianism and Plato, and that Plato introduced Zoroastrian dualism into the *Laws* in the form of the conflict between the good world-soul and the evil world-soul." Anastos, *ibid.* n. 500, cites "*Laws* 10 896E; cf. Plutarch, *De Iside et Osiride*, 48 (370F); J. Bidez, *Eos ou Platon et l'Orient* (Brussels, 1945) *passim*; Werner Jaeger, *Aristotle*, fundamentals of the history of his development (Oxford, 1934), 132f." (The Myth of Er in the *Republic* is also considered to be of Iranian origin.) Cf. also Wallis, *Neoplatonism* 35. Dillon says that "the dualism of Plutarch comes out in the description of the Ideas being 'seized by the element of disorder and confusion which comes down from the region above'. This seems to imply not just the rather negative unruly principle of the *Timaeus*, but a positive force, a maleficent soul, which has at some stage itself broken away from the intelligible realm. We seem thus to be brought close to Gnostic beliefs, but Plutarch can claim the authority of Plato on this matter, as indeed he does later in the essay (370E)." Dillon further says that "in Plutarch's metaphysics, in place of the more traditional Platonic triad of principles—God, Matter, and the Ideas or the Logos—we seem to have as many as five entities: a pair of opposites, God (monadic intellect) and an evil principle (indefinite dyad), represented for Plutarch by the Persian pair Ahuramazda and Ahriman (*De Ins.* 369E), as well as the Soul of Osiris and Seth-Typhon, then the immanent Logos, represented by the body of Osiris, and the World Soul-cum-Matter, Isis; and finally, their offspring, the sensible cosmos, Horus."

28. Empedocles, Fr. 121 *DK* ἔνθα φθόνος τε, κότος τε καὶ ἄλλων, ἔθνεα κηρῶν / Ἄτης ἐν λειμῶνι κατὰ σκότον ἠλάσκουσιν.

29. See Nicolosi, 81–104, who finds passages of *De Providentia* paralleling Homer, Hesiod, Pindar, Herodotus, Aratus, Plutarch, Plato, Aristotle, Iamblichus and Porphyry—in short, only Greek sources.

overcame Manichaean dualism—he remains squarely in the Platonic tradition.[30]

On Providence also acquaints us with certain ideas held by Synesius necessary to an understanding of his relationship to both Greek philosophy and Christianity. He held that the universe was interconnected by a central unifying force, which operated through a network of hidden sympathies. These sympathies connected things apparently without connection much as radio waves connect the listener with their point of origin. This theory, put forth by the Stoics and also found in the Timaeus of Plato,[31] goes back to the mythic roots of early Greek philosophy. It is usually referred to in Greek as the sympatheia ton holon. With this doctrine in mind, Synesius, following the Timaeus, one of the favorite dialogues of the Neoplatonists, proceeds to discuss the actual workings of the cosmos:

> Let us consider the cosmos to be one whole plenum complete with parts; we shall then conceive of it as confluent and conspirant; for in this way it could preserve its unity, and we shall also affirm that its parts have "sympathies" toward one another. Proceeding to the problem with this hypothesis, we may, according to reason, posit as the cause of things happening about our own sphere the blessed body (i.e., of the cosmos) moving in a circle. . . . Indeed, if anyone should propose with astronomy leading the way, the belief that the orbits of the stars and spheres are recurrent . . . such a man would recognize that, when the same motions returned, effects on earth would be the same as those of the distant past, as well as births, upbringings, opinions and fortunes. We should not be amazed, then, if we see very ancient history come to life now. . . .[32]

30. Nicolosi, 124, believes that Synesius' language, if understood in mythical terms—as he thinks it should be—does not imply Manichaean dualism: "Ma una simile concezione e quanto mai lontana dalla lettera e dallo spirito della filosofia sinesiana. La difficolta sta proprio nella stressa formulazione della dottrina, che nella teoria delle due fonti lia una espressione mitica e non filosofica, che deve essere 'tradotta' e inquadrata nella coerenza con le altre dottrine del sistema." See also 125: "Sinesio riprende l'immagine plutarchiana delle due fonti e quella omerica delle due giare, per tentare una soluzione del problema del male. Nonostante certe forzature di espressione, comprensibili dato il carattere allegorico e politico del'opuscolo, un dualismo radicale, di tipo gnostico o manicheo, sembra lontano dal pensiero sinesiano, ma c'e la concezione, di sapore dualistico, che la materia e l'elemento cattivo, che con la sua irrazionalistica resiste all'azione benefica degli dei, cosi come aveva dello Platone nel mito del Demiurgo, e dopo di lui, nelle forme piu varie avevano ripetuto tanti filosofi del periodo ellenistico."

31. 39E–43E.

32. De Prov., 11.7, 127B–128A (Terzaghi ed.): τὸν κόσμον ἓν ὅλον ἡγώμεθα τοῖς μέρεσι συμπληρούμενον· σύρρουν τε οὖν καὶ σύμπνουν αὐτὸν οἰησόμεθα· τὸ γὰρ ἓν οὕτως ἂν σῴζοι, καὶ οὐκ ἀσυμπαθῆ πρὸς ἄλληλα τὰ μέρη θησόμεθα. πῶς γὰρ ἂν ἓν ὦσιν, εἰ μή τοι . . . πείσεται . . . μετὰ τῆσδε τῆς ὑποθέσεως ἐπὶ τὸ σκέμμα βαδίζοντες, κατὰ λόγον ἂν αἰτιασόμεθα τῶν περὶ τὰ τῆσδε τὸ μακάριον σῶμα τὸ κύκλῳ κινούμενον. . . . εἰ δή τις τοῦτο προσβάλοι χορηγούσης ἀστρονομίας, τὰς πίστεις ἀποκαταστατικὰς

This theory of cyclical time and the eternal recurrence of events, in general patterns if not in exactly repeated individual occurrences, is characteristically Hellenic. Time in Judaeo-Christian thought is linear—it runs in a straight line which is divided, and given meaning, by a central unique historical event, the Crucifixion and Resurrection of Jesus Christ. Of course, in this period, when dogma was not yet firmly fixed, some Christians accepted the idea of recurrent time patterns (Origen was later accused of this). This doctrine was eventually condemned, but the idea behind it—the idea of the harmony of the cosmos—was to have a long future in the history of Christian thought. At any rate, Synesius, even with the Hellenic outlook he expresses in *On Providence*, seems to leave a certain amount of room for accommodation with Christianity.

The room he left for accommodation may be defined through analysis of two levels of ideas expressed in *On Providence*. If the work is a political allegory of contemporary events at Constantinople, the idea of divine providence itself must somehow include Christianity; i.e., if it is a theological tract describing the workings of the divine power in human affairs on one level, and an allegorical tract on contemporary history on another, then it must be taken on the latter level as a description of the workings of divine providence *in a particular case*. And that case involves Christianity; thus Synesius makes room for Christianity in a work that puts forth an essentially Hellenic world view.

Synesius' idea of the cosmos allows for the divine energy of the sublunary world to run down and require periodic renewal. This is accomplished when the gods in charge of the lower regions of the cosmos, perforce, leaving aside for the moment the bliss of contemplating pure Being, come down to earth and renew its supply of divine energy for another aeon. In this matter Synesius is still pagan in outlook. It is true that certain pagan thinkers held more rigid conceptions of providence, but the sublunary world and its relationship with the divine—especially divine providence—was still an open issue of debate among the Hellenes.[33] Besides, it can be reconciled with Plato's myth of divine governance in the *Politicus*, with its cycles of alternating ages in which the world is and then is not under the direct guidance of the divine hand.[34] However, Synesius

---

εἶναι περιόδοις ἀστέρων τε καὶ σφαιρῶν, . . . ὁ τοιοῦτος οὖν οὐκ ἂν ἀπογνοίη τῶν αὐτῶν κινημάτων ἐπανιόντων συνεπανίεναι τὰ αἰτιατὰ τοῖς αἰτίοις, καὶ βίους ἐν γῇ τοὺς αὐτοὺς εἶναι τοῖς πάλαι, καὶ γενέσεις καὶ τροφὰς καὶ γνώμας καὶ τύχας' οὐκ ἂν οὖν θαυμάζοιμεν, εἰ παμπάλαιον ἱστορίαν ἔμβιον τεθεάμεθα, . . .

33. For discussion of the different opinions of the Neoplatonists and their predecessors concerning providence see Wallis, *Neoplatonism*, 25, 28, 31, 70, 142, 148–50, 154.

34. 269B–275A.

goes a step further: he allows the intervention of the divine before the preordained time if the preestablished harmony of things here below is destroyed by evil men and forces before that time.[35] If one is not philosophically rigid, it is even possible to reconcile this doctrine with Neopythagorean or other types of Hellenistic paganism that allow for periodic renewals of the cosmos. Intervention by the epiphanies of savior gods found an important place in later paganism. Significantly, this was the kind of Hellenistic religion from which syncretistic bridges to Christianity could be built.

Eunapius tells us that, in order to celebrate the liberation of the capital from the Goths, the city prefect of Constantinople did not have a traditional military fresco made, but a great hand represented as coming out of the clouds bearing the inscription, "The Hand of God Routing the Barbarians."[36] Synesius himself expresses awe at the miraculous nature of the victory over the Goths: "Without it [Divine Providence] the better army would not have gained the victory." The event demonstrated to unbelievers the direct action of the mysterious force of providence.[37] Synesius, if we are reading the allegory correctly, also seems willing to call orthodox Christianity "our religion": when he speaks of the Arian Goths he says that they wish "to revolutionize everything which pertains to our religion" (τὰ περὶ τὰς ἁγιστείας ἡμῶν καινοτομεῖν), and that they bring with their heresy "a sort of ill counterfeit of religion, a debasement of what is holy" (πονηρόν τι κόμμα θρησκεύματος καὶ παραχάραγμα ἁγιστείας).[38] That Synesius speaks of "our religion" is clear evidence that he moved closer to Christianity at this juncture. What interests us is the nature of his accommodation.

Another important aspect of Synesius' theory of divine revivification of the cosmos is its potential for bringing Synesius to a point at which he would at least accept a symbolic theory of the Incarnation; for if spontaneous divine epiphanies by a deity are possible in times of great need, and this savior figure comes to renew the world, one may identify him with Christ. We shall see that the *Hymns* of Synesius portray a Hellenistic Christ as one needed to come down and redeem a world that has become too closely identified with the negative forces of matter to extricate itself. Synesius would not be able to accept literally the Incarnation of Jesus Christ as a historically verified unique event; but given the outlines of Synesius' theory of providential action, any personification of Jesus

35. *De Prov.*, 1233C; cf. Plot. III.2.8 and 37.
36. Dindorf, *Eunapii fr.* 263–264.
37. *De Prov.* 1260B; cf. Lacombrade, *Synésios* 119.   38. *De Prov.* 1256C.

Christ as a Logos-descended divine force would set the stage for a compromise with the Christian camp.

Thus Synesius, in his work *On Providence*, gives Christianity a place in universal history (which is providentially ordered) and allows for a conception of divine intervention. In a work Platonic in its conception and sources, and "gnostic" in outlook, he was able to find room for building potential bridges to the religion of his Christian allies. Perhaps the identification of Christianity with the Greco-Roman national cause gave Synesius his first emotional impetus for doing so. But he was willing to continue his efforts long after the great crisis had passed and he had had ample time for reflection.

Synesius' temperament must also be taken into consideration in this respect. He was naturally tolerant of philosophical heterodoxies and was opposed to all fanaticism, whether of Jews, Christians, monks, or pagan philosophers. Generally he tried to adopt ideas on their own merit without regard to the creeds of the men who held them. His political experience probably helped him assess the nature of events like the destruction of the Serapeum and the victory of Theodosius: for those who had eyes to see, it was clear which religious direction the world was taking. Synesius sincerely believed that the best way to preserve Hellenism was to bring it into the Church.

In addition to his metaphysical and spiritual concerns, Synesius displays a Stoic ethical conception in *On Providence*. All social roles are equally good and can be used as vehicles for the expression of virtue. The lives we receive from the divinity, like those in a tragic drama, can be played equally well in purple robes or in rags—seen for example, in the famous pair, Marcus Aurelius, the emperor, and Epictetus, the ex-slave. In the great drama of the universe, it is better to play one's role well than complain about one's lot: the actor who plays an old woman well is lauded by the audience, while he who plays a king poorly is booed and hissed. In this sense, all roles are equal: the lives we are given should be put on and taken off as if they were garments.[39] This eloquent passage could have been written by Marcus Aurelius himself. It is, of course, further evidence of Synesius' Hellenic attitude of cosmic affirmation in contradistinction to gnostic depreciation of the cosmos. It is even more interesting, however, when taken in the context of his existence, as an indication of the spiritual conflict which Synesius felt throughout his life: that between the active life and the contemplative.

39. *De Prov.* 1241B–1244. Stoic ideas had long since been incorporated into Neoplatonism.

Perhaps the stoicizing passage just discussed represents a rationale for and reinforcement of the strong sense of duty to society that he must have felt as a member of the old nobility. Synesius was called upon to play at least two important roles of which he wanted no part, that of ambassador to Constantinople, and that of Bishop of Ptolemaïs. He complains bitterly of the years he lost at Constantinople,[40] and in several places his correspondence reveals his aversion to episcopal office. He goes so far as to say that he would "rather die many times over" than become a bishop.[41] Here undoubtedly is an element of *persona*-building: to exercise power really effectively in late antiquity, one had to pretend that one was profoundly unsuited for it. The *nolo episcopari* of Synesius conformed to the studied pretense of distaste for public office among the ruling classes of the empire.[42] *Otium* was preferable to the involvements of public office: Western senators would send each other letters of congratulation upon leaving public office.[43] But such affectation was combined with a deeply felt sense of respect for office and political responsibility.[44] In any case, senators had a sense of service (*angaria*) and realized that in or out of office they were great public figures, the benefactors and patrons of smaller communities.[45] At times the real desire for power became obvious. For example, Ammianus Marcellinus[46] tells us that the distinguished head of the noble *gens Anicii*, Petronius Probus, gasped after prefectures like a fish out of water. Christian bishops did not always affect this aristocratic posture with respect to the obligations of office: they often took their responsibilities quite seriously.[47] But Synesius, of course, was closer in spirit to his senatorial counterparts in the West. He had the old Greek sense of the *leitourgia*: service to the *polis* as a member of the *boule*, benefactor, ambassador, or magistrate. In line with his general strategy, he transferred this sense of obligation—and the responsibilities that went along with it—to the office of bishop. But his obligatory gentleman's protest over becoming a bishop must be distinguished from his real intellectual concern over differences of doctrine.

Even so, one still senses that part of Synesius wanted to solve the problems of philosophy while living in a leisurely manner that did not force him into a strong attachment to the world. His ideal was to pursue the life of a country gentleman, a life he knew well. And as worldly and venerable as this old aristocratic way of life seems to us, I believe it con-

40. *De Insomniis* 1309A.   41. *Epp.* 11, 57, and 95.   42. Matthews, 9.
43. *Ibid.* 10.   44. *Ibid.* 12 and 30.   45. *Ibid.* 26f.
46. *Ibid.* 11, quotes Amm. Marc. 27.2.3 on Petronius Probus: *ut natantium genus, elemento suo expulsum, haud ita diu spirat in terris, ita ille marcebat absque praefecturis.*
47. Cf. e.g., Brown, *Religion and Society*, 79, on St. Augustine and *licentiosa libertas.*

ceals a tendency toward a kind of escapism and a contradiction in the personality of Synesius that on another level are closely connected with that side of Neoplatonism given over to flight from the world and that must have appealed to Synesius in his most deeply felt moments of metaphysical pathos. For to him Cyrene represented an idyllic and archaic "Arcadian"[48] landscape, in which he could dwell in a combined golden classical age and Homeric age of heroes. The main evidence is contained in letter 148, addressed to Olympius, and written as late as the year 408, perhaps shortly before Synesius' own villa was ravaged by barbarian tribes from the desert and he had to flee from Cyrene to Ptolemaïs. This letter is filled with wonderful allusions and comparisons of the Cyrenaic countryside to an ideal Homeric landscape. Some passages also bring to mind the idealized pastoral life described by many ancient authors in works praising agriculture. Synesius describes his native place, far from the city, roads, commerce and complicated ways.

> For we have leisure to philosophize, but none to do evil. All our meetings are also social gatherings for everybody, since we depend on one another for farming, shepherds, flocks and game, all sorts of which the land provides. We have barley—groats for lunch—sweet to eat and drink—of the kind Hecamede mixed for Nestor.[49]

After boasting that his country, if not best in any one thing (such as the production of honey or olive oil), is never less than a close second, he goes on to speak of the rustic music of this area in terms of its natural nobility:

> The Anchemachetae play a simple homemade shepherd's lyre, which has both a pleasing and adequately masculine tone, suited for the rearing of children in Plato's city.[50]

But the most telling passage of all appears toward the end of the letter. In it Synesius portrays his home town as living at an almost incomprehensible distance from the contemporary world and the problems of a complex imperial society:

---

48. Brown, "The Philosopher and Society," 15: "The only two factors that might seem to pry the philosopher loose from that (social) role—his mystical experiences and the occasional yearning of a sophisticated man for the pristine clarity of an Arcadian existence—had no meaning except in reference to an enduring bedrock of traditional learning." For the love of the countryside as a reservoir of the old traditions, and linked to the call of a god, see *Inscriptions grecques et latines de la Syrie*, no. 1410 (reign of Constantine): Abedrapsas of Frikiya is led by his guardian god to buy an estate and be relieved of the necessity of going into town; cf. Festugière, "Proclus," 1589f. See Marinus, *Vita Procli* 15 for Proclus' "cult hunting" while on a visit to Asia Minor.

49. *Ep.* 148, 1545D.   50. *Ibid.* 1548D.

But the emperor, his *amici*, and the wheel of Fortune, which we hear
about at our gatherings, are just names that, like flames, have been
kindled up to the height of splendor and then quenched; for the most
part these matters are not spoken of here, and our ears have rest from
such reports. Certainly people have distinct knowledge of the fact
that there is always a living emperor, for we are reminded of this
every year by the imperial agents who collect taxes; but exactly who
he is is not clear. Indeed, there are certain men among us, even at
this late date, who think that Agamemnon, son of Atreus, is still in
power, the same noble hero who attacked Troy. For we have been
traditionally taught from childhood that this is the king's name. The
good herdsmen say that he has a certain *amicus* named Odysseus, a
bold man, but clever at handling practical affairs and finding his way
in difficult circumstances. And indeed, they laugh when they speak
of him, believing that he blinded the Cyclops last year. . . . Thanks to
this letter you have been with us in spirit for a short time; you have
observed our land; you have seen the simplicity of our institutions.
"Life at the time of Noah," you will exclaim, "before justice became
enslaved."[51]

Synesius' mention of the "time of Noah" is interesting here. It was a Jewish, then Christian, way of expressing the idea of a natural law, linked to a
natural innocence that is somewhat surprising to find in Synesius. The
"seven laws of Noah" were considered in Rabbinic tradition to be incum-
bent upon all of the gentiles. These laws derived exegetically from commandments addressed to Adam and Noah. Thus they were regarded as
universal: a kind of revealed natural law.[52] Christians considered Noah as a
symbol of the Just Man (2 Pet. 2:5). He was also the originator of vinicul-
ture (Gen. 9:20), and the recipient of the blessing that assured the stability of the natural order (Gen. 8:20–23, 9:9–16).[53] Perhaps this brief
literary aside is not unrelated to Synesius' Christianizing activities.

In any case, it is clear that although Synesius smiled at the rustic
and mythical mentality of his compatriots, he found their way of life
charming. He was able to feel as though he were a member of the old
Homeric nobility even though he knew differently. Obviously, I do not

51. *Ibid*. 1549A–C.
52. See *Encyclopedia Judaica* 1189–1194. These were regarded as natural laws as
early as the Talmudic period: at least five of seven laws would have been mandatory even
had they not been revealed. Maimonides thought that the "righteous gentiles" who have
a share in the world to come are those who obey these laws. But they must be accepted not
only on their own merit, but also as divinely revealed. It is interesting to note that the
Aufklärung rationalist Moses Mendelssohn and the Neo-Kantian idealist Hermann Cohen
emphasized the Noachide conception as the common rational, ethical ground of Israel and
mankind and Noah as the symbol of the perpetuity and unity of mankind.
53. *Encyclopedia and Dictionary of Religion* 2545: Noah was also a "type" of the
Christ in later Christian tradition; the dove from the Ark, of the Holy Spirit, etc.

suggest that Synesius was a mythomaniac who acted out his fantasies. I say merely that the part of him that felt at home in the classical and epic past was brought into contact with those past realities, insofar as that is possible in this world, through sensual images evoked by a rural life that preserved immemorial and archaic traditions, as well as through reading the classics and attempting to write in the Doric and Attic dialects. The unity and simplicity, the Arcadian tranquility free from the cares and woes of the chaotic political and social world of his time, were perhaps analogous in some sense to the metaphysical unity and simplicity that Synesius sought in contemplation of the noetic realm. Perhaps the forces that motivated Synesius, the country gentleman, were the same as those that motivated Synesius, the Neoplatonist. Flight from the world and retreat were tendencies of the age. Even Hellenes were not immune to them. Yet, as a rule, they maintained their spiritual balance with more grace than many other groups.

On the other hand, Synesius proved himself more than competent when action was required of him. Whether it was a question of pleading his city's cause or that of Aurelian and the anti-Gothic party during the crisis at Constantinople, Synesius was there; whether he had to lead the people of his home town against the barbarians, or as bishop of Ptolemaïs deal with the tyrannical governor Andronicus, or placate the warring factions of his volatile Christian flock, Synesius was there. We should avoid thinking in one-sided clichés about Neoplatonic immaterialism and otherworldliness. It must be remembered, for instance, that Plotinus, that well-known escapist, quite efficiently turned his home into a kind of orphanage. Indeed, Peter Brown has recently shown us the important and sensitive social role that philosophers played among the classically educated elites of a now fragile and changing empire.[54]

Given Synesius' tolerant and syncretistic outlook, we should not be surprised to see Christian elements becoming more prominent in his writing. This is certainly true of the period from 402, after he returned from Constantinople, to 409–410 when he entered the episcopate.

---

54. Porphyry, *Vit. Plot.* 9; Brown, "The Philosopher and Society," on the complexities and paradoxes of late antique thought. Philosophers may appear completely otherworldly, as did many in that era. But they also played an important *social* role. Brown's article has gone beyond the clichés about "immaterialism," etc.; in doing so he has given us a new perspective on an important social phenomenon; see especially p. 2 ". . . the philosopher was expected to concern himself with the affairs of his home town and even, if need be, with the world of the Imperial Court. . . . contemporaries did not see the inconsistency which modern scholars tend to assume between such activity and the supposedly 'otherworldly' nature of the teachings to which the philosophers are committed."

IV

The Middle Years:
The Trinity and the *Hymns*

It would be worth our while to look closely at the *Hymns* which, with those letters in which he makes explicit statements about Christianity or gives us important information concerning his spiritual state at the time he wrote them, are, in this respect, Synesius' most important works. All the *Hymns*, with the exception of I, were written in the period between 402 and 408,[1] a period in which Synesius' exact relationship to the Church is difficult to discern.

The order of the *Hymns* established by Lacombrade is as follows: I, A.D. 396–397; III, 402; II and IV, 407–408; VI and V, 408–409; VII, VIII, and IX, 408–409.[2] As we shall see, they demonstrate Synesius' progressive accommodation with Christianity and his creation of the role of "philosopher-bishop."

In his recent edition of the *Hymns*, Lacombrade has followed the traditional manuscript order in which *Hymn* III = I and *Hymn* I = IX.[3] He believes that in later life Synesius edited and numbered the *Hymns* in this revised order, although he had originally composed them in another order; e.g., *Hymn* IX (I) in the 390s. If so, this would lend support to our view of Synesius' religious evolution, for IX (I) is the work of a pure Neoplatonist. The "power of three summits" and the "first engendered Form" spoken of in IX (I) are Chaldaean conceptions. They need not refer to the Christian Trinity nor to the Logos, although it is possible to make these associations. But Synesius does use them in this specific Christian sense in his other *Hymns*. Thus, if he thought of IX (I) as both his first and his last statement, he must have been saying: "I am a Neoplatonic 'philosopher-bishop.'"

Hymn III was written in 402, shortly after Synesius returned from

---

1. Lacombrade, *Synésios* 170–198. See now also *Les Hymnes de Synésios*, ed. Lacombrade.

2. For a detailed discussion of the true order of the *Hymns*, see Lacombrade, *Synésios* 183–198.

3. *Les Hymnes*, ed. Lacombrade, 98ff.

Constantinople.[4] It is one of the few *Hymns* that can be dated with some certainty, since it sings of the pilgrimages that he made to the temples of Constantinople and Thrace (see above, pp. 64–65). In addition to the political experience that made him receptive to Christianity, as an intellectual and a mystic he attempted to reconcile the two doctrines whenever possible. Our analysis of *Hymn I* and *On Providence* has introduced us to his method. Let us now analyze the later *Hymns* to try to discern just how Synesius harmonized his Hellenism with some of the major theological doctrines of the Church.

Hymn III contains several passages that strongly suggest Synesius was attempting to reconcile the Christian doctrine of the Trinity to similar concepts in Neoplatonism. This tendency also appears in *Hymns IV, V, VI,* and *VII.*[5] But before discussing the doctrine of the Trinity found in the *Hymns,* a few remarks on the relationship of the Christian Trinity to the Neoplatonic trinity of the One, Nous and Soul might prove useful.[6] Comparison of these ideas is commonly made on the basis of Plotinus' hierarchical scheme of procession from higher to lower realities, which takes place through the three hypostases.[7] The One, perfect unity-in-itself needing nothing and source of all things, is analogous to the Father. Wallis writes that, "Since lower realities tend naturally to reproduce themselves, we cannot, Plotinus argues, suppose that the One, the most perfect of beings, would grudge others a share in its perfection (V.1.6.39ff, V.3.15.1–11)."[8]

Nous or the Intelligible world (*ho noetos kosmos*) contains all the eternal Forms of things, which it contemplates in a timeless vision subsumed under the unity of the One. This stage of Reality may be thought

---

4. *Ibid.* 188; Lacombrade thinks that *Hymn III* was written soon after *Hymn I* because of the almost word-for-word correspondence of certain poetic formulas: "Ἰ ἔνι μὰν, ἐνι τι φέγγος / κεκαλυμμέναισι γλήναις. de I (v. 100–101) fait pendant le ἔτι μὰν ἔνι μοι βαιόν, τι μένος / κρυφίας γλήνας de III (v. 576–580). L'exhortation de Ἰἄγε μοι ψυχὰ (v. 128) sert à l'*Hymne* suivant de prélude. Au δνοφερὰν ἤρυσε λάθαν de I répond, dans III, ἔπιεν λάθαν (I v. 96, III, v. 658, Terzaghi 660)."

5. I am here following the order of composition suggested by Lacombrade in *Synésios.* (In referring to the Terzaghi edition, however, I have given the *Hymn* number that reflects the true order of composition; I [in Terzaghi's text] = III; II = IV; III = V; IV = VI; V = II; VI = VII; VIII = IX; IX = I.)

6. This is not the place to discuss the general history of the doctrine of the Trinity and its relation to Greek philosophy; for a concise and up-to-date account, which draws on all the sources, see Pelikan, 1.172–225; for a special study on the relationship of Athanasius to Neoplatonism, see Meijerling, *passim.* For the Trinity and its relationship to the Greek philosophical tradition from Plato to Bessarion, see Anastos, *DOP* 4.290 and n. 543, and Wind, 241–255.

7. Cf. *Enn.* V.1.   8. *Neoplatonism* 61f.

of as the divine mind and equated with the Creator-Logos of Christian theology. Finally, in a further breakdown from unity to plurality Nous gives birth to Soul. Soul does not contemplate the Forms *totum simul* but moves from one object to another (Plot. V.I. 4.10–25) and thus time is brought into being.[9] One might say that Soul represents the "power" of the Forms to be actualized in time and space; it is the connecting link between Being and Becoming, as it were, and is sometimes considered analogous to the Holy Spirit:

Neoplatonic	*Christian*
Hen	Pater
Nous (noetos kosmos)	Huios, Logos
Psyche	Hagion Pneuma

Anyone who is familiar with orthodox Christian doctrine will immediately see discrepancies between the Neoplatonic and orthodox Christian Trinities. First of all, the Plotinian view of reality is hierarchical: *Nous* is subordinate to the One, as Soul is, in turn, subordinate to Nous; on the other hand, all the persons of the orthodox Christian Trinity are equal: distinct as Persons (*hypostases*) yet of the same substance (*ousia; homoousios*, etc.). In short, they are distinct but not separate entities. It would seem, then, that a Neoplatonist moving in the direction of Christianity would lean toward semi-Arianism or "Origenism," doctrines in which the Son is subordinate to the Father.[10] In fact, studies have been devoted to demonstrating just how serious Neoplatonists, who became orthodox Christians, altered Neoplatonic doctrines in order to harmonize them with those of their new religion.[11] Synesius' *Hymns*, however, reveal a conception of the Trinity closer to the orthodox doctrine than to Origenism or any other type of subordinationism. Given Synesius' strong pagan Neoplatonic background, how is this possible? *Hymn* III is still replete with pagan imagery (as are the other *Hymns*). Even the terminology employed to describe the Trinity is not typical of Christian usage of the period.[12] Yet the conception of the Trinity seems close to the orthodox and remains substantially the same throughout the *Hymns*. Why? In the celebrated *Ep*. 105, written on the eve of his episcopal appointment,

9. *Ibid.* 53.

10. Arianism, strictly speaking, was not a real possibility for Neoplatonists; for in that doctrine the Son is a creature, although in a sense divine and above all creatures: a kind of super-creature, "there was a time when he was not." But emanation is eternal, not temporal, therefore Nous is eternal, so that some kind of "Origenist semi-Arianism" is a more likely prospect. (E.g. *homoiousios*, i.e., eternal but of *similar*, not of the *same*, substance.)

11. A well-known example is Henry, *JTS* n.s.1.42–55. Henry believes that "Marius Victorinus had to become somewhat original in order to remain orthodox" (p. 55).

12. Cf. Lacombrade, *Synésios* 189.

Synesius clearly states his disagreement with Christian dogma when it clashes with Neoplatonic doctrines concerning the preexistence of the soul, the eternity of the cosmos, and the Resurrection. Why, then, is Synesius orthodox with respect to the doctrine of the Trinity if he was to hold reservations about Christian dogma for years to come, if not for his entire life? Why be so scrupulous about one dogma while being skeptical about others? Synesius was both too sincere in his attempt at reconciliation and too honest to gloss over differences of doctrine. One might expect Synesius to hold subordinationist views, but from a certain point of view it is possible to consider the Neoplatonic hypostases in a way that brings them closer to the orthodox conception of the Trinity.[13] J. N. Findlay has suggested that the view of the hypostases as reified entities, too often reinforced by the Neoplatonists themselves, can become too rigid and scholastic. In the spirit of "mystical logic" the hypostases can be viewed as three aspects of the same reality: the One is unity; Nous is the specification of unity (i.e., Form [as the Son is the first manifestation of the Father]); Soul is merely the "power" of Form to be instantiated in time and space. On another level, it is also the "power" of the One to be both specified and have its specifications instantiated.[14] From this perspective, the hypostases have been conflated with the One: "The essence of the One, indeed, is not distinct from its power and its power contains undivided the totality of intelligible essences which are indivisibly divided while being reflected in the sensible and intellectual world."[15] Is this way of understanding Neoplatonism—especially the system of Plotinus—merely the whim of modern metaphysicians with monistic leanings, or is it in fact something that was rooted in the historical practice of the Neoplatonists themselves? The work of several important mod-

13. Marius Victorinus, whose conception of the Trinity appears to be similar, was converted to Christianity without reservations—at least after he announced his conversion; therefore, it is possible to explain his embrace of the orthodox version of the Trinity in terms of his conversion. For the story of Marius' conversion, see St. Augustine, *Conf.* VIII.2.3–3.5 (156–158); for similarity to Synesius, cf. Hadot, *Porphyre et Victorinus* 461–474; Ladner, 81–82 n. 76.

14. See Findlay, *Rel. Stud.* 2.157 and "Toward a Neo-Neoplatonism" in *Ascent*. Findlay applies his logic of mysticism to Plotinus' philosophy.

15. *Les Hymnes de Synésios*, ed. Meunier, 173 n. 11; cf. Wallis, *Neoplatonism* 69: "The World-Soul, possessing as she does the task of administering her own particular body, is herself an individual soul (albeit the most powerful of all); in fact, both she and the other individual souls are manifestations of Universal Soul—the Unparticipated Soul of later Neoplatonism (*Enn.* IV.3.2.1–10, 54–59, 4, 14–21; and p. 126ff). Now what is Universal Soul if not that Power of Being to give Life to beings—the Form of Soulness as it were—without extension (or only with potential for extension). For this reason Porphyry telescoped Soul into the Intelligible order and therefore he was confident that she could deliver herself unaided through moral virtue and philosophical contemplation."

ern scholars has demonstrated the latter to be the case. Furthermore, we shall see that it was probably the anti-Christian Porphyry, or one of his followers, who viewed the hypostases in this way.

Porphyry, following Plotinus, suggested the horizontal trinity *on* (Being)-*zoe* (Life)-*nous* (Intelligence) as ontologically comprising the Intelligence.[16] If he is the same man as the anonymous commentator on the *Parmenides* he also went beyond Plotinus in suggesting that the stage of Intelligence itself may be another way of viewing the One.[17] For the anonymous commentator identifies the moment of the Triad's Existence (*hyparxis*) with the One.[18] Thus some confusion arises as to the nature of the One: Plotinus saw it as beyond Being (*ousia*). But from Porphyry on, the term *hyparxis* (existence) is often used for what is beyond *ousia*. Thus a Porphyrian view could also equate the One with Absolute Being.[19] Furthermore, the anonymous commentator places Nous within the One, as the One is immanent in Nous.[20] Life or Power is the mediating principle between the two. If this is understood as a real ontological description, the Power (*dynamis*) can also be hypostasized—exactly as Synesius did. Thus, in a sense, he arrived at the idea of One Being with three distinct hypostases.

This is already implied in the procession of Nous from the One. In traditional Platonic terms, the "power" of the One is here really nothing more than the indefinite dyad, the One's "spiritual matter" (*noetike hyle*).[21] The One remains the One (*mone*). It proceeds "downwards" through "spiritual matter" (*proodos*). The end of the procession is a "looking back" to the One; a "reversion" or "conversion" (*epistrophe*). This last stage unifies and "solidifies" Nous which then becomes hypostasized. Nous in turn goes through this three-stage process with respect to Soul, and so on. Synesius merely compresses the entire procession of Nous back into the One, which, in any case, already implies it. He then hypo-

---

16. See Wallis, *Neoplatonism* 116f; Smith, *Porphyry's Place* 5; and n. 22 below.
17. Smith, *Porphyry's Place* xii, doubts whether Hadot's ascription of the anonymous commentary to Porphyry can be absolutely proven. But, in any case, this type of thinking is characteristic of Synesius. On the equation of Intelligence and the One, see Wallis, *Neoplatonism* 117.
18. Wallis, *Neoplatonism* 116.
19. *Ibid.* 116.
20. Smith, *Porphyry's Place* 16.
21. *Ibid.* 16, n. 27 points out that an Ennead is actually implied here:

hyparxis	dynamis	nous	(The One)
hyparxis	*dynamis* (dyad)	nous	
hyparxis	dynamis	*nous*	(Nous)

Synesius both "compressed" and hypostasized all the moments.

stasizes the three moments of the One into the trinity, *hyparxis-dynamis-nous*.

A. C. Lloyd, who speaks of a "monistic tendency" in Porphyry, has called this intellectual process "telescoping" the hypostases:

> Plotinus was dogmatic that there were neither more nor less than three hypostases above matter (whose reality was illusory); and this dogmatism has little meaning unless those hypostases are stages of existence which exist in their own right even though they are not, except for the highest, independent; they must not be mere appearances of the One. But the *opposite* is also suggested, for he seems often to care little whether it is Intellect or Soul which he is talking about. This, as it were, telescoping of the hypostases is prominent in Porphyry.[22]

Thus the monism of Porphyry, which makes it possible to see the hypostases as aspects of one reality, also makes it possible to bring Neoplatonism closer to Christianity: for, if the hypostases now may be viewed as equal to rather than subordinate to the One, little more than name separates them philosophically from the persons of the Trinity. Therefore, one need not be an orthodox Christian to accept such a version of the Trinity. It was perfectly possible for Synesius to see in Porphyrian Neoplatonism, of which he was a student, a potential bridge to the Trinity, while at the same time still refusing to accept those doctrines with which he could not harmonize his philosophy.

The Chaldaean Oracles, as interpreted in the Porphyrian tradition, were also used extensively by Synesius to bridge the gap between the two religions.[23] Especially interesting is their similar description of the "Father" as a trinity-in-unity, including the Father's existence (*hyparxis*), His power (*dynamis*) and His intelligence (*nous*).[24] "For Christian Neoplato-

22. Lloyd, 287f; for full discussion, see 287–293 and Wallis, *Neoplatonism* 110ff. The anonymous fragments on the *Parmenides* (by Porphyry or a Porphyrian) go well beyond Plotinus in telescoping the Intelligence with the One. For a critical view of Lloyd, see Smith, *Porphyry's Place* 47.

23. Cf. Theiler, *Orakel, passim*; Wallis, *Neoplatonism* 100–110; Hadot, *Porphyre et Victorinus* 461–474.

24. As Theiler, *Orakel* 9 puts it, opposing the vertical (*senkrechten*) emanation to the horizontal (*wagerechten*) "row" of emanation: "Das Synesios sich der einfachen wagerechten Reihe des Chaldaisierenden Porphyrios anschliessen muste wenn er Chaldaisches und Christliches in philosophischer Symphonie zusammenschloss. . . ." Theiler schematizes the emanations of the hypostases in this way:

	Father	Holy Spirit	Son
οὐσία of God	Πατήρ	Δύναμις	Νοῦς (πατρικός)
NOHTON	ἓν ὄν	ζωή or Ἀιων	αὐτοζῷον
NOHTON KAI NOEPON	ὑπουράνιος τόπος	οὐρανός	ὑπουράνιος ἄψις
NOEPON	Κρόνος	Ῥέα	Ζεύς

nists, such as Synesius, or the Latin theologian Marius Victorinus, such a trinity was of course far more attractive than Plotinus' hierarchically subordinated three Hypostases."[25] Let us now attempt to analyze some trinitarian passages in the *Hymns* themselves to see if our thesis holds up.

Hymns III and IV describe the mystical and ineffable generation of the Son, Who is the world-creating wisdom of the Father:[26]

III 1.202–206:

For you have been poured out,	Σὺ γὰρ ἐξεχύθης,
ineffable parent	ἀρρητότοκε,
in order to beget a child,	ἵνα παῖδα τέκῃς
your renowned world-creating wisdom.	κλεινὰν σοφίαν
	δημιοεργόν

IV 1.106–116:

For, in order that	ἵνα γὰρ προχυθῇ
the father be poured out	ἐπὶ παιδὶ πατήρ,
upon the son	αὐτὰ πρόχυσις
the pouring-out itself	εὕρετο βλάσταν
has been actualized	ἔστη δὲ μέσα,
and holds the median	θεὸς ἔκ τε θεοῦ
God from God	διὰ παῖδα θεόν·
because of God the Son;	καὶ διὰ κλεινάν
and because of the	πατρὸς ἀθανάτου
famous pouring-out	πρόχυσιν πάλι παῖς
of the immortal Father	εὕρετο βλάσταν.
the Son, in turn, has	
been actualized.	

Even after the pouring forth of the Father, the unity of the Godhead is maintained:

III 1.207–209:

Although you have been poured forth	προχυθεὶς δὲ μένεις
you remain in yourself	ἀτόμοισι τομαῖς
giving birth through	μαιευόμενος.[27]
indivisible divisions	

And this unity is a unity-in-trinity:

Theiler, *ibid.* 8–9, also points out that in Proclus, *In Crat.* 265.28 "Rhea ist μήτηρ τοῦ δημιουργοῦ" and in Marius Victorinus *Adv. Ar.* 1084C *sanctum spiritum matrem esse Jesu*; cf. Lewy, 193 n. 144.

25. Wallis, *Neoplatonism* 106.

26. Cf. *Hymn* VI, 1.6–7ff: ὃν βουλάς πατρικᾶς ἄφραστος ὠδὶς / ἀγνώστων ἀνέδειξε παῖδα κόλπων, κτλ., where the Father's will (i.e., Holy Spirit) is the medium for the generation of the Son. The phrase ἄφραστος ὠδὶς refers to the *ineffable* birth pangs of the

III 1.210–213:

I sing to you monad	ὑμνῶ σε, μονάς·
I sing to you triad	ὑμνῶ σε, τριάς
You are monad, while being a triad	μονὰς εἶ, τριὰς ὤν,
You are triad, while being a monad	τριὰς εἶ, μονὰς ὤν

IV 1.117–119:

You are monad, while being a triad	μονὰς εἶ τριὰς ὤν,
A monad which remains a monad	μονὰς ἅ γε μένει,
and yet a triad	καὶ τριὰς εἶ δή.[28]

We are immediately reminded here not only of the Christian Trinity, but also of the triads in the Chaldaean Oracles, "Orphic" and Pythagorean writings.[29] Damascius, the last head of the school of Athens, who was critical of those who would "telescope" the hypostases to such an extreme degree—he and the other late pagan Neoplatonists surely saw the potential of this doctrine to achieve a reconciliation with Christianity—credits Porphyry with doctrines similar to the above: "following Porphyry we will call the single principle of all things the Father of the Intelligible triad" (κατὰ τὸν Πορφύριον ἐροῦμεν τὴν μίαν τῶν πάντων ἀρχὴν εἶναι τὸν πατέρα τῆς νοητῆς τριάδος·); but the Oracles also say: "a triad which a monad rules, shines in every order" (πάντι γὰρ ἐν κόσμῳ λάμπει τριὰς, ἧς μονὰς ἄρχει).[30] The main theoretical issue was whether the Father (monad) was to be conflated with the triad over which he rules or remain completely transcendent. In short, we have here a pagan quaternity that maintains a monad presiding over a triad, as opposed to the Christian Trinity.[31] This critique implies that pagan Neoplatonists were combating

Spirit. Cf. also Hadot, *Porphyre et Victorinus*, 467. *Hymnes de Synésios*, ed. Meunier, 171 n. 1, observes that "cette première forme qui se manifeste, est le Fils, le premier né du Père autrement dit l'Intelligence qui organise et dirige le monde . . ." (Cf. also *Hymn* III, 1.152, προανούσιε νοῦ, i.e. mind before substance, or the mind of the One, the preexistent *Logos*). Cf. Proclus, *In Parm*. IV.115.

27. Cf. also *Hymn* III, 1.200–222 (esp. 1.214–216); *Hymn* IV, 1.120ff.

28. Cf. also *Hymn* II, 1.25ff: μία παγά / μία ρίζα / τριφαὴς ἔλαμψε μορφά.

29. Cf. *Hymni*, ed. Terzaghi, 179 n. 117: "Sententiam fortasse non tam Christianam quam orphicam secutus est Synesius: Cf. e.g. *Orph*. fr. 194, Procl., *In Crat*., p. 96, 15 Pasq.: ἡ μὲν (sc. κόρη) γὰρ ἕνας ἐστιν τῆς μέσης τριάδος τῶν ἀρχῶν, καὶ ζωογονικὰς προβέβληται δυνάμεις, ἀφ᾽ ἑαυτῆς. ὁ δὲ (sc. Ἀπόλλων) τὰς ἡλιακὰς ἀρχὰς εἰς μίαν ἕνωσιν ἐπιστρέφει, κατέχων τὴν τρίπτερον ἀρχήν, ὡς τὸ λόγιον φησί, scil., unum ex chaldaicis oraculis (cf. Kroll, 36) illis, ut liber de insomniis ostendit, cognitissimis," and p. 180 n. 142 ss: "miram vides consensionem inter stoicos neoplatonicos orphicos gnosticos aliquatenus vero christianos, et Synesium in cuius hymnos quodammodo omnes eorum doctrinas confluxerunt."

30. *Oracles Chaldaïques*, fr. 27 = Damascius I.87.3, II.87.14.

31. Pelikan, 1.222: "In opposition to the danger that the distinctiveness of the three hypostases would dissolve in a Platonically defined *ousia*, the Cappadocians, with varying

the idea of a trinity with dangerous implications for paganism and suggesting as an alternative a quaternity in which the One keeps its complete transcendence and superiority over the noetic realm. This argument is not without weight; e.g., the Cappadocians always had difficulties in their trinitarian speculation because they were forced to rationalize the paradoxes of the doctrines by appealing to the superior unity of the Father.

The pouring out of the Father into the Son is accomplished by means of the "wise will" of the Father, which springs forth as a "middle nature" or medium between the Father and the Son:

III 1.217–221:

Having been poured out upon the Son	ἐπὶ παιδὶ χυθείς
through your wise will,	ἰότατι σοφᾷ
and the will itself,	αὐτὰ δ'ἰότας
an unspeakable median nature,	βλάστησε, μέσα
brought forth	φύσις ἄφθεγκτος
the Being before Being	τὸ προούσιον ὄν

degrees of emphasis, found the guarantees of the unity of the Godhead in the Father. . . ." Whoever needs to "find the guarantee of the unity of the Godhead in the Father," and for whatever reason, is already in danger of ending up with a quaternity rather than a trinity. Pelikan also speaks of some of the metaphysical difficulties involved: "This puzzling, indeed frustrating, combination of philosophical terminology for the relation of One and Three with a refusal to go all the way toward a genuinely speculative solution was simultaneously typical of the theology of the Cappadocians and normative for the subsequent history of trinitarian doctrine . . . which was defiant of logical consistency and metaphysical coherence" (1.223). This brings to mind an interesting question: would a "genuinely speculative solution" necessarily lead to paganism in this case? Cf. Wallis, *Neoplatonism* 106. Ralph Cudworth, in his *True Intellectual System of the Universe* (1678), believed that the late pagans were deliberately using this criticism for anti-Christian purposes and thereby distorting both Plato and Plotinus, both of whom he considered to have held notions of a trinity very close to the Christian. Thomas Taylor, that modern Romantic pagan Neoplatonist, who absorbed their doctrines to such an extent that in some ways he was more like a late ancient or possibly a Renaissance figure than a nineteenth-century one, was aware of the quaternity issue, and is always very careful to point out the differences between Neoplatonic and Christian triadic ideas, as well as to state his preference for the former. Wilamowitz, 285, believes that: "Ihm wurden die metaphysischen Abstraktionen des Neuplatonismus an die sein Verstand glaubte, in der christlicher Trinität Konkreta, und danach verlangte seine Religiosität," but, as modern scholarship has demonstrated (1) the religiosity of the Chaldaean Oracles is also involved, (2) this fact *and* the terms of the solution which it imposed on Synesius make the rather straightforward scheme suggested by Wilamowitz too simple to apply adequately to the question. For more on this "school" issue of Trinity vs. quaternity, cf. Proclus, *In Parm.* 1070, 15: πολλοῦ ἄρα δεήσομεν ἡμεῖς, τοῦ νοητοῦ τὴν ἀκρότητα λέγειν τὸν θεὸν τὸν πρῶτον, ὥσπερ ἀκούω τινῶν ἐν θεολογίᾳ πρωτευσάντων, καὶ τὸν ἐκεῖ πατέρα ποιεῖν τῷ πάντων αἰτίῳ τὸν αὐτόν· and *In Parm.* 1091, 12: καὶ μέχρι ταύτης ἤδη τινὲς τῆς τάξεως (sc. τῆς τοῦ νοητοῦ) ἀναδράμοντες τὸ ἀκρότατον αὐτῆς εἰς ταὐτὸν ἤγαγον πρὸς τὸ "Εν, *In Crat.* 59, 14 Pasq.: τὸν Κρόνον διὰ τὸ ἀμέριστον αὐτοῦ καὶ ἑνιαῖον καὶ πατρικὸν καὶ ἀγαθουργὸν ἐν τοῖς νοεροῖς εἰς ταὐτόν τινες ἄγουσι τῇ μιᾷ τῶν πάντων αἰτίᾳ.

III 1.227–231:

Holy labor	ὠδὶς ἱερά,
ineffable childbirth	ἄρρητε γονά,
you are the limit	ὄρος εἶ φυσέων
of natures	τὰς τικτοίσας
which generate	καὶ τικτομένας.[32]
and are generated	

And in *Hymn* IV this median nature, the "limit of natures, engendered and engendering" is invoked among other things, as the Holy Spirit:

IV 1.94–105:

and the Father's	καὶ τὰν ἐπὶ σοί
labor over you	ὠδίνα πατρός,
the median principle	γόνιμον βουλάν,
the Holy Spirit	μεσάταν ἄρχαν,
center of the Generator	ἁγίαν πνοίαν,
center of the Son	κέντρον γενέτου,
herself mother . . .	κέντρον δὲ κόρου, / αὐτὰ μάτηρ . . .
herself daughter	αὐτὰ θυγάτηρ,
who gave birth	μαιωσαμένα
to the hidden root.	κρυφίαν ῥίζαν.

The Holy Spirit, then, is here openly identified with the "birth pangs" of the Father, his "creative will" through which the Son is engendered; it is both a medium *and* a primal nature (*mesatan archan*).[33] Although the basis for his trinitarian ideas is the Porphyrian interpretation of the Chaldaean noetic triad, Synesius' doctrine coincides with the orthodox Christian account of the Godhead's self-manifestation and has been interpreted as such by some scholars; for instance, Ladner says:

> Some Platonizing Christian theologians in fact went far beyond Basil or Cyril. They tried to strengthen the Trinitarian dogma above all by attempting to demonstrate that the doctrine of the Holy Spirit could explain how the one God could generate a second hypostasis which is not inferior to Him. The Third Person, the mutual spiration of divine love, could be construed as maintaining divine unity. See, for instance, Synesius, *Hymn* II (IV) 95 ff. See also *Hymn* I (III) 210 ff. [!][34]

32. Cf. *Hymn* III, 1.236–253.

33. For an interesting discussion of Synesius' method here in the context of Porphyry's, see Smith, *Porphyry's Place* 18: Porphyry's understanding of the "activity" within the hypostases and of *dynamis* "places him in a line of development which may well have culminated in a system of thought such as that displayed by the Parmenides Commentator."

34. Ladner 81 n. 76.

But Synesius' similarity to Patristic authors is incidental. He worked from a purely philosophical tradition. Nor should his use of liturgical terminology deceive us. It was inconsistent and not essential to his thoughts.

In *Hymn* III Synesius makes it quite clear that he is not speaking of a subordinationist form of emanation; in fact, the language he employs might be construed as a warning against tritheism:

III 1.223–226:
it is not lawful	οὐ θέμις εἰπεῖν
to speak of a second arising from you	δεύτερον ἐκ σοῦ,
it is not lawful	οὐ θέμις εἰπεῖν
to speak of a third	τρίτον ἐκ πρώτου
arising from the first	

It is in keeping with Synesius' Hellenism that he uses the Homeric *themis*—a word with oracular overtones in late antiquity—in a passage that maintains the religious correctness of the idea of the unity of the Godhead, as opposed to a conception that would posit emanated "gods" within the Godhead (the second, the third) as completely separate and subordinate entities.[35] It should be becoming clear by now that Synesius, despite his use of terminology from several religious traditions, has a general plan in mind: the *Hymns* are not a reflection of religious confusion, as some scholars believe, but rather the result of a great conscious effort to harmonize some of the most subtle aspects of the mystical theologies of paganism and Christianity.

Hymn II presents the Trinity in terms of Chaldaean imagery:[36] the paternal depth of the Chaldaeans (*ho bythos patroas* 1.2), is the source of the Son (*kydimos huios* 1.28) and the Holy Spirit (*hagia pnoia* 1.32). At the same time much pagan cosmology, such as chains of procession, encosmic gods, etc., is employed in the *Hymn*.[37] The paternal depth must

35. *Hymni*, ed. Terzaghi, 226 n. 1, says: "Hic mihi videor aliud indicium Synesii iam Christiani facti deprehendere: cum enim adfirmet nefas esse tertium dicere quod a primo illo procedat, neoplatonicis repugnat;" cf. Plot. IV.4.4 (which he quotes). But Terzaghi does not take into account (1) "telescoping" (2) of the Hypostases (2) triadic developments which make Neoplatonism compatible with the orthodox Trinity. Other passages could be found, even in Plotinus, to the opposite effect. This is no evidence of a rejection of Neoplatonism, and the next (cosmic) section makes such a rejection less likely; for religious and especially oracular associations of θέμις and related words see Du Cange and Sophocles, *Lexicon of Later Greek*, and Lampe, *Patristic Greek Lexicon*, s.v. θεμιστεία, θεμιστεύω, θεμιστονόμος, θεμιστοπόλος, θεμιστώδης.

36. See lines 1.59–74 which are particularly striking for their "gnostic" tone. For Chaldaean imagery, cf. Theiler, *Orakel* 1of and n. 3; Hadot, *Porphyre et Victorinus* 474 n. 7; *Oracles Chaldaïques* 38–39; Wilamowitz, 285.

37. Cf. *Hymn* II, 1.25–58 on the description of the Trinity, emanation, encosmic gods imposing intelligible patterns on matter; 1.21 presents an interesting problem: can

be identified with the "one source, one root" of line 25, which in the Chaldaean scheme as interpreted by Porphyrians contains the entire noetic being (*noeton*) within it. It might seem that Synesius was moving in a decidedly Christian or at least Christianizing direction. But it is also evident that he maintained his cherished pagan beliefs and displayed no signs of giving them up as part of a process of conversion.

Hymn VI (next in the order of composition) designates the Son as a median Intellect (*mesopages nous*). The phrase seems to be Porphyrian and is reminiscent of St. Augustine's well-known remark that Porphyry "calls God the Son the paternal intellect or paternal mind." This syncretism is even more striking in *Hymn* V, which contains the first actual reference to Jesus Christ in the series.[38] It also has an extensive section on the Trinity (1.48–65) yet it still contains a Neoplatonic prayer for release from the toils of matter (*hyle*) and earth, along with other pagan philosophical elements.

In his praise of the Trinity (1.58–65) Synesius, quite strikingly, alternately names the Father in terms of (i.e. the qualities of) the Son and the Son in terms of the Father, devoting one verse to each three times. Thus he very neatly allows us to see their reciprocity—the fact that they belong to the same Godhead—as well as their distinctiveness. The Holy Spirit is left for the last two lines, but is called, again in Porphyrian terminology, the center of the Father and the Son.[39] The purpose of Synesius in these lines will be more clearly seen by means of a table giving the basic meaning of the verse, an English translation of the poetry, and the Greek original:

Meaning	Translation	Greek
Hail to the Father	Hail Source of the Son	χαίροις, ὦ παιδὸς παγά,
Hail to the Son	Hail Form of the Father	χαίροις, ὦ πατρὸς μορφά,
Hail to the Father	Hail Foundation of the Son	χαίροις, ὦ παιδὸς κρηπίς,
Hail to the Son	Hail Seal of the Father	χαίροις, ὦ πατρὸς σφραγίς,
Hail to the Father	Hail Power of the Son	χαίροις, ὦ παιδὸς κάρτος,

πνεῦμα here be the Holy Spirit? No, because Synesius associates it with the "vehicle of the soul" (cf. *De Ins*. 1297A–D) and uses πνοία when speaking of the spirit. Here it seems to be connected with Soul as emanated life principle.

38. Cf. *Hymn* V, 1.1–9 and 1.4–5: Ἄρρητοι πατρὸς βουλαὶ / ἔσπειραν Χριστοῦ γένναν.

39. Cf. St. Augustine, *De Civ. Dei* X.23.

Meaning	Translation	Greek
Hail to the Son	Hail Beauty of the Father	χαίροις, ὦ πατρὸς κάλλος,
Hail to the Holy Spirit	Hail Pure Spirit	χαίροις, δ' ἄχραντος πνοιά,
Center of each One	Center of Father and Son	κέντρον κούρου καὶ πατρός.

Such poetic locutions as these reveal a striking potential compatibility between certain aspects of Christianity and Neoplatonism. The last two lines are especially interesting because they bring to mind St. Augustine's identification of Porphyry's "medium" between Father and Son with the Holy Spirit: *Quamuis quem alium* (i.e., the Holy Spirit) *dicat horum medium, non intellego.* St. Augustine clearly sees the difference between the usual Neoplatonic hierarchy and Porphyry's: "For if, like Plotinus when he is discussing the three principal hypostases, Porphyry too meant us to understand by the third term, the elemental soul, he certainly would not use the words 'midway between these two,' that is, between the Father and the Son. For Plotinus considers the elemental soul inferior to the intellect of the Father, but Porphyry, when he says 'midway between' places it, not below, but in between the Father and the Son. So then . . . he must have meant . . . the Holy Spirit."[40] Had St. Augustine known the Porphyrian interpretation of the Chaldaean Oracles, he would have realized that this doctrine did not depend upon Christian belief, and therefore would have been less confused.[41]

Synesius, then, understood the Christian Trinity through a Porphyrian interpretation of the Oracles. Hadot believes that a conception of the Trinity thus arrived at is somewhat atypical of the period—although not necessarily unorthodox—and can only be found in Synesius and Marius Victorinus, who also identified the Chaldaean triad with the persons of the Christian Trinity and used Porphyry's exegesis as the basis for his Trinitarian theology.[42] Because of the exigencies of Porphyrian Neoplatonism, they had to conceive of the Trinity as the manifestation of an unmanifest preexistent state of being in which the hypostases were conflated but not yet really distinct. In short, the development of the "internal" monad into an "external" triad had to be justified. In this way, modalistic monism could be avoided without falling into subordinationism. Nor is this method surprising in a Christian context if one considers, for exam-

40. *Ibid.*

41. For an explanation of St. Augustine's confusion here, see Wallis, *Neoplatonism* 106.

42. See Hadot, *Porphyre et Victorinus* 496f.

ple, the difficulties that the Cappadocians had in maintaining the unity of the Godhead.[43] It also follows that his unique approach to the Trinity makes it difficult to compare Synesius to such fourth-century theologians as Athanasius, for whom the issues were not exactly the same. The trinitarian dispute within the Church, with its confusions of terminology and concepts and its soteriological emphasis was conducted on a different level.

Having discussed this important point, we must also keep in mind that Synesius remained a good Neoplatonist. He never abandoned the Plotinian doctrine that the hypostases also became *manifest* in vertical descending order as the One, Nous and Soul. Each entity was subordinate to its prior cause. This remained the ontological basis of the cosmological scheme of things.

Another minor mystery of the *Hymns* is Synesius' apparent use of the technical Christian terminology for baptism. In *Hymn* III (1.620–621) he says: "now let my suppliant soul bear the seal of the Father" (*sphragida patros*), a technical term for baptism. The term itself (*sphragis patros*) had a long history of identification with both the Logos and the Spirit.[44] For instance, even before Christianity Philo makes this identification quite clearly in *Opif. Mundi* 25: "The archetypical seal, which we have identified with the intelligible world, is the *Logos* of God" (ἡ ἀρχέτυπος σφραγίς, ὃν φάμεν νοητὸν εἶναι κόσμον, αὐτὸς ἂν εἴη ὁ θεοῦ λόγος). Synesius himself makes the same identification at *Hymn* V, 1.61. Is this then merely an example of Synesius' adopting Christian terminology in a purely logical attempt to identify Christ the Logos with Nous, or does the term have any special significance beyond this? The latter, surely. For the Chaldaean Oracles provide us with the connection for which we are looking. The Chaldaean term *synthema* is a synonym in the Oracles for *symbolon*;[45] both refer to occult symbols which enable the theurgists who know them to achieve union with a divine being. Although it appears that Synesius did not advocate acts of ritual theurgy, he accepted theurgic symbolism and metaphor as an integral part of his mysti-

43. See n. 29 above.

44. See Lacombrade, *Synésios*; Marrou in *Conflict* 140. On this subject see also Dölger, esp. pp. 156–169, "#2 Σφραγίς und σφραγῖδα τηρεῖν und das Mysterienwesen" (for a discussion of the term in pagan mysteries, Orphic fragments, Apuleius, Gnostic hymnology, etc.); Lampe, *passim*; cf. Theiler, *Orakel* 296 and n. 150.

45. *Oracles Chaldaïques* 40, whose editor Des Places considers σφραγίς to be a Chaldaean term; he has also made the connection between it and other Chaldaean terms in *Hymn* III: see *ibid.*, frr. 108 and 118; e.g., fr. 108: Σύμβολα γὰρ πατρικὸς νόος / ἔσπειρεν κατὰ κόσμον, ὃς τὰ νοητὰ νοεῖ καὶ κάλλη ἄφραστα / καλεῖται. For additional commentary see Lewy, 191 and nn. 255–256; Proclus, *Timée*, ed. Festugière, 2.32 n. 2; cf. Theiler, *Orakel*, 296 and n. 150.

cal theology. Perhaps he believed that through study and contemplation of the Oracles themselves, philosophically interpreted, the purified philosopher could achieve union with the noetic realm.[46] In *Hymn* III (1.539–540) *synthema* is used interchangeably with *sphragis*: "grant me your token, your seal" (*Synthema didou, sphragida tean*). This phrase, if understood as theurgic symbolism, would mean: "allow me to achieve union or contact with the divine mind by means of secret knowledge granted as a kind of revelation to initiates." Synesius, then, need not have been talking about Christian baptism. It is likely, however, that he employed a certain type of language that specifies our connection with the noetic realm through a type of grace.[47] The seal of baptism is a symbol of Christian "initiation," but as the seal of the secret Chaldaean tokens or signs, it is a symbol of theurgic initiation. Yet these terms, or the experiences they represent, are not simply interchangeable. There are considerable theological differences between the Christian idea of the grace of baptism and the Chaldaean idea of the "grace" of secret symbols that enable the theurgist to approach the divine. For the purposes of Synesius, however, whose attitude toward Christianity was in any case somewhat unusual, there was enough similarity in the concepts. Such ideas would certainly make it possible to express the content of the old Hellenic beliefs through Christian symbols. Synesius seems to have been following a pattern here similar to that of his trinitarian speculation: he discovered another potential bridge—albeit a rather occult one—between paganism and Christianity. His profound interest in the Oracles also suggests that he might have been attempting to develop a purely intellectual "higher theurgy."[48]

46. Cf. Iamblichus, *De Myst.*, ed. Des Places, Ch. II.11:

Ἔστω μὲν γὰρ ἡ ἄγνοια καὶ ἀπάτη πλημμέλεια καὶ ἀσέβεια, οὐ μὴν διὰ τοῦτο ψευδῆ ποιεῖ καὶ τὰ οἰκείως τοῖς θεοῖς προσφερόμενα καὶ τὰ θεῖα ἔργα, οὐδὲ γὰρ ἡ ἔννοια συνάπτει τοῖς θεοῖς τοὺς θεουργούς· ἐπεὶ τί ἐκώλυε τοὺς θεωρητικῶς φιλοσοφοῦντας ἔχειν τὴν θεουργικὴν ἕνωσιν πρὸς τοὺς θεούς; νῦν δ' οὐκ ἔχει τό γε ἀληθὲς οὕτως· ἀλλ' ἡ τῶν ἔργων τῶν ἀρρήτων καὶ ὑπὲρ πᾶσαν νόησιν θεοπρεπῶς ἐνεργουμένων τελεσιουργία ἥ τε τῶν νοουμένων τοῖς θεοῖς μόνον συμβόλων ἀφθέγκτων δύναμις ἀντίθησι τὴν θεουργικὴν ἕνωσιν.

Synesius never belonged to the Iamblichean school, though his study of Porphyry's work on the Oracles would certainly make him aware of matters such as the above, which are perfectly capable of being interpreted symbolically without necessarily insisting on special rite and ritual as the only means by which they can be effective.

47. For the conception of grace in Iamblichus see Wallis, *Neoplatonism* 118–123.

48. See Smith, *Porphyry's Place* 91, "Lewy argues 'that Iamblichus thought theurgy and philosophy are two distinct ways to the same goal.' He adds that there is a mystical theurgy or metaphysical theurgy in the philosophical way, and to justify it, the philosophers employed some of the seemingly more intellectual passages of the *Oracles*. . . ." Smith denies that Iamblichus held this view. But such a position is still a possibility for Synesius.

V

The Middle Years:
The Incarnation and the *Hymns*

Up to this point we have been dealing with Christian doctrines perfectly compatible with the integrity of Synesius' beliefs and principles as a convert to philosophy. Furthermore, as we have seen, he had only to change the names of the moments of Neoplatonic horizontal emanation in order to identify them with the moments of spiration and filiation in the development of the Christian Trinity. But what if Synesius were faced with a Christian doctrine that Neoplatonists found hard to accept? *Ep.* 105 is clear evidence that Synesius took such problems seriously. His method always was reconciliation with such doctrines wherever possible and philosophical objection when reconciliation was not possible or was very difficult. How then does Synesius deal with the Incarnation, which was not usually accepted by Neoplatonists? He acknowledges it symbolically in the *Hymns* and raises no objection to it either in *Ep.* 105 or any other of his writings. It does not appear until *Hymn* VI, but becomes a continuous theme thereafter. Thus the problem is worth discussing at some length.

Nock points out that the idea of God having a son was not wholly repellent to a pagan.[1] After all, this was a commonplace of ancient mythologies, as of all mythologies. Historical as well as mythological figures were said to have divine parents: Plato, Augustus (and other emperors) and Alexander are well-known cases. In addition it was possible to have both a divine and a human father: "No one questioned that Alexander was the son of Philip and Olympias, and yet the oracle of Ammon in Libya hailed him as the god's son." This is also true of Heracles, the Pharaoh and the child in Virgil's *Fourth Eclogue*. A god could die; Asclepius was killed by Zeus' lightning and later restored to life. "Heracles died on the pyre of Oeta, and, having purged away his mortality in its flames,

---

1. *Conversion* 232: the following section is largely a summary of Nock's views. He discusses several important developments of Christian doctrine which might tend to make it more acceptable to pagans; e.g., Justin Martyr guarded against the physical interpretation of the begetting of Jesus; Origen denied emphatically that any holy man ever celebrated His birthday.

lived thereafter on Olympus. A god could have a passion and resurrection—Zagreus, Attis, Adonis, Osiris." Often this was considered a cyclical event, which took place yearly. Sallustius interprets this belief: "All this did not happen at any one time but always is: the mind sees the whole process at once, words tell of part first, part second."[2]

Even the idea of the uniqueness and historicity of Jesus was not wholly strange; most ancient cults had founding legends.[3] Also, since the high god of all religions of the age was the cause of all things behind phenomena, was transcendent, was impassible, and was not to be approached directly through prayer or sacrifice, the idea of mediation between man and God was widespread.[4]

After having pointed out all the things that would seem to make the Incarnation acceptable to pagan minds, Nock attempts to show some inherent difficulties: Gregory of Nyssa's Catechetical Oration (c. 383) bears witness to a widespread objection to the idea of incarnation.[5] The year gods Attis and Adonis lived in the mythical period and were not aspects of the divinity but largely the expression of natural processes. Both, like Mithras, had divine not human cycles of life. That ancient kings were supposed to be avatars of deity was true only in the case of Pharaoh. When Horace said Augustus was Mercury in human shape this was an epiphany in a shape assumed for the moment, like the appearance of Athena to Telemachus in the guise of an old friend; it was unlike the coming of a Bodhisattva. The idea of incarnation was not godlike: "None of the heavenly gods will leave the bounds of heaven and come down to earth," says the writer of *Corpus Hermeticum* X.25, expressing the general view of antiquity. Humanity in its essential nature and quality was regarded as a liability rather than an asset.[6]

Several points here should be briefly discussed. First of all, the fact

<hr>

2. *Ibid*. 234: "These ideas were in time applied to Christianity. The Eucharist, a meal and thanksgiving linked to the symbolic act by which Jesus made his disciples willing partners in his death, became the re-enacting of that death. Medieval piety developed the drama of Holy Week with increasing realism and in the domain of the Greek Church the popular attitude is still that at every Eastertide Christ rises, and that if he did not rise, the crops would not grow." Χριστὸς ἀνέστη, ἀληθῶς ἀνέστη, as the Greeks still say at Easter.

3. *Ibid*. 235: "Most of these were not firmly fixed, but in Mithraism, indeed, the sacred story was definitely fixed at the beginning of the world order and Mithras, unlike other gods, had a complex *Vita*, shown in a sequence of scenes in art and corresponding to the Gospel story; but Mithras did not die."

4. *Ibid*. for some examples. Differences: paganism had cosmic links and therefore a Christ-like mediator was not necessary in the same way as in Christianity. On this idea, see Wallis, *Neoplatonism* 121.

5. Nock, *Conversion* 236.   6. *Ibid*. 237.

that year-gods had divine not human cycles of life is not completely impossible to reconcile with a view of the Incarnation that does not emphasize its historicity. Here Nock fails to point out that pagans of the fourth century, especially such pagans as Sallustius or Synesius, would regard the year-gods as aspects of divinity and not exclusively as natural processes. Nor does he take into account the *theios aner* or "divine man" conception, in such pagan "gospels" as Philostratus' *Life of Apollonius of Tyana* and Iamblichus' *Life of Pythagoras*; indeed, the paradoxical nature of the beliefs, activities and wonders of these figures, as portrayed in pagan hagiography, often leads one to believe that they themselves are not men, but divine epiphanies of the transcendent; i.e., sons of God. In fact, if one views them neither as mere men nor altogether as gods, one arrives at a Hellenistic version of the paradoxical nature of the man-god that is compatible to some degree with a mystical or paradoxical understanding of the Incarnation. As is well known, the pagan idea of *ho theios aner* had messianic overtones, and Apollonius and Pythagoras were often considered pagan alternatives to Christ. In these late Hellenistic "gospels," both were portrayed as historical figures playing wonder-working roles.[7]

Nock also underrates the idea of the king as a divine figure. In the West, the divinity of the Roman Emperor may not have been taken seriously, but the East is another matter. The ruler might not have been a manifest Olympian but he was at least in close touch with the divine Logos, as such titles as *Soter, Euergetes*, and *Epiphanes* tend to indicate. An extensive Hellenistic Neopythagorean literature, studied especially by Goodenough,[8] deals with the king as a Platonic imitation of divinity, a mediator between mankind and the Logos. In the later Roman Empire this idea would have been more acceptable to pagans. By 270, the Roman Emperor was closely associated with *Sol Invictus*, the Unconquered Sun. The sun itself was interpreted as a visible manifestation of the divinity.

Although, as Nock says, the human nature was regarded as a liability rather than an asset, there is another side to the picture: the sense-

7. For a fascinating discussion of the influence of the Hellenistic *theios aner* on the Gospels see Jonathan Z. Smith, 190–207. He believes the Gospels of Mark and John to be generically related to lives of "divine men" by authors such as Philostratus and Iamblichus—who worked from earlier traditions. The hero is always paradoxical, intangible, ineffable. Any literal reading of such works leads to a cul-de-sac, which is usually written off by the "uninitiated" as nonsense. Such works attempt to demonstrate transcendence which has become manifest in a savior figure, a great metaphysical-theological paradox. "*A 'gospel' is a narrative of a son of god who appears among men as a riddle inviting misunderstanding*," p. 204.

8. See above, Chapter II, n. 47.

world is the best possible copy of the ideal cosmos and therefore both good and necessary (e.g., *Enn*. II.IX); humanity is therefore good and necessary and not merely the result of a "fall."[9] Humanity also conceals divinity within, and as a microcosm, can descend into matter, ascend to the divine or remain, as most do, in between. Pico della Mirandola sees *dignitas* in this chameleon-like human flexibility and potential to achieve great, mediocre, or base things. Man is in a sense superior to the angels, for they must remain fixed while man—although he can sink, although his existence is problematical—can reach divinity and become godlike himself. I would not argue that this dynamic optimism, more characteristic of the fifteenth than the fifth century, was held by pagans of our period; but the potential for it was there and its roots are in some tracts of the *Hermetica* and the Platonic conception of the cosmos found in the *Timaeus*. It is often argued that the idea of the Incarnation was needed to resolve the problems of Greek dualism; it seems to me that *Timaeus'* cosmology already satisfies this function within the Platonic tradition.

Though the author of *Corpus Hermeticum* X.25 says that the heavenly gods would not come down to earth, Synesius himself saw them descending when needed to restore the world, even though they would rather contemplate the ideal realm in tranquility. Pagan Platonists in general during the late period provided for divine protection even down to the lower reaches of the cosmos through complicated chains of gods, which include the creators, preservers and guardians of the visible universe.[10] True, these gods did not always assume human form, but if we think of figures like Asclepius and Heracles, we begin to approach the Savior idea; and if we combine this with the idea of the *theios aner*, we come even closer to the idea of divine incarnation.

Having discussed some possible general views of incarnation in antiquity, let us first review the specific complaints against the Incarnation of Christ put forth by the Neoplatonists.[11] Purists among philosophers rejected the doctrine of the Incarnation as metaphysically absurd and inconsistent, and theologically impure. They criticized the Christian claim to Christ's uniqueness and historicity: why should God, a perfect being, ignore all the generations until the first century A.D., and then send the

9. For views on the "fall" of the Soul in Neoplatonism and its unfallen level in Plotinus, see Wallis, *Neoplatonism* 73, 76, 82, 92, 95, 120, and 153; on Neoplatonic attitudes toward the body, 9, 11, 20, 35, 83, 104, 108, 111, and 178; on the relation of body to soul, 17, 24, 28, 41, 50–52, 61 n. 1, 73–79, 92, 98, 108, 111, 120, 126–129, 167, and 173; on the Narcissus motif and descent of the Soul, 78.

10. For cosmic gods who guard the visible cosmos see Sallust, *De Diis et Mundo* 6. Proclus, *Elem. Theol.* prop. 113–165, outlines the "chains" of gods.

11. For a convenient summary of these, see Wallis, *Neoplatonism* 104.

Savior of mankind in a lowly role to some out-of-the-way province of the Roman Empire?[12] The idea that the Incarnation was a once-and-for-all event in time contradicted the Neoplatonic idea of many subordinate gods, perpetually manifesting the different aspects of divinity from one end of the cosmic chain to the other.[13] The idea of the suffering god was a direct contradiction of the idea of divine impassibility;[14] consequently the Crucifixion was considered absurd as well as shameful.[15] The lamentations of Jesus on the Cross were unfavorably compared with the ancient sage's idea of *apatheia* or indifference to suffering.[16] The miracles performed by Jesus were looked down upon as the kind of magical practice which any magician who knew his business could perform.[17] The philosophical idea of the impurity of the Incarnation is well summed up by Porphyry (fr. 77):

> If any Hellene is so light-headed that he thinks the gods dwell in stat-ues, he still possesses a much purer notion than the man who be-lieves that the divinity entered the womb of the Virgin Mary, became a foetus, and was wrapped in swaddling clothes after he was born, all full of bloody afterbirth and bile—and still other things which are much more absurd.[18]

In another fragment (fr. 84) Porphyry questions the meaning, value, and validity of the Incarnation, Crucifixion and Resurrection. He con-cludes his argument with a concise criticism of the notion (contradictory to a Greek philosopher) of the suffering man-god: "And how, if he was im-passible, did he come to suffer?"[19]

Synesius was well aware of these objections. Although he himself was never vituperative when questioning Christian doctrine, he did not hesitate to criticize it if he felt that it contained philosophical inconsisten-

---

12. Origen, *C. Cels.*, IV.7 and VI.78; Porphyry, *C. Chr.*, frr. 81–82; Aug., *Ep.* 102.8; Jerome, *Ep.* 133.9. The standard work is Labriolle, *La réaction païenne*; see also W. Nestle, *Arch. f. Rel.* 37.51–100; Hulen, *passim*; and Geffcken, 56–77.

13. Cf. *Enn.* II.9.9.26–42; Porphyry, *C. Chr.* frr. 75–78 = Macarius Magnes IV.20–23.

14. Porphyry, *C. Chr.* fr. 84; Dionysus, for example, might be brought in as a counter-example here—Hölderlin, for instance, identified Dionysus and Christ; but meta-physical purists would deny that Dionysus was God Himself Incarnate. See Ladner, 154 and n. 3.

15. *C. Cels.* II.31ff, VII.13–15, etc.

16. *C. Cels.* II.24; Porphyry, *C. Chr.* frr. 62–63 = Macarius Magnes III.1–2.

17. *C. Cels.* I.6; Porphyry, *C. Chr.* fr. 4 = Jerome, *Tract. de Psalm.* 81.

18. Porphyry, fr. 77: Εἰ δὲ καί τις τῶν Ἑλλήνων οὕτω κοῦφος τὴν γνώμην, ὡς ἐν τοῖς ἀγάλμασιν ἔνδον οἰκεῖν νομίζειν τοὺς θεούς, πολλῷ καθαράτερον εἶχε τὴν ἔννοιαν τοῦ πιστεύοντος ὅτι εἰς τὴν γαστέρα Μαρίας τῆς παρθένου εἰσέδυ τὸ θεῖον, ἔμβρυόν τε ἐγένετο καὶ τεχθὲν ἐσπαργανώθη, μεστὸν αἵματος χορίου καὶ χολῆς καὶ τῶν ἔτι πολλῷ τούτων ἀτοπωτέρων. *Script. Pag. I–IV Saec. de Christ. Test.*, p. 24.

19. *Ibid.*

cies. After all, a literal reading of the idea of the *entire* Nous or Logos (i.e., God himself and not just an "aspect of divinity") becoming incarnate in one man would provide difficulties even for a pagan seeking accommodation with Christianity. Synesius' Christological concerns and meditation upon the Incarnation, then, must be studied in the light of the long history of pagan criticism of the doctrine.

Let us now analyze Synesius' view of the Incarnation as he presents it in the *Hymns. Hymn* VI (composed before V) deals with the "birth" of the Son in the Godhead and his cosmological function as the mind of God ordering the universe; the soteriological function of the Son is also alluded to:

> You dance around perishable nature and divide
> undivided spirit throughout the earth
> and you reunite with its source that which the source has given
> freeing mortals from the necessity of death. (VI, 1.20–23)

> Σὺ δὲ καὶ φύσιν φθιτὰν ἀμφιχορεύεις,
> ἀμέριστον περὶ γᾶν πνεῦμα μερίζεις,
> καὶ παγᾷ τὸ δοθὲν πάλιν συνάπτεις,
> θνατοὺς ἐκ θανάτου λύων ἀνάγκας.

However, in the following lines (1.26–27), this liberation is conceived in "Orphic" terms as a liberation from matter. The return to the source of 1.22 is reminiscent of the Neoplatonic doctrine of *epistrophe* (the return of all things ultimately to the One, their cause) and uses the verb, *synaptein*, of the noun *synaphe*, which is a Neoplatonic technical term for union with the divinity. He prays to the Son in a very personal way (1.24–27), but such prayers were common among pagan Neoplatonists. He also calls upon the Son to "dry up the destructive billows of matter."[20] A Christ who breaks through matter has "Orphic" associations and is somewhat reminiscent of the Christian Gnostic idea of a Christ who crashes through the Cosmos on the (ahistorical) mission of bringing the message of the "Alien God" to mankind.[21] At any rate, *Hymn* VI stresses the mystical and metaphysical rather than the human side of Christ.

In *Hymn* V we are presented with Christ Incarnate: "the Son of the Bride, the Bride not promised for marriage beds destined for men" (1.1–3); "The ineffable counsels of the Father caused the generation of Christ. The sacred labor of the Bride manifested the form of man, who arrived among mortals, the conveyor of light from the source" (1.4–9). In 1.12, He Himself is the "light from the source," like the Light of the

20. *Hymn* VI, 1.26–27; cf. also *Hymn* III, 1.539–540 and 548–550.
21. See Jonas, 264.

Logos which is the Life of men in the Fourth Gospel, and the Life and Light of the *Hermetica*.[22] The imagery is Chaldaean. Christ, "light from the source," is close to the Oracles' *patrogenes phaos*.[23] The "ineffable counsels" and "sacred labor" echo oracular phrases from other *Hymns*, which depict the begetting of the Son. He portrays the birth pangs of the Virgin and the Incarnation in language analogous to descriptions of the cosmologically productive activities of the Chaldaean goddesses Rhea and Hekate, usually identified with the World Soul.[24] Given this evidence, it is not unlikely that, in order to facilitate the working out of doctrines acceptable to a Hellene, Synesius applied Chaldaean ideas to the Christian ideas of the Virgin Birth and the Incarnation. Moreover, he could have proceeded by analogy as follows: as the begetting of the Son in the Trinity resulted from the ineffable labor of the Father's Will, which showed forth a child from his unknowable depths (*kolpoi*), and as the World Soul (Rhea-Hekate) gives life to the cosmos from its ineffable depths (*aphrastoi kolpoi* or sometimes *zoogonos kolpos*), so the Incarnation results from the "ineffable counsels of the Father" and the "sacred labor" of the Virgin. In short, Synesius probably brought his Chaldaean-influenced mystical notion of filiation into play with respect to the Incarnation. However, here he displays originality, since he makes use of Chaldaean-inspired imagery to express an important Christian doctrine with no exact parallel in the Oracles. Furthermore, his sense of the ineffable paradox of the event has strong overtones of Chaldaean religiosity. Thus, a theologically creative use of the Oracles, along with an adaptation of the pagan "divine man" and related ideas, could have provided the means to help Synesius deal with the "stumbling block" of the Incarnation.

Although there is Christian language here, there is much that reflects Chaldaean and other non-Christian ideas of salvation. Line 14, for

22. Light imagery is prominent in both the Oracles and *Hermetica*; cf. *Oracles Chaldaïques*, frr. 21, 1; 49, 1; 51, 3; 55; 59; 71; 111; 115, 1; 118, 1; 121; 145; 146, 4, 5; 147, 3; 155; Index Verborum *s.v.v.* φῶς, πῦρ; *Corp. Herm.* I.9 νοῦς as ζωὴ καὶ φῶς, 12, 17, 21, 26; VII.2; XII.9, 17, 19. Theiler, *Orakel* 286, points out that φῶς "steht für πῦρ gelegentlich auch in den Orakelen;" *ibid.* 287: "Bei Synesios ersetzt es, wie in ζωηφόριον φῶς 1, (111) 602 für ζωηφόριον πῦρ;" 265: "Zu φῶς παγαῖον für Vater und Sohn, 3, 9.12 vgl. die πηγαῖοι πατέρες . . . , oben S. 12 φῶς kann gerade die höchste göttliche Aufgipfelung wie auch ἄνθος ἀκρότης heissen; . . . Proclus mal. subst. 11, 23 summitates . . . et velut flores et supersubstantialia lumina Dion. Areop. *div. nom.* 645b (von Jesu und dem hl. Geist): βλαστοὶ θεόφυτοι καὶ οἷον ἄνθη καὶ ὑπερούσια φῶτα."

23. *Oracles Chaldaïques*, fr. 49, 1.

24. For parallels to κόλποι θεοῦ cf. Theiler *Orakel* 284; e.g., "auch 4, 6 f. von der Geburt des Sohnes ὃν βουλᾶς πατρικᾶς ἄφραστος ὠδὶς ἀγνώστων ἀνέδειξε παῖδα κόλπων und *or. Chald.* (30) bei Proklos *Crat.* 81, 7 ('Ρείη) δυνάμεις κόλποισιν ἀφράστοις δεξαμένη γενεὴν . . . προχέει; ζωόγονος τῆς 'Εκάτης, κτλ."

example, depicts Christ having broken through dark matter in order to illuminate pious souls.[25]

Synesius does not forget the cosmological role of the Logos: He is founder (*ktistas*) of the universe, fashioner of the spheres, root of the centers of earth, as well as the saviour of man, *autos d'anthropon soter.*[26] Thus he was aware of both the creative and soteriological functions of the Logos. Synesius is apparently attempting to harmonize doctrines by a juxtaposition of the imagery of late Hellenistic-Roman ways of salvation with that of their Christian counterpart. The important question is: has he departed from pagan conceptions by accepting an idea of the Incarnation?

It is not until *Hymn* VII that the familiar "offspring of the Virgin, *Jesus*" appears (1.4). The poem also alludes to the Christmas star, the Nativity scene and the gifts of the Magi.[27] The opening lines suggest that Synesius found a Jesus of the Hellenistic mysteries: "I am the *first* to have discovered the mode, for you, blessed, immortal, glorious offspring of the Virgin, Jesus of Solyma, to strike the strings of my lyre with newly formed harmonies."[28] Christ is conceived of in the paradoxical manner of the Hellenistic "gospel." Like the mythical Heracles he is a "God among the heavenly beings and *nekys* among the race below earth" (i.e., the dead); (τὸν ἐπουρανίοις θεόν / τὸν ὑποχθονίοις νέκυν). He has been poured out upon the earth and "born *of a mortal womb*" (ἐχύθης ὅτ'ἐπὶ χθονὶ βροτέας ἀπὸ νηδύος).[29] This "pouring out" is an image associated with not only the Christian "emptying" of the Logos, but also with the Chaldaean World Soul (Rhea-Hekate) "pouring forth" the living world of generation.[30] The magus wondered "what manner of infant had been born, who might be this god concealed, god, or nether shade, or king" (τί τὸ τικτόμενον βρέφος / τίς ὁ κρυπτόμενος θεός / θεὸς ἢ νέκυς ἢ βασιλεύς 1.23–26). It is interesting to note that Synesius does follow traditional

25. *Hymn* V, 1.14–15:

> Ῥήξας δ' ὀρφναίαν ὕλαν
> ψυχαῖς ἐλλάμπεις ἁγναῖς

26. *Ibid*. 16–20.

27. For a skeptical opinion of Synesius' relationship to the mythology of the Nativity, see Wilamowitz, 288.

28. *Hymn* VII, 1.1–6:

> πρῶτος νόμον εὑρόμαν
> ἐπὶ σοί μάκαρ ἄμβροτε,
> γόνε κύδιμε παρθένου,
> Ἰησοῦ Σολυμήϊε,
> νεοπάγεσιν ἁρμογαῖς
> κρέξαι κιθάρας μίτους

29. *Hymn* VII, 1.18–19; cf. *Les Hymnes*, ed. Meunier, 234.

30. See above, n. 24.

Christian usage when describing the gifts of the Magi: incense for Christ as God, gold for Christ as King and myrrh for His mortality. This is surely not enough to indicate orthodox intentions. It is, however, probable that Synesius learned of this order from hearing Christian sermons in which this theme was often expounded.[31] The poem concludes with a prayer (1.30–42) to the king who has purified the land, driven out the demons and come to the aid of the dead in Hades (φθιμένοισι βοηθόος / θεὸς εἰς Ἀίδην σταλείς).[32] On the pagan side this imagery brings to mind the figure of Heracles, who also descends to the underworld on missions of salvation.[33] The Heraclean theme, as we shall see, is prominent in *Hymn IX*. In *Hymn VII* Synesius meditated on the story of Christ and adopted some of its traditional language and imagery. The continued presence of pagan imagery and concepts is less a sign of his religious confusion than of his religious position and literary habits.

Hymn VIII is important not only for its religious content, but also because it provides biographical information and important clues for the dating of the *Hymns*.[34] It is a personal prayer on behalf of the members of Synesius' family, and for his own personal health, good fortune, and freedom from the anxiety and the toils of earthly life.[35] Wilamowitz, however, claims that although the poem is in the form of a personal prayer and the Virgin and Son of God appear as playing a powerful role in the destinies of individuals, it is not directed to an individually determined intervention; he sees strong parallels with the theme of salvation in the *Hymns* of Proclus.[36] We have already seen that pagans in this period often wrote per-

31. I am indebted to Professor Gerard Caspary of the University of California at Berkeley for discussing Synesius' views on the Incarnation with me, and pointing out that, although he is unorthodox and hard to pin down on this issue, he does follow the orthodox Christian description of the gifts of the Magi; see also *Les Hymnes*, ed. Meunier, 234 for the symbolism of myrrh; further, Villard, 92–98, which shows that for the Syrian world and some Greeks also, myrrh meant medicine of Christ the Good Doctor; so that Synesius was perhaps making a conscious choice of symbolism here.

32. *Hymn VII*, 1.38–39.

33. Cf. *Hymni*, ed. Terzaghi, 250 n. 1.33–39: "Iesus quasi novus Hercules laudatur qui terram mare caelum inferorum sedes lustraverit, qui, deus ad Orcum cum Hercule comparato, cf. *H*. 5.55." Terzaghi also provides a pagan parallel for 1.16, p. 248: *Orph.* fr. 247.33:

> ἔστι τι δὲ πάντη αὐτός
> ἐπουράνιος, καὶ ἐπὶ χθονὶ
> πάντα τελευτᾷ, ἀρχὴν αὐτὸς ἔχων καὶ μέσσην ἠδὲ τελευτήν;

34. For dating of *Hymn VIII* and a discussion of the biographical information which it provides see Lacombrade, *Synésios* 193.

35. For a discussion of this prayer, see Wilamowitz, 281.

36. For a comparison with Proclus, see *ibid*. 282.

sonal hymns to gods, on the theory that prayer could better focus one's personal consciousness on the divine.[37] Indeed, as Festugière has shown, classical Greek piety had a personal side, which became more pronounced in late antiquity.

Hymn VIII also addresses Christ as the glorious offspring of the Virgin (1.5), as does *Hymn* IX, in which Synesius sustains the theme of the Son's saving mission. What is most unusual about the latter is its almost riotous mixture of pagan and Christian imagery. Lines 4–6 depict the chthonic serpent's expulsion from the great garden of the Father, the same serpent who offered the forbidden fruit to the primal youth (not to Eve).[38] Christ descends to Hades (1.13–27), which is also called Tartarus, where *Thanatos* reigns over nations of souls in thousands (1.17–18); he then makes Hades and his man-devouring hound shudder: "Hades, the ancient, and his hound, the devourer of man, draw back from the threshold . . ." (1.20–23). Having made his Heraclean journey to Hades, Christ delivers the righteous souls (1.24–27) and raises hymns to the Father with them.

One of the exact phrases Synesius uses for the Incarnation (1.15), "bearing a mortal body" (*broteion pheron demas*), seems to be associated by Macrobius with the "Orphic"-Pythagorean-Platonic idea of the body as the tomb or prison of the soul: "For a creature to have existence, it is necessary that a soul be confined in the body; for this reason the Greek words for body are *demas*, that is a 'bond,' and *soma*, a *sema* as it were, being the tomb of the soul."[39] Synesius, as a Neoplatonist, conceives of the Incarnation in a manner analogous to that of a soul taking on a body. This is to be expected: he always tried to rationalize his beliefs philosophically.

What, then, was Synesius' conception of the Incarnation? He clearly speaks of the Virgin birth, but locates it in Jerusalem. In conformity with pagan tradition he calls the city Solyma. Tacitus, for example, believed that the Jews were descended from Homer's Solymi.[40] He

37. Cf. Iamblichus, *De Myst.*, V.26 (237–240); see Dillon's remarks in *Iamblichi Chalcid. in Plat. Dial. Comm. Frr.* 405–409 and n. 338.

38. *Hymn* IX, 1.7–9: ὃς κάρπον ἀπώμοτον / τροφὸν ἀργαλέου μόρου / πόρεν ἀρχεγόνῳ βοράν·

39. Macrobius, *Comm. in Somn. Scip.* XI (3), tr. Stahl, 124–125; but this section is problematical: the line δέμας φέρων βρότειον does not appear in Migne's text and is bracketed by Terzaghi. If it is a later addition, the scholiast showed a good grasp of the way Synesius, given his philosophical position, had to approach the Incarnation. Stahl, *ibid.* 264 n. 4, provides some convenient references for the body-soul relationship described in this passage: "see *Phaedo* 62B; *Tusc. Disp.* 1.74; Phil. *De Somn.* 1.138; Plot. IV 8.1.3; Ath. *Deipnosophist.* 157C; Porphyry, *Sententiae* 8; Proclus 64B (Diehl)."

40. Cf. e.g. Tacitus, *Histories* 5.2. Those who held this view gave the Jews a distinguished Homeric origin. They named their city Hierosolyma after the Homeric Solymi.

describes the descent into Hades and the ascent to the Father's realm, although he does avoid what is anathema to Hellenes: the god who suffers on the cross. Other famous scenes from the traditional Christ story are also included in the *Hymns*. But the fact that Christ is depicted several times as saving mankind from "matter," and carries out his mission in a traditionally pagan setting, is clear evidence that Synesius was attempting to maintain his Hellenic ideas of salvation and savior figures. Synesius was unconcerned with the historical mission of Jesus: his view of Christ is basically cosmological, soteriological and mythical. In tune with his resolve to mythologize outwardly and philosophize inwardly (*Ep.* 105), he used the familiar settings of the Christ story symbolically; it must be remembered that *Hymn* IX also depicts the Resurrection, the literal idea of which he openly entertained doubts.

The Incarnation never took on the central role for Synesius that it did for a Gregory of Nyssa and the Greek Fathers,[41] but at least he does seem to have felt that pagan and Christian soteriology could be harmonized to some extent. The noetic realm could not become incarnate. But he does not hesitate to allow the Sun God to call the cosmological Christ "offspring of God/Mind the best-artificer, source of his own (Sun-Titan) fire." Thus Christ becomes a manifestation of the *noeric* realm: Synesius' Christ-Helios could have the same function as Julian's Helios-Mithras, center of the Intellectual Gods.

Thus Nous may be equated with the Logos. Yet the literal incarnation of the Logos is another matter: Synesius must have thought that if Greek mythology could be allegorical, then so could Christian. If the uninitiated take the Christ story literally, are they indeed any worse off than pagans who believe gods dwell in statues?[42] A more detailed discussion of the pagan "gospels" and some of the ideas of the Greek Fathers will deepen our perspective on Synesius' position on this important question.

First, let us return to the pagan "gospels" and look at them more carefully. Eunapius says that Apollonius of Tyana "was not just a philosopher, but something midway between the gods and man."[43] He believes that although Philostratus called his book the *Life of Apollonius* "he ought to have called it *The Visit of God to Mankind*."[44] Philostratus' life of the

---

41. See Ladner, 154, who speaks of the central role of the Incarnation in the thought of Gregory of Nyssa and other patristic authors; cf. below, p. 116.

42. Porphyry, *C. Chr.* fr. 77, believes even these pagans to be superior to Christians; see above, n. 18.

43. Eunapius, *Vit. Soph.*, ed. Boissonade, p. 454: ἀλλὰ τὸ μὲν ἐς τοῦτον ὁ Λήμνιος ἐπετέλεσε Φιλόστρατος, βίον ἐπιγράψας ᾿Απολλωνίου τὰ βιβλία, δέον ᾿Επιδημίαν ἐς ἀνθρώπους θεοῦ καλεῖν. Cf. *Enn.* IV.4.7.

44. Eunapius, *ibid.*

philosopher is filled with allusions to his divine origin. Sometimes Apollonius claims to be a mere man, but at other times he seems to acknowledge his divinity. The *Life* contains prophecies of a divine and miraculous birth. A divinity appears to his mother and informs her that she will give birth to himself, "Proteus, the Egyptian God" (1.4). The birth is accompanied by divine portents (1.5). The natives of Tyana are said to have thought that he was the son of Zeus (1.6). But Philostratus says that in this instance Apollonius referred to himself as the son of his *human* father (1.6). This is typical of the ambiguity and paradoxical nature of these numinous heroes, characteristic of the Hellenistic "gospels." In one place humanity is emphasized, in another, divinity. When his follower Damis offers to act as an interpreter on the way to Babylon, Apollonius asserts that he knows all languages, even those he has never learned. At this point Damis worships him as a divine being (1.19). When, without any religious rites or invocations, he removes his leg from a chain in Domitian's prison, Damis clearly understands that Apollonius is really a god (7.38).

Apollonius himself advocates a purified paganism based on a philosophical solar monotheism, in which Apollo plays an important role.[45] In fact, Philostratus' depiction of his famous trial scene presents us with evidence of a direct connection with Apollo. During the trial the prosecutor asks Apollonius why men call him a god. He replies that all good men are given that name. But when he presents the conclusion of his defense, an amazing reversal of his identity occurs. At first, in the manner of a Stoic sage, he invites the tyrant to destroy his body if he will, for he cannot destroy his soul. He then declares that Domitian cannot even destroy his body: "For you shall not kill me, since I am not mortal." Having said this, he vanishes (8.5). Morton Smith points out that these are the very words uttered by Apollo when he has been threatened by Achilles (*Il.* 22.13).[46]

Porphyry, in his *Life of Pythagoras*, reports stories of the divine nature of the philosopher without any philosophical explanation or justification. He tells us that some people believe Pythagoras was really a son of Apollo and Pythaïs, and in name only the son of Mnesarchus (2).[47] In Magna Graecia the cities received laws from him as if they were commandments of the gods, among whom they numbered Pythagoras (20). When Abaris, as priest of the Hyperborean Apollo, believed him to be

45. Cf. e.g. *ibid.* 8.13.

46. Hadas and Smith, *Heroes and Gods* 250 n. 3.

47. Porphyry, *Opuscula Tria*, ed. Nauck, 14–39. For Christian Gospel parallels to Porphyry's *Vit. Pyth.*, see Hadas and Smith, *Heroes and Gods* 107.

that very god, Pythagoras showed him his golden thigh, "*confirming that this was true*" (28).

Iamblichus also relates many tales associating Pythagoras with divinity in general and Apollo in particular.[48] He mentions a certain Samian poet who says that Pythagoras was a son of Apollo. His beauty and godlike appearance and actions made it reasonable for many to assert that he was the son of a god (2.10). He convinced a group of sailors with whom he was travelling that he was a divinity (3.14–17). The people of Magna Graecia numbered him among the gods; some considered him the Pythian, others the Hyperborean Apollo. Still others thought that he was Paeon, a daemon from the moon, or one of the Olympians who had come to earth and "appeared to the men of those times in human form for the benefit and correction of the mortal life" (6.30). The story of Abaris also appears in Iamblichus' account. Here, too, Pythagoras shows the priest his golden thigh in order to confirm his opinion that he was Apollo (19.92; 28.135, 140). He also tells Abaris that he had assumed human form "lest men becoming disturbed by his strange divine nature, should avoid his teaching" (19.92). The Pythagoreans themselves thought that their philosophy was true because it was originated by a god. They often asked the question "who was Pythagoras?" To which they replied that he was said to be the Hyperborean Apollo (28.140). They also used to speak enigmatically, "saying that man, bird and another third thing are bipeds; *Pythagoras is the third thing*" (28.144).[49]

In one place Iamblichus is critical of the tradition he is reporting. When Mnesarchus, the father of Pythagoras, receives an oracle at Delphi that tells him his son will be a wonder child, he begins to call his wife Pythaïs instead of Parthenis, and names his child Pythagoras to signify that he was predicted by the Pythian Apollo (2.6–7). Here Iamblichus declares that we must reject the views of Epimenides, Eudoxus and Xenocrates, when they conjecture that Apollo had caused Parthenis to become pregnant and then predicted the birth through his prophet: "Surely, this is in no wise to be admitted" (2.7–8). It is possible that here Iamblichus tried to sharply distinguish the pagan "divine hero" from Christ by criticizing the idea (*in the pagan tradition*) of a virgin birth. This is understandable: Iamblichus was the foremost pagan ideologue of his age. He was held in the highest regard by the Emperor Julian. On the

48. Iamblichus, *Vit. Pyth.*, ed. Nauck; *Life of Pythagoras*, tr. Thomas Taylor (London, 1818).

49. Cf. ch. 6.31, where he attributes to Aristotle the Pythagorean dictum that of rational animals one kind is a god, another man, and another such as Pythagoras.

other hand, outside of this critical passage, even Iamblichus' descriptions of Pythagoras are ambiguous enough to be of use to a pagan in sympathy with the Church if he really wanted to assimilate such figures as Apollonius and Pythagoras to Christ. In this work Iamblichus only lays the groundwork for a carefully developed pagan position; he does not systematically establish it. For instance, after his observation on the virgin birth, he does not hesitate to connect Pythagoras closely with Apollo:

> Yet, having inferred the fact from his birth and the all-encompassing wisdom of his soul, no one would dispute that the soul of Pythagoras was sent down to men from the imperium of Apollo, either as an attendant or organically connected with the god in yet another more intimate way. (2.8)

It is not difficult to see how a sympathetic pagan might adapt this idea to Christianity. It is but a short step from this position to a theory of incarnation not completely unlike that of Origen; i.e., the "more intimate way" of connection with the god might be conceived of as a "fusing" of the soul of Pythagoras with the intelligible "Apolline principle" before it is "emanated" or becomes incarnate. This principle need not stand for the whole Logos, but it could represent a partial aspect of the noetic realm.

There is no doubt that pagans such as Julian would, unlike Synesius, avoid being flexible on this issue and dogmatically try to adopt principles that would preclude the building of bridges between the two religions. For this reason, Thomas Taylor, a devout Romantic pagan revivalist,[50] attempted to explicate the philosophical meaning of Iamblichus' criticism of a virgin birth. Hoping to revive the religion of Julian and Proclus, in his view the true light of wisdom, Taylor opposed both Christianity and modern empirical and scientific thinking. If one reads between the lines of his interpretations, one can often discern an anti-Christian theological position. Taylor thinks that it would be "absurd in the extreme" to believe that Apollo was literally connected with Pythaïs.[51] The assertions of Epimenides and company "should be considered as one of those mythological narratives in which heroes are said to have gods and goddesses" for their parents. The real meaning of the doctrine can be found in the Platonic theology of the ancients. In order that the "chain of Being" should have no "gaps" between "those perpetual attendants of a divine nature called essential heroes, who are impassive and pure, and the bulk of human souls who descend to earth with passivity and impurity, there should be an order of human souls who descend with impassivity and purity." In

---

50. For an interesting discussion of Thomas Taylor and his connection with the Romantics, see Raine in *Le Néoplatonisme* 475–483, and in *Thomas Taylor the Platonist* 3–48.

51. Iamblichus, *Life of Pythagoras*, tr. Taylor, 31 n. 1.

other words, the "chains" of daemons and spirits, which connect divinity with humanity,[52] would be incomplete without this order of souls:

> For as there is no vacuum either in incorporeal or corporeal natures, it is necessary that the last link of a superior order should coalesce with the summit of one proximately inferior. These souls were called by the ancients *terrestrial* heroes on account of their high degree of proximity to such as are essentially heroes. Theseus, Pythagoras, Plato and C[o]. were souls of this kind who descended into mortality both to benefit other souls, and in compliance with that necessity by which all natures inferior to the perpetual attendants of the Gods are at times obliged to descend.[53]

Thus, according to Taylor, who bases his arguments on a strictly "scholastic" Procline conception of emanation, Pythagoras, and those like him, are incarnate divinities of a lower order, but not the Logos (Nous) Himself, who has "emptied" into a man. He is a specific being with a definite rung on the ladder of emanation. In this way humanity and divinity can be connected without disturbing the metaphysical eminence of the intelligible realm or the transcendence of the One. Yet Iamblichus himself only opposes a literal conception of the virgin birth. His critique of literalism is much like that of Porphyry in fr. 77. Synesius himself pictures the Incarnation in a Chaldaean manner, which stresses the mystical ineffability of Christ's birth. In the Neoplatonic thought-world in which Synesius moved, such ideas were acceptable.

Many of Iamblichus' other statements leave room for interpretation. The Hyperborean Apollo might only be a partial emanation of the god, but Pythagoras was also supposed to be the Delphic Apollo, an Olympian, etc. These different aspects of Pythagoras give us a sense of the *multiplex numen* behind phenomena which manifests itself in different ways throughout the cosmos; i.e., of the pagan idea of the High God manifesting Himself in many "gods." Nor does Pythagoras discourage Abaris from thinking that he himself is Apollo. If one tones down the scholastic view of such a figure, one at least begins to get a sense of the paradox of the very notion of divinity becoming incarnate in humanity that is not completely at odds with a genuinely Christian mystical sense of such a phenomenon. He is a man, and yet (somehow) he is also Apollo. What is most important for our study is that the pagan thought-world of late antiquity at least in-

52. *Ibid.*; the standard middle and Neoplatonic source text for daemonic chains is Plato, *Symp.* 202E. The pagan and Christian problems on this point are in a sense ultimately the same—the Christian asks: "How does the Logos remain impassible having become incarnate?"; the pagan: "Having become incarnate, how can this pure and impassive order of human souls remain in this condition?"

53. See n. 51. For idea of divine descent, cf. Synesius, *De Prov.* 1229A–1231D.

cluded within its framework the idea of gods incarnate who were also historical men: of course, one need not emphasize their historicity, but be-
neath the accretions of legend these figures were believed to have lived in
historical time.

Eunapius (though perhaps not a very good example of pagan thought
at its best) seems to go even further than other Greek hagiographers. He
attributed to Plato the idea that divine as well as human *bodies* could exist
with souls. Speaking of the philosopher Alypius, he tells us that his cor-
ruptible element was actually divinized.[54] This sounds almost like a Christian doctrine of the divinization of the flesh in Christ through the activity
of the Logos. Julian himself believed in the incarnation of Asclepius. Taylor, further explicating the position of Iamblichus, quotes Julian (*apud*
Cyril) in this connection:[55]

> From what has been said respecting the divine origin of Pythagoras,
> it follows that he was a terrestrial hero belonging to the series of
> Apollo. Thus too the Esculapius who once lived on earth . . . pro-
> ceeded from the God Esculapius; i.e., was a lower embodiment of
> the "intellectual" Asclepios. "For Jupiter, in intelligibles, generated
> from himself Esculapius; but he was unfolded into light on the earth
> through the prolific light of the sun . . . he appeared uniformly in a
> human shape about Epidaurus . . . became multiplied . . . and ex-
> tended his saving right hand to all the earth."

Despite Taylor's Procline insistence on the exact ontological status of
these divinities, Julian's words also lend themselves to an interpretation
not totally incompatible with the more flexible views of Synesius. Without altering the Porphyrian Neoplatonic schema, he might have proceeded by analogy in the following way: "As Pythagoras is to Apollo and
the manifest Asclepios is to the Asclepios who subsists in Zeus (i.e., the
active [*noeric*] side of the demiurgic mind)—so Christ is to the Nous
(Logos). As incarnate he is (in Chaldaean phraseology) the "bringer of
light-from-the-source to mortals" (*Hymn* V, 1.8–9); as a "portion" of the
Logos Himself (Nous) he *is* "the light-from-the-source / the beam that
shines along with the Father" (*Hymn* V, 1.12–13, again Chaldaean
phraseology).

That Pythagoras *is* Apollo is true for pagans in one sense because of
the principle that "all things are in all things, but in each according to

54. *Vit. Soph.*, ed. Boissonade, 460: . . . οὕτω τὸ φθειρόμενον οὐκ ἐπέδωκεν εἰς
μέγεθος, δαπανηθὲν εἰς τὸ θεοειδέστερον. Perhaps this represents an attempt to provide a
pagan equivalent to certain forms of Christology from a position that has become defensive.
55. Iamblichus, *Life of Pyth.* 15 n. 1.

their proper nature."[56] Since in an "organically interpenetrating universe,"[57] all causes and effects reflect each other, the fact that Pythagoras
is a special manifestation of the Apolline series makes it possible to call
him Apollo from our point of view. Yet, because "a god is more universal
as he is nearer to the One, more specific in proportion to his remoteness
from it,"[58] Pythagoras is still to be thought of as a derivative emanation. It
is possible that on these grounds, Synesius, if pressed for a strictly philosophical answer, would have admitted that Christ was for him not unlike
the derivative order of gods who descend to purify the world in his *On
Providence*. On the other hand, his Chaldaean trinitarianism explains the
fact that Synesius associates Christ so closely with the Son of the Trinity.
Formally, then, the soul of the Savior might still proceed along a chain,
but perhaps it would have a special status not completely coincident with
the ontological rank of a terrestrial hero.[59] For when, in Chaldaean language, Synesius portrays Christ as the "ineffable offspring" of the "ineffable counsels of the father," he seems to attribute to him direct contact
with the Source. It is not simply a question of Platonic participation in
divinity at a rank just above that of the human soul. The soul of Christ
would, in this case, be so pure because of its complete fusion with the
divine mind, that even a journey into the lower realms would not stop
him from bringing the source light to earth. Even in his doctrine of the
Incarnation, Synesius is most interested in the saving power of Nous. But
any connection with the ideas of Origen here is coincidental or secondary.
There is no evidence that Synesius read the Alexandrian Christians.
There is much evidence that he worked primarily in the Neoplatonic and
Chaldaean traditions.

Synesius read Philostratus and was familiar with the *Lives*, but we
cannot prove that he studied the hagiographies of the pagan "divine men"
in order to apply the ideas therein to the problem of the Incarnation.[60]
Although he certainly knew about Pythagoras and was familiar with his
thought,[61] it is significant that if Synesius was interested in the idea of the

56. Proclus, *Elem. Theol.*, prop. 103. The qualification is the central issue here; for if
we accept it, then we can only claim the man-god is ontologically a terrestrial hero just
above the human on the "chain" of emanation.

57. Rosàn, "Proclus" 450, uses this descriptive phrase for the philosophy of Proclus.

58. Proclus, *Elem. Theol.* prop. 126; cf. props. 129 and 133, and for a principle of
incarnation, 140.

59. Cf. *Hymn* IX, 1.31–71 (as a return journey through the "Heliac chain").

60. *Dion ad init.* and ff.

61. For references to Pythagoras, see *Epp.* 137–146; for Apollonius, see *Calvitii Encomium* 68B–C (ed. Terzaghi).

theios aner, he was primarily interested in its cosmological and soterio-logical aspects. He tells us nothing of Christ's life and teachings, although pagan hagiographies provided him with sufficient parallels to the Gospels.

Our purpose has been to form a picture of the pagan thought-world at the time of Synesius and to try to imagine how he might have dealt with the problem of the Incarnation in the context of that thought-world. His failure to discuss the doctrine philosophically suggests that he preferred metaphysical poetry where a strictly philosophical account presented dif-ficulties. The tone and imagery of his poetry indicate that the most impor-tant sources of his inspiration were the Chaldaean Oracles and other Hellenistic mystical writings. Here he showed himself a typical Neoplato-nist, resorting to the language of the mysteries when faced with an insolu-ble philosophical problem.

Having analyzed Synesius' position on the Incarnation in connec-tion with pagan thought, let us now review the development of some of the basic Greek Christian concepts of the Incarnation and Christology to see if they are at all compatible with his views. "The problem of Christol-ogy, in the narrow sense, is to define the relation of the divine and the human in Christ." [62] The generally held Christian view that Jesus is Lord was elaborated by the New Testament authors, who believed Christ was preexistent to the Creation. They attributed a twofold order of being to Him, as man "according to the flesh" (*kata sarka*), and as God "according to the spirit" (*kata pneuma*). This formulation became the "foundation datum of all later Christological development." [63] However, many views were expounded before the issue was finally resolved.

The heretical doctrine of Docetism (from *dokein*: to seem), which first appeared in the second century, asserted that Christ's manhood and His sufferings were unreal. "There are some who declare that Jesus Christ did not come in flesh but only as spirit, and exhibited an appearance (*phan-tasian*) of flesh." [64] Although a docetic interpretation of the Incarnation would help Synesius get around standard pagan objections, he makes no statement in the *Hymns* that is clearly docetic. His first presentation of the Incarnation (*Hymn* V, 1.6–7) might seem docetic, but we are not compelled to read it in this way: "the sacred labor of the bride / man-ifested the form of man" could indicate a real human figure rather than a

---

62. Kelly, 138. He also says: "For a full dress attack on the issues involved we must wait until the fourth century; it was the decision promulgated at Nicaea, that the Word shared the same divine nature as the Father, that focused attention upon them." But, as we shall see, due to his unique position, Synesius seems to be closer to second-century Christological confusion than to the hair-splitting refinements of the fourth century.

63. *Ibid.* 141.   64. *Ibid.*

phantasm.[65] We could also attempt semi-Platonic or Hermetic speculations on the *morphe anthropou* as the manifestation of the archetypal
man or *Anthropos*. There is not enough evidence here, however, to make
it possible to draw clear and definite conclusions. The phrase can simply
be taken as a periphrasis for the god-man; it tells us nothing about the
status of Christ's human nature. We need not discuss more complicated
Gnostic theories, for Synesius presents no defense of his view of the Incarnation. The "gnostic" tone of his poetry can be understood as part of
the religious heritage of the age. It does not necessarily indicate borrow-
ings from such Alexandrian Gnostics as Valentinus. The Chaldaean Oracles, for all their "gnostic" imagery, were studied by men who—theurgy
notwithstanding—basically agreed with Plotinus' famous attack against
Gnosticism (*Enn.* II.IX).

In many ways Synesius appears closer to the early Apologists than to
the Christian theologians of his own time. "Preoccupied with the *Logos*,
they evince surprisingly little interest in the 'Gospel Figure.'"[66] They
speak of him as God in the form of a man, or as descending from heaven in
the Holy Spirit (*en pneumati hagioi*) and taking flesh from a Virgin, but
they stressed his preexistence and identification with the Godhead. "Justin himself was usually content to reproduce the familiar affirmations of
the rule of faith. He is satisfied that the Word became man by being born
from the Virgin."[67] Synesius affirms this much in *Hymn* VII, 1.18–19:
"When you were poured out on earth / from a mortal womb." However,
he stops at this affirmation, whereas Justin "insists on the reality of the
Messiah's physical sufferings;"[68] a doctrine that Synesius the Hellene
scrupulously avoids.

Kelly points out that Justin's doctrine of the *logos spermatikos*
might help us to understand his Christological position.

> Since we agree that the *Logos* manifested Himself in various forms to
> Abraham, Isaac, and Moses (he [Justin] is thinking of the Old Testa-
> ment theophanies), why should we shrink from believing that He
> could be born as a man from the Virgin? The *Logos*, moreover, has
> been active in all men, imparting to them whatever goodness and
> knowledge they possessed. The idea lurking in his [Justin's] mind
> seems to be that His presence in Jesus Christ should be understood
> as similar in kind to this universal presence, though much greater in
> degree.[69]

65. For a Neoplatonic definition of μορφή, see Proclus *In Tim.* xi, tr. T. Taylor.
66. Kelly, 145.   67. *Ibid.*
68. *Ibid.*: "yet for Justin he did not cease to exist as Word, being, in fact, at once God
and man."
69. *Ibid.* 145f.

Synesius' general conception of the saving power of Nous was similar to Justin's. Yet he never states his case with even this much clarity; we must, therefore, attempt to reconstruct it from our analysis of his other works in addition to his *Hymns*.

As a Christianizing Platonist associated with Alexandria, one would expect that Synesius studied the writings of Clement and Origen in order to facilitate his construction of hermeneutic bridges. Though there is no evidence that he consulted their works, the common heritage of Platonism justifies a discussion of some of their ideas.

Clement speaks of the Logos as descending from heaven, entering into or attaching Himself to human flesh and creating His own humanity in making Himself visible. He clothed Himself with a man, was God in the form of a man. Nevertheless, Christ really suffered.[70] Consequently, Clement was not a docetist and believed in the reality of the Incarnation. There were, however, certain docetic elements in his thought: ". . . many of his statements, e.g., that Christ was no ordinary man with physical passions, have a distinctly docetic ring." Although Clement attributed a human soul to Christ, the real directive principle in him (the Stoic *to hegemonikon*) was the Logos, of which the human soul was merely a copy. "*Soteriologically* considered the *humanity* of Jesus had little theological importance in his scheme." Here we begin to approach a position that Synesius could have held: for whether or not a human soul or mind is seen as a *metaphysically* necessary constituent of the incarnate god-man, it is of secondary importance to its role in the economy of salvation. The Christ of Synesius becomes incarnate, descends on a mission of salvation to Hades and ascends in triumph; but did "He dwell among us"? We shall have occasion to analyze this theme carefully in the following pages.

Clement's "docetic tendencies" stem from the Greek philosophical side of his thought. "The problematical element in his picture of Him springs from the way he allowed it to be coloured by the Greek ascetical ideal of *apatheia*, or emancipation from passion." Clement was convinced that the Lord must have been exempt from all desire since His constitution was sustained by "divine power." Such a description of the Messiah would appeal to a pagan convert trying to come to grips with the problem of the Incarnation. One could easily envision Synesius developing his thought along the same lines as Clement, insofar as the latter's orientation remained Hellenic.

Origen's original solution to the problem is, at bottom, designed to

70. Cf. *ibid.*, pp. 153. The following discussion of Clement's relation to docetism and Origen's view of the natures of Christ is based on Kelly, 154–157, and the quotations are drawn from those pages.

allow one to retain Christian belief without falling into philosophical absurdity. The main idea is that in the preexistent spiritual world there was a fall in which all souls, Christ's excepted, fell away from the Logos through the exercise of free will. The soul of Christ remained with the Logos and became "fused" with Him through pure mystical devotion.

> The union is as complete as that of a lump of iron into the fire into which it has been plunged, becoming red-hot; and Origen quotes 1 Cor. 6.17 as Scriptural proof that it formed "one spirit" with Him. But since his soul, while thus cleaving to the *Logos*, properly belonged to a body, it formed the ideal meeting point between the infinite Word and finite human nature.

Thus in Christ "godhood and manhood were inextricably united." Although Origen speaks of the two natures in Him as a real union and not a mere association—although he allows for the "sufferings of the flesh"—his theory is not completely successful from a soteriological point of view. "However intimate the relationship established by the soul's loving adhesion to the Word, it can in the end be no more than a *special case*, differing in *degree* but not in *kind*, of that union of affection and will which the saints can attain with Him." The soul was so fused with the divine wisdom in Him that "the Word had in effect taken over the role of *hegemonikon*, or governing principle in Christ."

Thus "the Incarnation as such stood outside the logic of Origen's system." Although he gives a place to the Incarnation in his thought, the Son's participation in human nature is not permanent or essential. The simple Christians are attached to Christ's manhood; the gnostic Christian "strains upward to the *Logos*, the soul's authentic life from which it originally fell away." The true mediator is in the last analysis not the God-man Jesus Christ but the "Word Who bridges the gulf between the unoriginate Godhead and creatures."

As we have already suggested, a theory of the Incarnation like Origen's could help a philosophical pagan work out a solution to the vexed question of how the entire Logos became a man. The soul perfectly fused with the Logos was also destined for a body. Thus, it being at one and the same time unifically the Logos and an individual soul, one might even be able to conceive of it as somehow emanating through, for example, the "Heliac series" before assuming a body. Having avoided the pre-Creation "fall" of the other souls, it could act as a pivot-point between the human and divine without displaying any of their inherent weaknesses. Origen's cosmological emphasis on the Logos rather than the Incarnation would fit in well with Synesius' general conception of divinity. That the Incarnation is for Origen ultimately a special case differing in degree but not in kind

from His union with the saints parallels Synesius' syncretistic view that
Amos, Antony, Hermes and Zoroaster were perfect autodidacts in direct
contact with Nous. Thus Synesius exempted them from the need for traditional *paideia* because of their saintly or deified natures. Origen's division of the Christian camp into simple and "gnostic" Christians is made to
order for Synesius. He himself conceived of Christianity in a similar way:
the simple Christians who are attached to the person of Christ accept a
kalon pseudos as the truth; the "gnostic" or the Platonic philosopher-
bishop understands and aspires to the life of Nous, the truly divine life.

The doctrines of Synesius and Origen, then, are in many ways
potentially compatible; but one may arrive at such ideas from a purely
philosophical angle. Both the lack of evidence of any direct connection
between them and the ambiguity of Synesius' statements about the Incarnation compel us to make speculative suggestions rather than arrive at
definite conclusions.

If Synesius' ideas of the Incarnation and Christology seem incomplete when compared with those of the Apologists and Alexandrian Christian Platonists, they should hardly be worth discussing in the context of
the complex Christological controversies of the fourth and early fifth centuries. This criticism notwithstanding, we shall see that an attempt to
focus on certain themes which were emphasized in this period will help
us form a clearer picture of how Synesius' thought stands in relation to
contemporary Christian thought. Even negative results will serve to un-
derline the uniqueness of Synesius' position.

After the Council of Nicaea, the stage was set for the Christological
controversies of the fourth century. Although the Nicenes largely ignored
the Christological issue, they agreed upon a creed stating that the Son
was made flesh, becoming man. "The Nicenes . . . in affirming the homo-
ousion, inevitably confronted themselves with the problem of combining
deity and manhood in the Saviour." [71] Exactly how that combination was
to be understood was only resolved by the Church after a long, subtle and
complicated controversy. While Churchmen were developing involved
theological arguments about the nature of the God-man, we shall see that
Synesius of Cyrene did no more than to give poetic expression to the basic idea of the Incarnation. Thus, he appears to us an isolated figure: he
was more open to Christian influences than most pagans, but he was not
learned in Christian doctrine. His sensitive historical position as a pagan
collaborating with Christianity and his high social standing made it in-
cumbent upon him to approach Christianity in his own way.

71. *Ibid.*, 280.

The basic Christological discussions during the fourth century were centered on what have become known as the "Word-flesh" and "Word-man" types of Christology. The "Word-flesh" view had as its basis a reaction to the teachings of Origen and the "dualist" Antiochene doctrines.

> Making no allowance for a human soul in Christ, this viewed the incarnation as the union of the Word with human flesh, and took as its premise the Platonic conception of man as a body animated by a soul or spirit which was essentially alien from it. In rivalry with this, however, we can trace the growing influence of a "Word-man" type of Christology, based on the idea that the Word united Himself with a complete humanity, including a soul as well as a body. Behind this lay the Aristotelian theory of man as a psycho-physical unity, and also the determination to do justice to the genuinely human character of the Figure delineated in the Gospels.[72]

Even thus stated, in a most general way, we can readily see the difficulty of demonstrating which theory, if either, Synesius preferred. For example, his phrase "bearing a mortal body" does have Platonic overtones, and would indicate a preference for the "Word-flesh" doctrine. On the other hand, his statement that the Virgin birth "manifested the form of man" could be taken to mean that the Logos became a real man with a real human soul; it could also mean that the Logos Himself simply assumed a human figure. Furthermore, even if Synesius found it convenient to attribute a human soul to Him to achieve metaphysical cogency, he might still have conceived of the Logos as the real "ruling principle" in Christ. Finally, there is simply no evidence that he ever attempted to do justice to the Figure delineated in the Gospels.

Had he been a mainstream Christian theologian, it is perhaps most likely that, as an Alexandrian and a Neoplatonist, Synesius would have adhered to either an Origenist or a "Word-flesh" theory. Synesius could even have appreciated the paradoxical "Word-flesh" Christology of Athanasius, who believed that the Logos was simultaneously present in Christ and "everywhere else in the universe, vivifying and directing it with his life-giving power"[73] (cf. *Hymn* V, 1.8–9, 16–18). Apollinaris, an extreme proponent of "Word-flesh" Christology, insisted on the unity of being between the flesh and the Logos. His main concern was soteriology: ". . . considered *merely* as a man Christ had no saving life to bestow; He could

72. *Ibid.*, 381.
73. *Ibid.*, 385; Athanasius, later in his career, accepted the idea of a human soul in Christ, see *ibid.* 288: "At the Synod of Alexandria . . . [presided over by Athanasius] . . . agreement was reached to the effect that 'the Saviour did not have a body lacking soul, sensibility or intelligence': (οὐ σῶμα ἄψυχον οὐδ' ἀναίσθητον, οὐδ' ἀνόητον εἶχεν)."

not redeem us from our sins, revivify us, or raise us from the dead."[74] Synesius had a different conception of salvation. He believed that a divinity, completely free from material defilements, had to purify the cosmos and the souls therein, *when they became too implicated in the hylic realm to extricate themselves.* Soteriological differences notwithstanding, however, Apollinarist doctrine is also well-suited to Synesius' "Orphic" salvationism: a fully real *and* separate human nature implies material pollutions that would neutralize the Savior's effectiveness.

The Cappadocian reaction to the docetic tendencies of Apollinaris resulted in a profound vision of the Incarnation that moves in a dimension foreign to the religiosity of Synesius.

> It was man's rational soul, with its power of choice, which was the seat; and if the Word did not unite such a soul with Himself, the salvation of mankind could not have been achieved. In a famous phrase of Gregory Nazianzen, "What has not been assumed cannot be restored, it is what is united with God that is saved." It was Adam's *nous* he recalled, which originally violated the commandment, so that it became imperative that the Redeemer should possess one too. According to Gregory of Nyssa, "By becoming exactly what we are, He united the human race through Himself to God."[75]

Much more could be said about the Cappadocians' doctrine,[76] but it should already be apparent that their meditation on the soteriological mission and nature of the Second Adam went far beyond anything attempted by Synesius.

There is, however, one passage in which Synesius does represent Christ as something like a second Adam. At the beginning of *Hymn* IX (1.4–9), he depicts Him as the one who "has driven . . . the treacherous source, the chthonic serpent from the gardens of the Father; the serpent who gave the forbidden fruit to the primal man (*Archegonos*)." But Synesius gives no indication that Christ had to become fully man, with a human will, to accomplish this. Thus presented, the myth does not require that Synesius alter his ideas of "sin" and "salvation." For instance, allegorically the "chthonic-serpent/treacherous-source" might be interpreted as the principle of the material defilements from which the Savior came to free us. The fall of the *Archegonos* could be analogous to that of the Hermetic *Anthropos*. Consequently, the phrase "nourisher of painful destiny" (*trophon argaleou morou* 1.8–9) might be interpreted as a refer-

74. See *ibid.* 291.

75. *Ibid.* 296; for Gregory of Nyssa's conception of the Incarnation and its connection with the Christian idea of reform, see also Ladner, 75–107, 154, and *passim.*

76. Cf. Kelly, 296–300.

ence to the *Heimarmene*, by which the *Archegonos* was subjected to conditions of the material world. Adam's "sin" is represented in cosmological terms, as if it were a determined fact of cosmic history. The Savior is not intimately connected with the *Archegonos*, he merely arrives to rectify man's fate through an act of divine power. Synesius does not bring up the question of the free will of the first man; on the contrary, he understood the myth as symbolic of an "Orphic fall-into-matter" rather than a "fall" brought about by the free choice of the first man. In addition to all of this, the fact that the serpent gives the fruit to *Archegonos*—why not Adam?— and not to Eve, indicates that Synesius' brief portrayal of the "garden" is a somewhat distant reflection of the Christian story rather than a meditation in the mainstream of Christian tradition.

It remains now to discuss the other crucial problem for a pagan: the potential conflict between the idea of the Incarnation and the doctrine of the impassibility of the divine nature.

Not only educated pagans, but also educated Christians, accepted the validity of the notion of divine impassibility. They were well aware of the philosophical difficulties to which the Incarnation gave rise.[77] The Fathers suggested many answers to the problem. Those who were most sensitive to the question either denied that the flesh was *in itself* a real nature, or deemphasized the "sufferings of the flesh." These sufferings did not affect the Logos and were to be given a "purely physical explanation."[78] It is important for our study that contemporary Alexandrian Fathers stressed emphatically the idea of divine impassibility.

Pelikan has focused on the importance of this problem for Christological doctrine.[79] In his view, "Alexandrians such as Apollinaris appear to have stressed the notion of impassibility without compromise." Moreover, "Apollinaris believed that 'the presence of the "sufferings of the flesh" could not in any way impair the impassibility of the divine nature;' therefore he attacked anyone who would attribute to the divinity in Christ such human things as development and suffering."

With respect to this question, Cyril of Alexandria is even more important than Apollinaris. Cyril stressed the contrast between the permanent unchangeable nature of God and the nature of created beings who

77. Cf. Pelikan, 1.229: "the early Christian picture of God was controlled by the self-evident axiom, accepted by all, of the absoluteness and impassibility of the divine nature. No one wanted to be understood as setting forth a view of Christ in which this definition was in any way compromised or jeopardized."

78. Kelly, 286.

79. 1.222–277, esp. 230–243. The following discussion, with quotations, is drawn from pages 230–232.

were subject to time and change. In discussing the Incarnation, Cyril denied that God had "become" something which He had not "been" in the beginning:

> He always remains what he was and ever is, even though he is said to have "become" a refuge (*Ps.* 94:22 and 90:1). In fact, the very mention of the word "God" made the interpretation of "become" as applied to God "stupid and altogether wicked" if it is supposed that this could refer to any sort of change in the unchangeable God.

Cyril could not believe that the Incarnation and the taking on of flesh could affect His impassible nature: "He was the *Logos* also in the beginning and proceeding from the eternal and immutable God and Father, He also had in His own nature eternity and immutability." So strong was Cyril's emphasis on this point that even the Incarnation could not be allowed to contradict it.

> This attribute of being "ancient and unchangeable" could not be set aside even in the Incarnation. Cyril allows that He took on a flesh that could suffer but did not suffer Himself insofar as He was God. He suffered in the flesh but not in the nature of His deity.

Pelikan clearly sums up the essential meaning of all these statements: "Even the Alexandrian insistence upon the reality of His sufferings and upon the unity of divine and human in His person could not be allowed to *qualify or endanger* the essential impassibility of the nature of God."

Athanasius also dealt with the problem of *apatheia* in his life of St. Antony. As one who had been saved, his "soul was imperturbed, and so his outward appearance was calm."[80] If a monk achieved *apatheia* it was because he imitated the *apatheia* of Christ.

> Antony, he meant to say, possessed in a very high degree Christian *apatheia*—perfect self-control, freedom from passion. Christ who was free from every emotional weakness and fault—*apathes Christos*—is his model.[81]

Needless to say, this was also the ideal of the pagan sage. Taken out of its Christian context it could be a description of the perfect sage (Antony) and the *theios aner* (Christ). Furthermore, if compared to Antony in a Hellenic-Christian scheme, Christ could be viewed as a special case with respect to the Logos: greater in *degree*, but not in *kind*.

Although Synesius surely would have been sympathetic to these no-

---

80. *Ibid.* 232, quoting *Athan. Vit. Ant.* 67 (*PG* 26.940).
81. *Ibid.*

tions of Christ's *apatheia*, it is difficult to believe that he could have accepted any notion of the "sufferings of the flesh" or Cyril's statement that it "was not an elder or an angel but the Lord Himself who saved us, not by an alien death or by the mediation of an ordinary man, but by His very own blood."[82] The attitude of Apollonius, when he disappears in front of Domitian, is much more representative of Hellenic sentiment. Even the sufferings of pagan gods were different from those of Christ.

> The Christian message of the Cross was that of a suffering God in a real incarnation which made effective in life's agonies the full depth of the co-suffering (sympathia) of God with his creatures. . . . The *pathe* of Dionysos were legendary; the *pathe* of Jesus were very real to Himself and His followers.[83]

Finally, let us look at the confession with which any Christology must come to terms:

> For the sake of us men and for the purpose of our salvation, Christ had come down, had become incarnate, had suffered and risen again on the third day, had ascended to the heavens, and would come again to judge the living and the dead.[84]

We can immediately see how far Synesius is from this Christian affirmation. He does not mention the Passion or the Resurrection on the third day; he combines the latter with the Ascension and does not deal with the Last Judgment. However, he did believe that Christ must become a *nekys* to visit the underworld. And, as has been seen, he follows traditional Christian usage when he allows myrrh to be given as a gift to the mortality of Christ. But his acceptance of Christ's mortality follows the pattern of the mysteries and certain Greek myths. Thus Synesius is able to deal with the mortality of Christ without becoming involved in a problematical depiction of the "sufferings of the flesh."

Synesius' combination of the Resurrection and Ascension, as well as his use of cosmic imagery, also have precedents in the Christian tradition. In his study of Jewish Christianity, Daniélou presents ample evidence in this literature of the theme of cosmic ascent. He discusses its similarities with Gnostic tracts such as the *Pistis Sophia* and its continuation in Justin, Origen, and the two Gregories.[85] This theme was preponderant in the literature of Jewish Christianity because Jewish Christianity had a cosmological rather than an anthropological point of view.[86] But there is little likelihood that Synesius patterned *Hymn* IX after this theme in Christian

---

82. *Ibid.* 227.   83. Angus, 307.   84. Pelikan, 1.229.
85. Daniélou, 1.248–262.   86. *Ibid.* 1.249.

literature. The similarity can be more reasonably explained by the fact that he also had a cosmological rather than an anthropological point of view.

Synesius had enough religious and philosophical flexibility to accept the Incarnation in a cosmological, metaphysical and mystical sense. Yet it is difficult to arrive at a precise understanding of how he rationalized the doctrine. Here, as elsewhere, his old beliefs remained the basis for his religious outlook. The Trinity was easier for him to accept than the Incarnation because it had clearer precedents in Pythagorean thought, Neoplatonism and the Chaldaean Oracles. The Incarnation also had pagan precedents, and the Christological debate provided some answers to standard pagan objections (e.g., the *apathes Christos*), but it remains an essential Christian dogma very difficult to harmonize with pure Hellenism. In the last analysis, Synesius' statement that the Resurrection was *hieron ti aporreton (Ep.* 105) might well be applied to his vision of the Incarnation. If his views on the matter are not completely intelligible, we can also blame both lack of evidence and the unsettled state of the issues, even among contemporary orthodox Christians.[87]

It is probable that the pagan idea of the divine man enabled Synesius to assent to the concept of incarnation *per se*. He transformed Chaldaean mystical notions in order to harmonize them with this concept. He had personal contacts among Christians and probably heard sermons in churches; thus he had a vague and general notion of both the Christ story and the Christian views of the Incarnation. But he remained outside of the mainstream of Christian tradition. This is all that the evidence allows us to affirm.

Let us now turn briefly to the pagan side of Synesius' religious sensibility as manifested in the *Hymns. Hymn* I (already analyzed), and *Hymns* III–IX are filled not only with pagan imagery, but also with theological concepts basic to the higher forms of pagan religiosity. Returning to *Hymn* IX, it will be remembered that after Christ had delivered the righteous souls from Hades, His Resurrection was presented as an ascent through the visible (pagan) cosmos all the way to the hypercosmic paternal realm. In the same *Hymn* (IX, 1.31–33), the daemons of the air tremble at his ascent; a chorus of immortal stars is seized with awe (1.34–35),

> and Aither laughing, wise father of harmony, blended upon the seven-stringed lyre [i.e., the spheres] a hymn of victory to thy might.
> . . . Titan spread his far-flaming hair under the ineffable track, and

87. See Pelikan, 1.247, who alludes to the difficulty for any one theology in settling the problem of John 1:14. He also discusses (p. 249) the way in which Syriac theology transcends or ignores the traditional polarization by use of ambiguous terminology.

recognized the offspring of God, Mind, the Artificer of all that is best, and the principle of his own flame.

This is clearly pagan cosmology, as the divinity of the cosmos, immortality of the heavenly bodies and the harmony of the spheres depicted therein attest. At the same time, the ascending Christ, recognized (by Titan) as the Son of God, the Demiurgic mind (Nous-Logos) and the principle behind the fire of the Sun (*idiou pyros archan*) suggests Chaldaean parallels and a solar theology similar to that proposed by Julian in his *Hymn to King Helios*.[88] The cosmic journey through the spheres is also typical of the late pagan "astral" religion.[89]

The hymn now passes from the visible cosmos to the hypercosmic noetic realm: the Son travels from the *visible divine* to invisible divine transcendent (1.55–71). He leaps over the back of the azure heaven (cosmic vault) and takes his place among the inviolate spheres of the intellectual realm[90] (σφαίρῃσι δ'ἐπεστάξῃς / νοεραῖσιν ἀκηράτοις), "out of the sea of light and the chords of the harmony of the spheres into timeless, motionless and activityless eternity."[91] This realm, free from time, "the silent heaven" which is the source of "goods" (*agatha*) in the Chaldaean Oracles, is paradoxically described in the terms of the "mystical logic" of the *coincidentia oppositorum*: "but eternity the ancient of days ageless itself, at once young and old is for the *gods* steward of their eternal mansion."[92] The gods are the intelligibles whose mansion is Nous. Indeed, this mystical sense can be found throughout the *Hymns* in which phrases are put together, one after the other, in such a way as to create a sense of the Absolute. By bombarding us with images, Synesius attempts to break through our everyday way of thinking to bring us a step closer to the ineffable. These superlative descriptions of divine reality are in the tradition of the great mystics.[93]

88. Cf. Proclus, *Hymn to Helios*; cf. also Fitzgerald, *Essays and Hymns* 493.

89. See Cumont, *After Life* 90–109 and 148–169; *Les Hymnes*, ed. Meunier, 249 n. 2.

90. Smith, *Porphyry's Place* 63, equates this with the Chaldaean *empyrean* realm.

91. Wilamowitz, 289, who also compares the mixed pagan and Christian imagery of this hymn to Correggio's dome painting of the Assumption of the Virgin at Parma.

92. *Hymn IX*, 1.67–71: ἀλλ' αὐτὸς ἀγήρως / αἰὼν ὁ παλαιγενής, νέος ὢν ἅμα καὶ γέρων, / τᾶς ἀενάω μονᾶς ταμίας πέλεται θεοῖς· *Hymni*, ed. Terzaghi, 269, seems to deny paganism here: "qui v. 71 nominantur, non gentilium dii sunt sed et caelestia corpora et animae, quibus ut penes Deum per saeculorum saecula manerent concessum est." But surely these are the "gods" of the *divine* cosmos as everything about them would indicate; cf. also the Orphic fr. 54 which mentions χρόνος ἀγήραος. Even in Terzaghi's interpretation a great concession to pagan cosmos-piety is indicated. The description of αἰών as both old and young is the type of metaphysical paradox that would fit the idea of the Hellenistic savior figure alluded to above.

93. Cf. e.g. *Hymn IV*, 1.60–80; *Hymn II*, 1.60–72; *Hymn I*, 64: σὺ μὲν ἄρρην, σὺ δὲ θῆλυς. There is a parallel in Valentinian Gnosis: as the myth tells it, before Creation

Terzaghi's[94] analysis of *Hymn* IX has proven that the major events of Christian sacred history are presented in three separate sections: the serpent in the garden, i.e., the Fall; the Incarnation; and the Resurrection. But, as Terzaghi himself recognizes, Christ is the new Heracles or Orpheus who beats back the hound of Hades in order to rescue the damned souls and bring them back to God. We are also presented with Chaldaean and other pagan religious ideas. For Synesius the great myths of the Christian history of Salvation are poetic metaphors, which have their setting within a cosmic scheme and frame of reference that is still pagan.[95]

All of the *Hymns* exhibit the major characteristic of pagan mysticism and cosmology, i.e. cosmos-piety,[96] including ideas of eternity and *divinity* of the cosmos. They depict the preexistence and *divinity* of the human soul and contain prayers for the purification of life and liberation from matter.[97] They describe deity in the mystical commonplaces of Neopythagorean–Neoplatonic thought.[98] There are also sections which are heavily influenced by the Chaldaean Oracles[99] and other pagan "scrip-

when all things were contained in the *Autopator*, God was conceived as both male and female . . . etc.; see Jonas, 179–182.

94. *Hymni*, ed. Terzaghi, 262: "Versus enim intercalares (1. 1–3, 10–12, 28–30) totum carmen in tres partes dividunt, quarum prima dracone terrestri paradiso eiectum memorat, altera Christi descensum in terras atque ad inferos laudat, tertia vero Christi resurrectionem celebrat."

95. Several scholars have remarked on this, e.g. Druon (with whom I disagree), quoted in *Les Hymnes*, ed. Meunier, 248: "Chrétien par les croyances, il reste, par l'imagination, néoplatonicien et presque païen." Also Geffcken, 220: ". . . reitet der Titan, die unauslösliche Quelle der Morgenrote, der löst der gehörnte Mond das nachtlige Dunkel, und in Geiste der echten Antike wird beschrieben, wie der menschfressende Hund von der Schwell zurückweicht, wie dann bei der Auffahrt des Herrn, gleichwie bei der Epidemie eines Hellengottes, ganze Schöpfung in hellen Jubel gerat." Meunier, *ibid*. 249 n. 1: "Toutefois, ce serait méconnaître le curieux attrait qui les caractérise que d'oublier qu'ils sont un des rares exemples parvenus jusqu' à nous, de cette audacieuse pensée qui s'efforça d'intégrer dans le Panthéon hellénique et dans la théologie néoplatonicienne, le Verbe qui nâquit d'une Vierge de Solyme . . . dans son ascension vers les sphères intelligentes et pures le Christ semble suivre d'après Synésios une voie analogue à celle que suivent les initiés aux Mystères de Mithra. . . ." (Meunier's notes on the *Hymns* are always lucid and show an excellent grasp of both Synesius' religious position and Neoplatonism.)

96. For cosmos-piety see e.g. *Hymn* III, I.266–280, 292, 301, 310, 312–315, 323–328, 339–342; *Hymn* IV, 1.60–79; *Hymni*, ed. Terzaghi, 1–4 and 5 n. 1; also 266–268 on astral religion and cosmos-piety.

97. For purificatory prayers and liberation from matter see e.g. *Hymn* III, 1.37–44, 51–71, 72–85, 89–94, 101–108, 577–579, etc. For a Neoplatonic conception of prayer, see Proclus *In Parm*. IV.68 (*conversion* of the intelligent soul towards God is indispensable for arriving at contemplation); Ps.-Dion. *Div. Nom*. III.1 (Comm. of Aquinas 1.3); Iamblichus, *De Myst*. I.12 and 15, V.26.

98. Cf. Fitzgerald, *Essays and Hymns* 2.482–484; *Les Hymnes*, ed. Meunier, 130–131 nn. 9 and 10.

99. For Chaldaean elements, see *Hymn* III, 61, 71, 78, 102, 104, 539–540, 620–622.

tural" writings. For example, a long section of *Hymn* III, which deals with hypercosmic–cosmic chains of emanation, follows the exact Neoplatonic order of descent and employs Chaldaean terminology.[100] In places, Synesius' archaizing classical viewpoint comes to the surface: "grant persuasion to my words and glory to my deeds, becoming to the ancient traditions of Cyrene and Sparta."[101]

In a prayer for the "grace" of *sophrosyne* (*Hymn* II, 1.85–91), Synesius represents the passions as being bad specifically because they are acosmic, i.e., disordered and out of tune with the cosmos.[102] Disorder is in itself a chaos, and this disorder of the passions prevents them from being a cosmos themselves, and therefore unable to harmonize with the rhythm of the greater cosmos by imitating its balance and perfection. Thus the uncontrolled passions are acosmic in every sense of the word. Noetic intuition is the power to overcome the *Até* of earth, ἵνα μὴ τὸ νοῦ πτέρωμα / ἐπιβρίσῃ χθονὸς ἄτα (1.87–88)—an expression rich in associations with classical epic and tragedy. The myth of Plato's *Phaedrus*—an influence here—also describes righteous souls, following in the train of the "chariots of the gods" to the "back of heaven," in order to view the intelligibles, whereas souls that fail to control the passions lose their wings, and through a "fall" are burdened by the weight of earth (*Phaedrus* 246C–248E). And the Chaldaean Oracles mention the weight of matter and the dark "amorphous abyss" that deter souls from the enjoyment of the "paternal intellect."[103] The tragic condition of man, the limitations of his earthly lot, may be overcome by a noetic experience, made available through a philosophy which has become a Hellenic mystical theology.[104]

Hymn X is the straightforward prayer of a believing Christian who seeks the help of Jesus Christ in his despair. Many scholars have taken it as evidence that Synesius was finally able to accept Christianity totally

---

100. *Hymn* III, 1.280–290.

101. *Hymn* V, 1.36–39. This almost Homeric prayer is placed directly after a section about Christ.

102. *Hymn* II, 1.85.

103. Cf. *Oracles Chaldaïques*, frr. 134, 155, 163, 180, and 181.

104. Both the Olympian and "Orphic" traditions of Greek religion have contributed to this idea. Festugière, *Personal Religion* 720, has pointed out one important difference: "In the Homeric-Aeschylean tradition, the Olympians, the heavens, etc., are contrasted in their serenity with the lot of man, but man can only look at them, or think about them, or perhaps long for them, but not establish an intimate spiritual connection with them; on the other hand, the 'Orphic'-Pythagorean-Platonic tradition, which had its greatest floreat in late antiquity, allows for the intimate connection of the human with the divine, the soul's salvation, transcendence of earthly limitations both here and hereafter." Thus the tragic is not final.

when he wrote it. Wilamowitz, however, rejects it as spurious on several grounds. There are, first, many uncharacteristic errors in meter; again, the word *pneuma*, which is used for (Holy) Spirit, is not characteristic of Synesius, who prefers its poetic equivalent *pnoia* in the *Hymns*.[105] Most modern scholars, including Lacombrade,[106] have accepted Wilamowitz' conclusions. The tone and content of *Hymn* X are so different from anything Synesius has done before that one must either reject it or accept the incongruous possibility that Synesius experienced a sudden and total conversion. *Hymns* I–IX, then, reflect a pagan religious sensibility. Although such Christian themes as the Incarnation become prominent in the later *Hymns*, they are prefigured in the earlier ones. In fact, with the exception of *Hymn* I, Synesius deals with Christian ideas in all the *Hymns*. But they are really a new means of expression for a Neoplatonist who views Christianity from the perspective of a philosopher. Thus, scholars must not focus on his transition from one religion to another, but rather on the Hellenic style, religious sensibility and framework in which he understood the new religion. Leaving aside theories of the secret inner workings of grace and the pattern of progressive salvation in the *Hymns* of Synesius, only the following conclusion seems fairly certain: at the time of the composition of the *Hymns*, Synesius, never a hostile enemy of the Church, and somewhat of a universalist in religion, was trying to harmonize his Neoplatonism with Christianity. To some extent he succeeded.

105. Wilamowitz, *Die Hymnen* 295. This Hymn also combines old Ionic forms with Doric forms in a mixed dialect like the Homeric: μνώεο, 1. 1; θειοῖο, ἀλιτροῖς, 1. 3, 5; ψυχᾶν, 1. 12.
106. *Synésios* 182.

VI

The Middle Years:
Hellenism, Philosophy, and Mysticism

The *Dion* and the Cultural Ideal of Synesius

Neoplatonic pagans of the late Roman Empire used the term "Hellenism" to represent an ideal in which the cultural, philosophical and religious aspects of existence are inextricably connected. Pious Hellenes were determined not to lose touch with the heritage of an incomparable past that, along with philosophy, helped to provide the key to an understanding of man's place in the cosmos. Thus, as far as they were concerned, Hellenism could not merely be a synonym for a Greek literary education, available to Christians as well as pagans, and often used to adorn the rhetorical showpieces of nominal pagans who had no serious religious commitments.[1] It must rather be a cultural ideal that had as its twin or reflection a religious ideal. No doubt Hellenism meant to many merely Julian's attempted revival of ancient glories. But a late pagan Neoplatonist would look upon it quite specifically as the unbroken thread of Greek thought derived from Plato, and even from Homer. For these men, Hellenism provided the only secure path to true knowledge and the correct interpretation of reality. Without it, they would live in darkness. It was no accident, then, that even Greek-speaking Christian writers often used the word Hellenism to refer to paganism.[2] Militant pagans appealed to the old culture in their defense of the old religion.

Julian himself, who best exemplifies this attitude, sums it up well in his law forbidding Christians to teach in the schools.[3] At the outset of his rescript, the emperor asserts that true education has for its end sound moral judgment rather than superficial rhetorical ability. Those who instruct the young must also be of sound character and not teach what they

1. On the distinction between the serious mystical Hellenism of the Neoplatonists and the more superficial Hellenism of the rhetoricians, see Bidez, *Julien* 47ff.
2. Cf. Coleman-Norton, 289 n. 3. Coleman-Norton, 1.324 n. 4, attributes the first extant Christian use of *paganus* to refer to the Greco-Roman religion to a mandate of Valentinian I and Valens issued in A.D. 370 (*Cod. Theod.* 16.2.18).
3. *Epistles*, 422A–424A.

themselves do not believe. If all the great classical authors were divinely inspired, how can certain impious atheists (i.e., Christians) who teach their writings be consistent when they attribute to these authors false opinions in religious matters? In short, those who would reap the fruits of Hellenic culture must also acknowledge its connection with the true doctrines of Hellenic religion. Gregory of Nazianzus well understood Julian's purposes when he attempted to demonstrate that it was preposterous for the emperor to exclude Christians from the benefits of Greek culture on the basis of an alleged identification of Greek language and literature with Greek religion.[4]

In addition to this rescript, many of Julian's other works demonstrate this attitude. His sixth and seventh Orations, *Against the Uneducated Cynics* and *Against the Cynic Heracleios*, are a defense of true Hellenism against the debased coinage of false contemporary Cynicism. His Oration V, *To the Mother of the Gods*, is an attempt to harmonize the myths of the ancient popular cult of the Magna Mater with the highest speculations of Neoplatonism. In his famous Oration IV, *To King Helios*, he tries to justify theurgic solar monotheism as the true religion of the Roman Empire. Throughout the hymn, Julian bases many of his interpretations on passages from Plato, Homer, Hesiod and other classical authors.[5] His work against the Christians presents the Greek tradition as superior to the Judaeo-Christian: the creation myth of the *Timaeus* surpasses in piety and understanding that of Genesis.[6]

Many other pagan Neoplatonists and Neoplatonic-influenced authors forged a strong link connecting Hellenic culture and religion. Porphyry felt perfectly free to interpret Homer according to what he thought to be the rules of Neoplatonic exegesis.[7] Proclus, aware of the importance of Homer to Hellenism, did not hesitate to comment on the famous problem of poetry v. philosophy presented in *Republic* X. His discussion resulted in a complete justification of the Homeric poems if understood according to Neoplatonic exegetical principles.[8] Even a superficial perusal of the same author's *Hymns* will result in the recognition of his debt to a poetic tradition that goes back to the *Homeric Hymns*.[9]

Eunapius' anxiety that the world-order would be threatened by the end of the mysteries was an anxiety about a world-order based on Greco-

4. *Contra Jul.* I. 103.   5. E.g. 132D–133A and 136B–137C.

6. *Contra Galil.* 96C–E, 49A–E, 57B–58D, 65A–66A, 99E.

7. Cf. Porphyry's *De antro Nympharum, passim*.

8. *In Remp.*, I. 14–16, 24, 118–119, 168–169, 178, 181, 182, 202–205.

9. *Procli Hymni* (ed. Vogt). These hymns are theurgic prayers written for a circle of initiates.

Roman culture and civilization.[10] Vettius Agorius Praetextatus' statement, that if the mysteries which hold the whole human race together were not celebrated life would become unlivable for the Hellenes,[11] was made with the idea in mind of the intimate connection between Greek culture, civilization and religion. The same Vettius delivers an eloquent discourse on syncretistic solar theology in the *Saturnalia* of Macrobius.[12]

Macrobius, who was himself influenced by Neoplatonism, presents us with the Roman counterpart of this type of Hellenism. His characters discuss with religious fervor the Latin classics, the ancient customs, and the divine significance of the city of Rome and its traditions.[13] Servius discourses on the poetry of Virgil, who was considered a sacred author along with Cicero as the composer of the *Somnium Scipionis* and the Platonic and Pythagorean philosophers. In Macrobius, then, an interest in antiquarianism and Roman tradition is found closely connected with pious paganism. This attitude was periodically revived in Roman circles until at least the sixth century.

Synesius' ideas were in many ways similar to those of these pagan authors. His religious views made it obligatory for him to find a way in which to bring Hellenism into harmony with Christianity. His uniqueness lies in the fact that even as a Christian bishop he was able to maintain his Hellenic religiosity and its theological background, as well as his Hellenic cultural posture. At the same time, he freed himself from a specific attachment to pagan cults.

Synesius' commitment to Hellenism as a cultural ideal appears most clearly in his work *Dion*, written c. 405–406. The *Dion* is a work on conversion to philosophy, the nature of rhetoric and philosophy, and an *apologia* for Synesius' own way of life. It is a prose work written in the form of a divinely inspired address to a son (yet unborn), which is meant to guide him on the path to wisdom through a proper approach to Greek literature and philosophy.[14]

The work opens with a depiction of the second-century (c. A.D. 40–

10. Eunap., *Vit. Soph.* 471 (ed. Boissonade). 11. Zosimus, *HN* IV.33.

12. Macr. 1.17. Praetextatus was Proconsul of Achaea under Julian (Amm. XXII.6.6). On Praetextatus' religious activities, see also H. Bloch, "The Pagan Revival in the West at the End of the Fourth Century," in *Conflict* 193–218 and plates, 195–197, 203, 207–210, 215.

13. For a brief but interesting description of the *Saturnalia* in its pagan context, see Bloch, 207–210.

14. *Dion*, or *On My Own Way of Life*, ad init. et passim. What follows is a summary of the work, its *skopos* and some of its main points. For a detailed analysis of Dion Chrysostom's influence on Synesius, see Asmus, *BZ* 9.85–151, and Fitzgerald, *Essays and Hymns*, vol. 1, notes on Dio, 211–241; Moles, *JHS* 98.79–100, argues against the idea of conversion to philosophy; he claims that the Dio Chrysostom of the *Dion* was himself a fraud. Synesius

after 112) orator and philosopher Dion Chrysostom's great sophistic rhetorical ability and his subsequent abandonment of sophistry for philosophy. But Dion, one of Synesius' models, did not abandon eloquence when
he embraced philosophy: rather he employed learning and letters as an
aid to true wisdom rather than as mere showmanship. Even as a sophist
attacking philosophy he displayed great power and eloquence. But following his sudden conversion, he became a philosophic "saint of culture."
Thus Philostratus, in his *Lives of the Sophists*, places Dion among those
students of philosophy who have been considered sophists because of
their beautiful way of speaking. These are to be distinguished from sophists in the negative sense of the term: those whom the Platonic Socrates
refuted. If one understands this, says Synesius, then it is possible to determine which works of Dion were the pre-conversion compositions of a
pure sophist and which the works of a philosopher who used eloquence to
turn others in the direction of the just state and the good life.

Synesius argues that the active life of a good Hellene concerned
with *paideia* and private and civic *arete* may be combined with the contemplative life. The philosophical mystic need not and should not abandon the enjoyment of culture. Socrates could discourse with all men on all
levels; this is most clearly seen in the *Phaedrus*, where he speaks in vi-
sionary terms of immortal souls' vision of Truth yet also plays the role of
a rhetorician who competes with the sophist Lysias. The wisest of the
Hellenes did not abandon eloquence, but employed it in the service
of the good. Socrates even practiced poetry at the behest of the Delphic god.

Synesius himself was also a poet, a rhetorician, a philosopher and a
mystic. This is the way of the true Hellene, the man for whom culture is a
determining force in both serious and playful pursuits. In this way he describes his own ideal of life. In thus avoiding spiritual fanaticism and spiritual excesses of all types, Synesius presents us with a picture of Hellenism that includes literary education as a necessity for the philosopher:

> For I think it right that the philosopher must in no way be rude or
> base, but rather an adept of fine and cultivated ways, a Hellene to the
> core, by which I mean a man who is able to communicate and deal
> with people by being a competent practitioner of all forms of literary
> eloquence.[15]

---

has deceived himself and us. But Moles at most brings into doubt an individual case of conversion to philosophy; he does not adequately deal with the perfectly valid general pagan
phenomenon of conversion to philosophy.

15. *Dion*, 1125A: ἀξιῶ γὰρ ἐγὼ τὸν φιλόσοφον μηδ' ἄλλο τι κακὸν μηδ' ἄγροικον
εἶναι, ἀλλὰ καὶ τὰ ἐκ Χαρίτων μυεῖσθαι, καὶ ἀκριβῶς Ἕλληνα εἶναι, τοῦτ' ἔστι δύ-
νασθαι τοῖς ἀνθρώποις ἐξομιλῆσαι, τῷ μηδενὸς ἀπείρως ἔχειν ἐλλογίμου συγγράμματος.

Philosophy is the art of arts, the science of sciences; therefore, the philosopher needs training in all branches of knowledge. He will acquire knowledge as a man of letters, but he will criticize each and every thing as a philosopher.[16] Philosophy harmonizing and supervising all the arts is represented by the figure of Apollo singing in harmony with the Muses.[17] The philosopher communes with himself and the gods through philosophy, but with men through the subordinate powers of language; therefore, the philosopher who despises literature is an incomplete human being. Here again we see an example of Synesius' practical and political side. Unlike Porphyry, who cared little for affairs, but like Dion Chrysostom, after whom the work is named, he did not hesitate "to busy himself with public affairs and participate in the running of the state."[18] Nor was this sort of thing completely foreign to all of the Neoplatonists, as is often asserted.[19]

Synesius cleverly combines the practical-rhetorical with the mystical by claiming that the true initiate who can guard the esoteric secrets of the Neoplatonists must also be an able public speaker:

> And if the man who is a consummate speaker is more suited to conceal divine matters and has it in his power to lead assemblies in any direction he so chooses, so also that man must needs fall short who has not previously completed a liberal education or cultivated the arts. For one of two proclivities overtakes him: either to be silent or to speak of things unlawful to mention.[20]

Being human and variable, we cannot always contemplate. We are not Nous undefiled, but Nous in the soul of a living creature. For this reason also we must seek out the more human forms of literature, for when our souls descend from contemplation they can be refreshed by letters without further descending into matter. Our nature tends toward plea-

16. *Ibid.* 1125C: ἐπιστήσεται μὲν οὖν ὡς φιλόλογος· Κρινεῖ δὲ, ὡς φιλόσοφος, ἕκαστον τε καὶ πάντα.

17. *Ibid.* 42D–43B (ed. Terzaghi, 246).

18. *Ibid.* 1125C: πράττειν τὰ κοινὰ καὶ πολιτεύεσθαι.

19. A few *topoi* usually in Porphyry are always quoted to prove how apolitical and otherworldly the Neoplatonists were. Cf. Wallis, *Neoplatonism* 7, 18, 23, 40, 136, 164. But Synesius, Julian and other men with active careers who were influenced by Neoplatonism certainly had what amounts to a political theory and practice. For an interesting comparison of Synesius with some practical Greek intellectuals of the Roman Empire, such as Dio Chrysostom, Plutarch and Themistius, see Lacombrade, *Synésios* 35. See now also Brown, "The Philosopher and Society" *passim*.

20. *Dion,* 1128A–B: εἰ δὲ καὶ κρύπτειν ἐπιτηδειότερος τὰ ἀβέβηλα ὁ παντοδαπῶς ἔχων τοῦ λόγου, καὶ περιβαλλόμενος δύναμιν τοῦ διατίθεσθαι τὰς συνουσίας ἢ βούλεται, καὶ οὕτω μειονεκτεῖν ἀνάγκη τὸν ἄνδρα ἐκεῖνον, ὃς οὐ προετελέσθη τῷ κύκλῳ, καὶ τὰ Μουσῶν οὐκ ὠργίακε. δυεῖν γὰρ αὐτὸν καταλαμβάνει τὸ ἕτερον, ἤτοι σιγᾶν, ἢ λέγειν ὅσα νόμος σιγᾶσθαι·

sure, since pleasure is what keeps soul united to body; therefore, literature can assuage this need without a further fall. Only God is free from the passions. Men are able to exchange evil for virtue by control of the passions; the flight from excess is a characteristic achievement of the sage.[21]

This brings us to one of the central points of the essay: Synesius' juxtaposition of his own balanced spiritual ideals against those of his more fanatic pagan and Christian contemporaries. In *Ep.* 154 to Hypatia, which is close to the *Dion* in spirit, he states his position succinctly:

> For some of those who wear the white mantle (i.e., philosophers) and some who wear the dark (i.e., monks) have called me a transgressor because I brought beautiful and rhythmic prose to philosophy, and thought it worthwhile to say something about Homer and about eloquent rhetorical figures of speech. Indeed, they think it fitting that the philosopher hate literature and concern himself exclusively with divine matters.[22]

In the *Dion*, we find an extensive criticism of the spiritual practices of these two groups, especially the monks. The first group, those who wear the white mantle of philosophy, are not specifically identified by Synesius and there has been some speculation concerning their identity. Fitzgerald, opposing Synesius to Plotinus and his followers, seems to think that Synesius is referring to the mainstream of Neoplatonism;[23] but this is impossible. Plotinus and his followers were great admirers of Hellenism; they read Homer as well as Plato, made great scholarly contributions to classical studies, and were generally the most learned people of their time. Porphyry, for instance, was an outstanding scholar who studied with Longinus as well as Plotinus. The mystical experience itself was only available after long years of ascetic preparation and philosophical discipline—not to mention that *Ep.* 154 was written to Hypatia, who herself was the head of a philosophical school.

21. *Ibid.* 1133A–1137B; this form of humanism balances the "otherworldly" tendencies of Neoplatonism. Synesius' Hellenism remains strong in this work and Hellenic imagery and analogies are employed throughout. See esp. Ch. VI.

22. *Ep.* 154, 1553A: καὶ γὰρ τῶν ἐν λευκοῖς ἔνιοι τρίβωσι καὶ τῶν ἐν φαιοῖς ἔφασάν με παρονομεῖν εἰς φιλοσοφίαν, ἐπαίοντα κάλλους ἐν λέξεσι καὶ ῥυθμοῦ, καὶ περὶ Ὁμήρου τι λέγειν ἀξιοῦντα καὶ περὶ τῶν ἐν ταῖς ῥητορείαις σχημάτων, ὡς δὴ τὸν φιλόσοφον μισολόγον εἶναι προσῆκον καὶ μόνα περιεργάζεσθαι τὰ δαιμόνια πράγματα. The last words reinforce the idea that humanism is a balance for exclusive concern with the divine.

23. See Fitzgerald, *Essays and Hymns* 1.232–234; cf. Lacombrade, *Synésios* 142–144, who suggests—as an alternative to Fitzgerald's notion—certain followers of Iamblichus. I tend to prefer other possibilities, although wonder-workers such as Maximus of Ephesus are perhaps a possibility.

Lacombrade's suggestion that Synesius was referring to certain followers of Iamblichus is perhaps more likely. Iamblichus was a poor stylist who, Eunapius tells us, failed to sacrifice to the graces of Hermes, the god of eloquence.[24] But Julian and his followers were champions of Hellenism in all of its aspects. True, they tended to be intensely mystical to the exclusion of other things; but is there any evidence that they felt it necessary to hate literature in order to be true philosophers? I think not. In addition to this, Proclus, greatest of the theurgic Neoplatonists, was a scholar of literature and science as well as "the most learned Hellenist of his day."[25]

It seems to me, however, that the best candidates for the types of philosopher and sophist that Synesius has in mind are, first, those authors in the *Corpus Hermeticum*[26] who insist on salvation at any cost, to the exclusion of all culture which can only be a hindrance when salvation is "the one thing needful;" and second, that group despised by Julian himself, the "uneducated Cynics."[27] It is these men who find all culture useless; and they are the ones who walk the streets cultivating their beards and proclaiming that "virtue" is all that is necessary for salvation. Besides, Synesius, in his other letters, alludes to philosophical charlatans who walk the streets professing philosophy without any real knowledge of its principles.[28] There he might be referring to a third group: professional Sophists who were not really philosophers but attached themselves to the mystique of philosophy and claimed to be able to teach men the way to wisdom. The Cynics of the late Roman Empire, however, who were well known in all the urban centers of the Greco-Roman world since the second century if not before, best fit the description of Synesius' "wearers of the white mantle." They promised a short cut to wisdom, despising and misunderstanding the knowledge, discipline, and effort required for the philosoph-

24. Eunapius, *Vit. Soph.* 458 (ed. Boissonade).

25. Dodds, xiii, of his edition of Proclus' *Elem. Theol.*

26. These might be the "silent" types Synesius alludes to in *Ep.* 154; the Cynics, then, would be the "loquacious" types; however, it must be remembered that Hermetic salvationists did preach. There is also a well-known statement of Epicurus to the effect that all culture should, if necessary, be abandoned for the sake of the pursuit of happiness. Nock, *Conversion* 3–4, discusses the *Poimandres* as a treatise of radical pagan salvationism; Epicurus, fr. 163 (ed. Usener): παιδείαν πᾶσαν φεῦγε.

27. But cf. *Dion* Ch. X, which implies a certain type of philosophical Sophist; Julian criticizes the uneducated Cynics for resembling Christian monks (ἀποτακτισταί) *Or.* VII, 244A–C. Those who have shown no capacity for rhetorical and philosophical culture rush straight to the profession of Cynicism; *Or.* VII.22: τῶν ῥητορικῶν οἱ δυσμαθέστατοι καὶ οὐδ' ὑπ' αὐτοῦ τοῦ βασιλέως Ἑρμοῦ τὴν γλῶτταν ἐκκαθαρθῆναι δυνάμενοι, φρενωθῆναι δὲ οὐδὲ πρὸς αὐτῆς τῆς Ἀθηνᾶς σὺν τῷ Ἑρμῇ, . . . ὁρμῶσιν ἐπὶ τὸν κυνισμόν.

28. Cf. e.g. *Ep.* 137–146 as well as 154.

ical life. Such men were just the type of vulgar counterfeiters and popularizers who would annoy a learned gentleman like Synesius.

Synesius criticizes Christian monks without the usual bitterness and vituperation of his pagan contemporaries. They have noble spiritual ideals and are intent upon the contemplative life, but they manifest a barbarous one-sidedness in their practice of virtue and their contempt of *paideia*:

> I have hitherto observed barbarous men . . . who have devoted
> themselves to contemplation; thus they have become uncivil and un-
> sociable, inasmuch as they continuously strive to liberate themselves
> from nature. They had their sacred songs, holy symbols and certain
> ordered paths to the divine. All this has prevented them from sinking
> back into matter. They also live apart from one another, so as to keep
> anything pleasant out of sight and out of mind, "for they do not eat
> grain, nor do they drink fiery wine."[29]

Knowing that they are human, and suspicious of their lowly terrestrial lives, they spend their time weaving baskets when they have descended from the heights.[30] In short, where the Greek employs *paideia*, the barbarian ascetic weaves baskets; men are not gods and the human must be taken into account.[31] The best, the few genuine "Bacchoi" whose first impulse was divinely inspired, can remain under the influence of the divine only as far as the limitations of human nature allow. Hence, the need—even for the mystic—of the human disciplines. The *Dion* in general is an appeal for humanist education, which was threatened by the barbarization of the empire and the more extreme tendencies of the new spirituality.

But although a part of us is to be involved with the things of this world, Synesius admits, the involvement should not be so strong as to drag us down and take complete possession of us. For this very reason, the monks practiced basket weaving as a form of avoidance:

29. *Dion*, Ch. VII, 45D:Ἤδη δὲ ἐγὼ κατενόησα καὶ βαρβάρους ἀνθρώπους ἐξ ἀμφοῖν τῶν ἀρίστων γενῶν, θεωρίαν μὲν ὑπεσχημένους, καὶ κατὰ τοῦτο ἀπολιτεύτους τε
καὶ ἀκοινωνήτους ἀνθρώποις, ἅτε αἴξαντας ἑαυτοὺς ἐκλῦσαι τῆς φύσεως· καὶ ἦσαν
αὐτοῖς σεμναί τε ᾠδαὶ καὶ ἱερὰ σύμβολα καὶ τακταί τινες πρόσοδοι πρὸς τὸ θεῖον· πάντα
ταῦτα ἀποκόπτει κατὰ τῆς ἐπιστροφῆς τῆς εἰς ὕλην· καὶ βιοτεύουσι χωρὶς ἀπ᾽ ἀλλήλων,
τοῦ μή τι χάριεν ἰδεῖν ἢ ἀκοῦσαι, οὐ γὰρ σῖτον ἔδουσ᾽, οὐ πίνουσ᾽ αἴθοπα οἶνον· See also
Ch. VII *passim* (ed. Terzaghi). Geffcken, 217, distinguishes Synesius' balanced criticism of
the monks from the opinion of the pagan enemies of Christianity; for an example of harsh
criticism of monks, cf. Eunap., *Vit. Soph.* 473 (ed. Boissonade).
30. *Dion*, Ch. VII, 46B (ed. Terzaghi); for a detailed exposition of Fitzgerald's opinion, see his *Essays and Hymns*, 1.230.
31. Synesius, when speaking of the inspired among the above groups, also quotes a
famous *topos* from Plato (*Phaedo* 69C): ". . . many of the Thyrsus bearers, but few the Bacchoi." Cf. also Olympiodorus' *Comm. In Phaed. ad loc.*

For they do not contemplate while they skillfully work on their wicker baskets. They also became suspicious of the leisure which our nature cannot endure, a nature which provides us with many sources of distraction. Therefore, lest they begin to stray from their goal by engaging in diverse activities, they have formulated a rule among themselves: to remain constantly occupied with their weaving; thus they keep their natural inclinations in check.[32]

The Greek is superior to the barbarian in this respect because, when forced to descend, he has first settled himself in the "neighboring area," for he has established himself in knowledge, and knowledge is the royal road (*diexodos*) to Nous.[33] Therefore, literature and other lower intellectual activities are both respites from contemplation and a preparation for further contemplation: intellectual pursuits adorn the spiritual eye within us and

> rouse it little by little until it is accustomed to its [proper] objects of vision, so that it may venture, at some time, to contemplate a higher object of contemplation, and not blink at all while looking intently upon the sun.[34]

Hellenism and the Path to Mystical Contemplation in the *Dion*

So far, we have seen that Synesius employed Hellenism as a general critique of the spiritual life of his age. He also made use of traditional Greek philosophical ideas in order to make some positive suggestions.

It is clear that Synesius' *itinerarium mentis ad Deum* is related to Plato's scheme of *paideia* in the *Republic*. First, there is the grounding in *paideia* as a form of general education. Next, there is the unity of *paideia* in philosophy: Apollo singing in harmony with the Muses. Under the guidance of philosophy, the art of arts, all culture becomes unified, the Muses are always found together. Thirdly, there is the dialectical ascent to intuition of the divine, which is analogous to the levels of *dianoia kai*

32. *Dion*, Ch. VII, 46C–D (ed. Terzaghi, 252).
33. *Ibid*. Ch. VII, 47B (ed. Terzaghi, 253).
34. *Ibid*. Ch. VII: ἀλλά τοι πάντα ταῦτα κοσμεῖ τὸ ὄμμα ἐκεῖνο, καὶ ἀφαιρεῖ τὴν λήμην, καὶ διεγείρει κατὰ βραχὺ προσεθίζοντα τοῖς ὁράμασιν, ὥστε θαρσῆσαί ποτε καὶ πρεσβύτερον θέαμα, καὶ μὴ ταχὺ σκαρδαμύξαι πρὸς ἥλιον ἀτενίσαντα. Cf. Plato *Rep*. 516B. This section might also mean that the "inner eye" is harmonized with the cosmos (because of the context); ἀτενίσαντα here has the same overtones as the scholastic *intentio*: the intense focusing of consciousness on the object of contemplation. On this passage see Fitzgerald, *Essays and Hymns* 231, who brings in parallels from Olympiodorus, Sallustius, Justin, Plato, and Philo.

episteme on Plato's divided line, the philosopher as Apollo singing by himself.[35] Finally, there is contemplation or the supra-rational experience of the divine, which is akin to Plotinus' union with the One or the Good; the Good is beyond Being (*epekeina tes ousias, Rep.* 509B) and thus transcends reason, which is identified with the essential or noetic realm. Therefore, contemplation of or union with the divine must be achieved by some supra-rational faculty.[36]

Unlike the Hellene's ordered path to mystical experience, the barbarian method is "like a Bacchic frenzy or the mad leap of one possessed by a god"—an arrival at the goal without running the course and an irrational motion to the realm beyond reason.[37] The state of fitness for revelation, as well as the process, has an irrational (or supra-rational) element which becomes even more pronounced because reason plays no part in the preparation. Thus mystical experience must be approached with caution because it is subject to this non-rational element. The descent also has no reason and is like a fall as the ascent is like a leap.[38] If we have no intelligible upward and downward path to the Real we are in danger of leaping too suddenly and looking upon the "sun" (i.e., the Good) without adequate preparation. On the downward path, the return from the noetic to the sense realm, we are likely to fall below our intended landing point. This situation, wherein we make sudden journeys from the pinnacle of Reality to the dregs of the universe, can lead to a condition of spiritual schizophrenia and cosmic disorientation.

The monk and the philosopher have the same ends but different means of achieving them. The crucial difference that makes the true philosopher superior is the means he employs:

> With respect to the middle stages of the journey, the Greek philosopher has made a more lucid inspection of the matter; for he has prepared himself a path and goes up it as if he were climbing a ladder, so that he accomplishes something by himself.[39]

There are a few autodidacts, however, both pagan and Christian, who can achieve the correct relationship with the divine; they are rarer than the

---

35. *Rep.* 509D–511E.

36. This concept is also found in the Chaldaean Oracles, where it is referred to as the ἄνθος τοῦ νοῦ, or the highest point of Nous, which can unify with the One. Cf. *Oracles Chaldaïques*, frr. 1, 1; 34, 2; 35, 3; 37, 14; 42, 3; 49, 2; 13, 4.

37. *Dion*, Ch. VIII, 48A (ed. Terzaghi, 254). Cf. Plot. II.9, to which this critique is similar in spirit.

38. *Ibid.* Ch. VII, 48B (ed. Terzaghi, 254): πῶς οὖν ταῦτα ἀλλήλοις ἂν πρέψειε, νῦν μὲν ἐπαφὴν ἔχειν τοῦ πρώτου, νῦν δὲ ἐπὶ ῥῶπας καὶ λόγους ἐστράφθαι; . . . The word ῥῶπας is appropriate here because the meaning of ὕλη was originally "wood."

39. *Ibid.* Ch. IX, 48D (ed. Terzaghi, 255).

phoenix. Notable examples are Amos the Egyptian, Zoroaster, Hermes (Trismegistus), and Antonius.[40] Others imitating these proficients will fail: the way is not open to all and we must not use an unintelligible method of reaching the intelligible and beyond. For mind is a temple, divinity's dwelling place within us.

For most men, the virtues are the necessary first step of the ascent. The masses should follow the middle course and cling to right opinion. If they must seek more they should go to a real philosopher for instruction. Initiates into philosophy must join the chorus before carrying the torch and carry the torch before becoming initiating priests, for the dangers and pitfalls are many and even Socrates feared them. Those who consider themselves worthy to grasp ineffable doctrines without proper education are terribly rash.[41] Average men who live temperately and without any pretense are preferable to those who do not even know that they do not know. As it is, their attempt is like that of "Icarus who refused to use his two feet, and straightaway failed to make contact with air and earth of which he hated the latter and was not able to reach the former."[42]

Synesius certainly remained an aristocratic Hellene in his conception of the spiritual life. Here he may be contrasted with St. Augustine and other Church Fathers, who claimed that the Christian could reach the truth through the Scriptures, which are more basic to Christian faith than philosophy. Synesius, on the other hand—with the exception of the four prophets Amos, Zoroaster, Hermes, and Antonius, and those like them—puts those who merely believe at the level of right opinion, that is, at the level of faith confirmed by experience, but without any real intellectual basis. As bishop, he continued to think this way. His conception of Christianity was always Hellenic: for him the vulgar, who comprise the congregation and follow the precepts of the Church, are inferior to the mystic and philosopher who "knows the reasons of things" and can have a direct experience of the divine.[43] Synesius' statement in *Ep*. 105 to the

40. *Ibid*. Ch. X, 51C (ed. Terzaghi, 259); the fact that Synesius criticizes the imitators of these specific sages makes it more likely that the counterfeit Greek philosophers he was talking about were would-be followers of Hermes Trismegistus; the thesis that he meant monks rather than Therapeutae or Essenes has more weight because of his specific mention of St. Antony; he is also Platonic in his criticism of "foreigners" who seek virtue by habit without knowing why they ought to be temperate. Is there an implicit criticism of simple Christian faith here, not as invalid, but as inferior to the informed religiosity of the philosopher-bishop?

41. *Ibid*. Ch. X, 52B–C (ed. Terzaghi, 261); cf. also Fitzgerald, *Essays and Hymns*, 1.239, who quotes Olympiodorus on philosophy and the initiations.

42. *Dion*, Ch. X, 53A (ed. Terzaghi, 262).

43. It should be noted that those Christian mystics who were most like the Neoplatonists, and even read their works thoroughly—e.g. Eckhart, Pseudo-Dionysius, Scotus Erigena, were often either in danger of condemnation or actually were condemned.

effect that he would mythicize publicly and philosophize privately becomes intelligible in this context.

One can readily see how he could assimilate the Platonic "common man" who follows the way of right opinion (*orthe doxa*) to the average Christian believer who was to adjust his beliefs to the doctrines of the Church (orthodoxy). Whatever the external demands of the Church with respect to the behavior and public pronouncements of its bishops, the philosophical bishop was to remain free to pursue his calling without hindrance. Like the Platonic philosopher, he would look upon the Forms and the Good, a reality transcending *any* temporal church or form of revelation—which must needs be something relative that points beyond itself.

Thus Synesius' cultural ideal was also a philosophical-religious ideal. To say that Hellenism merely meant *paideia* or Greek culture to Synesius, and to others like him, is misleading. If Synesius was to some extent confessionally neutral in matters of religion (he was not, like Julian, very attached to specific pagan rites and cults), he was nevertheless deeply religious. His non-attachment to cult *per se* is indicative of his religious universalism rather than any view of Hellenism as a cultural heritage only. Indeed, the latter view makes little sense in the case of Synesius. In fact, it leads to an artificial distinction, for, as we have seen, he viewed Hellenism as a culture that had as its unifying crown a philosophy possessing its own mystical theology. Hellenism as he understood it was a view of the world necessary and basic to the sanity of any religion, even Christianity. Again and again the point is brought home that in spiritual matters the Greek method is superior to the barbarian: is it too much to ask whether his criticism of the monks was in part an appeal for Christians to Hellenize? He is not harsh on the monks in the manner of Julian and Eunapius who merely hate and despise them; he even wrote a favorable letter to a friend who became a monk.[44]

His efforts seem to be aimed at improving the spiritual life of his times by means of a criticism of what he considered to be false and dangerous practices. It is hard to believe that he did not want the Church to move closer to Hellenic ideals. Nor was Hellenism something for which Synesius merely had a sentimental attachment: it was the basis of all truly human culture and civilization. In the *Dion*, he attempts to demonstrate that without it even the highest spiritual ends may become distorted. The battle for the Muses against those who are not participants in the gifts they bestow was undertaken against certain specific groups of pagans and Christians.[45] It was intended as a criticism of both groups. Although he

44. *Ep.* 147, to one Joannes.   45. Ch. XI *passim*.

was not yet a bishop, Synesius wrote the *Dion* about the same time that
he was in the process of assimilating the Chaldaean to the Christian Trinity. By this time some forms of Christianity had become a serious possibility for him, but a Christianity that abandoned the ideals of Greek
paideia would be intolerable to him. He had made many Christian friends,
specifically because he was able to share his interests and ideals with
them. Therefore, it was perfectly logical of him to want to bring to the
critical attention of his Christian friends those aspects of Christianity that
seemed barbarous and incongruous with Greco-Roman ideals. He believed Hellenism to be the most solid foundation on which to build and
preserve the relationship between the human and divine. The more
Hellenized the Church became, the better it would become. Synesius
might have been aware that the Church's authority was based upon different principles, but he hoped that Hellenism as he understood it would
be adopted in some kind of Christianized form. Synesius' recommendations indicate both social and spiritual priorities. Only a Church with a
commitment to Hellenism could preserve what was best in the old way of
life. To be sure, had not this process already begun, he probably would
have remained a pagan. After all, the Dion Chrysostom that he writes
about would have found much that was acceptable, even admirable, in a
new church two centuries removed from him in time.

Synesius and the Ideals of the Fathers

Before comparing the cultural and religious ideals of Synesius with
those of certain contemporary Church Fathers, it would be useful to outline the development of some important aspects of ancient culture. Our
purpose will be to provide a historical framework in order to clarify some
of the difficulties presented by later Hellenism in its relationship to
Christianity.

Philosophy and rhetoric, the two basic forms of ancient classical education, already had been perfected in Athens by the mid-fourth century
B.C.[46] The philosophical schools claimed to provide an exact theoretical
knowledge of the nature of reality. For Plato and Aristotle, all (or most)

---

46. Philosophy was represented by the Academy of Plato; rhetoric by the "school" of
Isocrates. For an interesting discussion of their early conflict see Jaeger, *Paideia* Vol. 3; see
especially Ch. 6, 132–155, and Ch. 8, 182–196. For the toning down of the conflict in the
Hellenistic age and beyond see Sallustius, *Concerning the Gods and the Universe*, ed.
Nock, *prolegomena*, Ch. 1. For a thorough discussion of these issues vis-à-vis the Cappadocians and Christianity, see Ruether, *Gregory, passim.*

things were basically knowable: metaphysics, cosmology, politics, ethics, aesthetics and the other sciences were all based on principles that were closely connected. Reality was intelligible: one could *know* the good, just, etc., live by them and rule political states by them. The universe was (insofar as possible) moral and purposeful. The highest knowledge and highest intelligibles were divine. The two great philosophers differed on many points, but both would agree to the foregoing when stated thus generally.

Rhetoric, as formally represented by the school of Isocrates, was quite different: scientific and specific knowledge of the kind taught by Platonic philosophy was at best dubious. General truths and valid opinions could be reached by consensus: this was "true philosophy." "Political science" was an illusion. Isocrates was skeptical about knowledge of the divine and knowledge of natural principles. It was possible to form reasonable opinions based on the agreement of reasonable men. One could train those of good intelligence in a wide range of skills, culminating in the ability to make persuasive political speeches and lead states in peace and war. The training of the well-rounded gentleman was more important than the highest end preached by the philosophers: *theoria* or contemplation. Isocrates summed up and systematized what had already been worked out by moderate sophists such as Protagoras in the fifth century B.C. Thus, the schools of rhetoric and philosophy were great rivals in the fourth century B.C. Yet any reader of Aristotle's *Ethics* and *Rhetoric* will also see that the Stagirite had to some extent toned down the opposition of the schools. Even Plato's guardians were trained to be flexible and adept at many things, not only philosophy. Thus the real school argument was over the ultimate nature of knowledge and the knowability of things.

During the Hellenistic age, these rival systems began to influence each other and, to some extent, teachers combined them. By late antiquity, we find many examples of philosophers who were also rhetoricians. Notable among these were, e.g., St. Augustine, Marius Victorinus, Themistius and Synesius.

By the second century B.C., rhetoricians were discussing general philosophical issues and even specific propositions such as "the mind of each individual is a god."[47] Quintilian saw the need for some philosophical training and Aelius Aristides had a working knowledge of Middle Platonism.[48] By the second sophistic period (second century A.D.), ability at both was common and "true philosophy" was important to rhetoricians as well as philosophers. Thus, both Dion Chrysostom and Epictetus attacked false philosophers. Dion later preferred philosophy and may even

47. Sallustius, *Concerning the Gods*, ed. Nock, xviii.
48. *Ibid.* xviii; cf. *Dillon*, 43–57.

be considered one of its converts. Yet he never devalued literary eloquence, an attitude that had great influence on Synesius. Marcus Aurelius, to the chagrin of his teacher, was converted from rhetoric to philosophy. Most rhetoricians praised philosophy; some more than others.
Callinus' work against philosophy was an exception.[49] Apuleius and Maximus of Tyre, two important Middle Platonists and religious syncretists,
were also excellent rhetoricians. Nor should we forget the great poly-
math, Middle Platonist and religionist Plutarch of Chaeronea.[50]

This tendency continued in the fourth century A.D. Libanius of
Antioch was primarily a rhetorician; but he had great respect for Plato as a
literary man and he praised Iamblichus, the theologian of Julian's pagan
revival. The Emperor Julian himself was both a rhetorician and a good
theurgic Neoplatonist. Indeed, his chief theurgic hymns (to Helios and
Magna Mater) are presented in the form of rhetorical orations. Himerius
was a good philosopher who studied Plato, and Themistius wrote commentaries on the works of Aristotle.

Thus, rhetoric and philosophy, which had begun as rival schools,
became compatible in late antiquity. A group of men more or less equally
adept at both disciplines flourished between the second and fourth centuries. It is to this group that Synesius belongs. Converted to Neoplatonism under Hypatia, he refused to abandon eloquence and literary taste:
he severely criticized those philosophers who refused to recognize these
arts. In late antiquity, rhetoric and philosophy were no longer rivals; they
were two aspects of the same Greco-Roman culture. Unfortunately, this
fact is often obscured in studies of Christianity and classical culture because we are usually presented with categories adopted from the thought
of the Fathers. For example, the Cappadocians identified classical culture
with the letters and rhetoric they learned at Athens; for them philosophy
was connected with the Christian *theoretikos bios*, Christian theology, or
the monastic life. But this was not true for Synesius: for him, rhetoric and
letters were on one level, philosophy and the contemplative life on another. The latter was identified with Neoplatonism.

A brief discussion of the Cappadocians will help us refine this important distinction. As we have seen,[51] several of the fourth-century
Greek Fathers studied with teachers of rhetoric, such as Libanius, Themistius, Prohaeresius (the one Christian among them), Himerius, and
others. Most important among these were the Cappadocians and St. John
Chrysostom. They absorbed the pagan rhetorical culture of their time

49. Sallustius, *ibid.*
50. For a thorough discussion of Plutarch's philosophy, see Dillon, 184–230.
51. See above, p. 44.

and by so doing greatly influenced Christian culture. Although they often made ambivalent and self-critical statements about their "classicism" and love of letters, the content of their personal, philosophical, theological and ecclesiastical writings reveals a profound classical influence. Thus, in some respects, Christians, such as Gregory of Nazianzen, were children of the revived Hellenism of late antiquity, as were pagans such as the Emperor Julian. The real difference was to be found in religion and philosophy. Julian's move to close the schools to Christians was meant to deprive them of the only possible means of expression in late antiquity: classical rhetoric. That is why Gregory of Nazianzus is so vituperative in his attack of Julian: if Greek rhetoric was an integral part of a Hellenism that included Greek religion, what would happen to Christianity? Rhetoric, of course, could be adapted to Christian usage. But it was not the rival of Christianity as such. Theurgic Neoplatonism was. Thus the logical Christian tactic would be to claim that rhetoric alone was Hellenism. It would also be logical to deny the validity of Greek religion and (partially of) philosophy and to claim Christianity as "true philosophy." Thus one could achieve the reverse of what Julian wanted: the Fathers separated classical rhetoric (for the most part) from the rest of Hellenism. Many modern scholars are still discussing Christianity and classical culture under the influence of polemical positions created in order to deal with the fourth-century conflict of religions. This procedure might be appropriate for the study of most of the Fathers, but not of Synesius. In addition, such views tend to distort the pagan position: they are at bottom modernized Christian views of another religion.

To return to the theme of Hellenic rhetoric and philosophy: it was easier for Eastern than Western Christians to separate them and claim Christianity as "true philosophy." This is because of the way in which Christian theology developed in the Greek world. Augustine had to make much more complex, contradictory and confusing moves in order to deal with similar problems.

In the Greek East, so-called Christian Platonism developed to some extent within the tradition of allegorical interpretation of the Scriptures.[52] This practice began at least as early as Philo Judaeus, who saw Platonic-Pythagorean meanings in Scripture correctly understood. A famous example in the Septuagint was God's answer to Moses: "I am He Who Is" (*Ho On*) which Philo equated with *to on* or Being in the Greek philosophical sense. Thus one of the great theological traditions began. The rabbis were not enamored of Philo, but his method was applied to Scripture by

52. See above, pp. 9–10.

the Christian Platonists of Alexandria, Clement and Origen. Although they were aware of a debt to Plato, Clement and Origen were also critical of certain aspects of his teaching. They modified their own teachings to fit a Platonic world-view without embarrassment, yet they also developed a tradition of Christian philosophy which they saw as their own. Perhaps the most important turning point in this development was Origen's *Contra Celsum*, a systematic defense of Christianity against a pagan Middle Platonist's powerful attack. In any case, by the fourth century it was easy to identify "true philosophy" with this Christian theological tradition and pay relatively little attention to Plato. Unlike Augustine—and this is important—the Cappadocians did not get their "Neoplatonism" directly from Plotinus and Porphyry, but rather from the Alexandrian Christians. Undoubtedly, their thought was indirectly influenced by the dominant Neoplatonic thought-world of their time, but they still could and often did identify philosophy with the Christian contemplative and monastic life.

For polemical purposes, the Cappadocians reopened the debate between rhetoric and philosophy. The old criticism that Plato leveled against the sophists was transformed into a Christian criticism of the superficiality of elegant style for its own sake.[53] "Philosophy" was part of Christianity; rhetoric was valid only insofar as it helped to enrich the religious life.[54] The love of literature for itself was seen as somewhat sinful, if unavoidable for the learned. The highest life was that of contemplation, which rose beyond rhetoric and discursive reason. This last idea parallels the goal of Greek philosophy, but the philosophers did not begin with revelation.

Synesius viewed monasticism as completely unphilosophical until late in his career.[55] The Cappadocians, who were "disciples of the Origenist monks of Egypt,"[56] viewed it as a new synthesis of Christianity and Platonic spirituality: "Basil as theologian and *nomothetes*, and Gregory of Nyssa, as mystical philosopher . . . bequeathed to the Christian tradition in a matured form both from the speculative and the social framework"[57] for the expression of *nostra philosophia*; i.e., Christian philosophy as Alexandrian Platonism. For the Cappadocians, Christianity could be understood in terms of monastic life, and monastic life in terms of Alexandrianism.[58]

There is no evidence that Synesius knew much about these devel-

53. Cf. e.g. Greg. Naz. *Carm. de Vita sua*, PG 37.1046–1047.
54. *Ibid.* PG 37.1039.   55. Cf. *Epp.* 137 and 143.
56. Ruether, *Gregory* 15.   57. *Ibid.*   58. *Ibid.*

opments. If he had, he would have respected monasticism more. But whether or not he would have adhered to it is doubtful. At best, he envied the monks their leisure for contemplation; late in life as a bishop he encouraged a friend who was a monk to contemplate philosophically. Thus he thought the monks needed philosophy.

On the other hand, Basil and the two Gregories often equate the monastic life and philosophy: for them, as for other Christian authors of the fourth century, the monk is the philosopher *par excellence*.[59]

Thus, from the pagan point of view, one might assert that philosophy and the social role of the philosopher were co-opted by Christians and transformed into that of the theologian, monk and holy man. Basil and Gregory planned to practice philosophy in a monastic community immediately after their student days at Athens.[60] As typical Christians from educated families, they studied in the great schools of rhetoric and were forced to adapt what was acceptable in the old culture to the new religion.

Gregory's celebrated conflict between the active (priest-rhetor) and contemplative (philosopher-monk) lives is typical of his age. He was ambivalent: at times he praised one or the other way of life. He predictably complained, when forcibly ordained by his father in 361, that he would have to deal with external affairs and abandon *hesychia*.[61]

Synesius also felt the tension of the active life (as civil servant and bishop) and the contemplative life (as country gentleman and philosopher).[62] Both tried to work out a synthesis of the two. Gregory would somehow serve the people and find time for contemplation.[63] Synesius would play the role of bishop in public, but philosophize in private. These ideas were typical of late antiquity and have the character of a *topos*. But simply because both men held the title of bishop does not mean they are necessarily comparable. Pagan philosophers also played a very special social role in late antiquity.[64] They were leaders of groups of spiritual disciples. For example, in the third century Plotinus' follower Rogatianus, a Roman Senator, was a Neoplatonic ascetic.[65]

The self-revelations of Gregory in his autobiographical poetry would be interesting to compare with those of Synesius from a psychological point of view. But from the point of view of the religious development of Synesius, the comparison is unimportant. Synesius can only be under-

---

59. Cf. e.g. Basil of Caesarea, *Sermo Asceticus*, PG 31.891; Eusebius, *HE* 6.3.9–12; Sozomen *HE* 6.33.

60. Greg. Naz. *Ep.* 1, PG 37.21.   61. Ruether, *Gregory* 32.

62. See above, pp. 74–77.   63. Ruether, *Gregory* 34.

64. Peter Brown, "The Philosopher and Society," *passim*.

65. Porphyry, *Vit. Plot.* 7.32–47.

stood correctly along the lines we have followed: he was a Neoplatonist without much knowledge of Christianity.

Misch has described the development of autobiography in late antiquity.[66] He deals at length with the personages of Christian Neoplatonism: Synesius, Gregory of Nazianzen, St. Augustine, and others.[67] He sees Synesius' *Hymns* and autobiographical works as expressions of a late Greek philosophical tradition drawing on Stoicism and Neoplatonism. Synesius prays to be lifted to a God who is the "highest good which eternally permeates the world" and the "innermost individual soul."[68] The self-scrutiny of Synesius is still close to the Stoic idea of personality; his personal attitude to God is not unlike that of Marcus Aurelius.[69] Although he "attains" a personal note, it is not that "individual inwardness" of the *anima Christiana*: deeper emotional (i.e., Christian) experiences and a genuine poetic talent, such as Gregory of Nazianzus possessed, were needed to produce a work embracing in consistent religious feeling both the individual biographical data and the metaphysical meaning of human existence. Synesius found for himself a compromise between mystical contemplation and an existence open to the world: this art of living he depicted as his *bios*.[70]

Writing from a point of view in which Christianity is seen as the culmination of the inner spiritual life, Misch views Synesius as a philosopher. Gregory's and Synesius' respective conflicts between active and contemplative lives are only superficially similar. Synesius' *bios* is not Gregory's celebrated middle way: the latter saw active and contemplative lives as equally Christian, and people involved in the active life as also deserving of our love. He himself would try to combine the serenity of contemplation with the practicality of activity.[71] But the compromise of Synesius was that of a philosopher: contemplation (*theoria*) is the highest activity; it is divine. But by necessity of our nature and the instantiated world, we are not completely divine (only our soul is). Thus we must learn practical as well as theoretical (contemplative) wisdom. This doctrine, after all, had already been clearly stated in Aristotle's *Nicomachean Ethics*.

The Cappadocian Fathers' philosophy was scripturally based. It was the philosophy of men who expressed the content of their faith in Platonic terms and at times speculated in the light of a faith that transcended their speculations.[72] When their philosophy and theology seem close to those of

66. Misch, Vol. 2; see Pt. 3, Ch. 2.   67. *Ibid*. 584–692.
68. *Ibid*. 594.   69. *Ibid*. 595.   70. *Ibid*.
71. Ruether, *Gregory* 1, 15–16, 29, 32–34, 54. Greg. Naz. *Ep*. 49, *PG* 37.101.
72. Sheldon-Williams, 425.

Synesius, it is rather because of their shared thought-world than because of specific common influences: their branch of Christianity had been Platonic for centuries. But their occasional similarity of ideas is more apparent than real. For example, on the Trinity: soteriology determined the position of the Logos in Cappadocian thought;[73] Synesius' Trinity was compatible with the Christian because he was able to reconcile it with purely Neoplatonic-Chaldaean ideas of horizontal emanation. Moreover, where these in turn are similar, it is because Christianity was indebted to Neoplatonism.

The Cappadocians were basically Christians who thought about their religion and tried to expound it in terms intelligible to Platonists.[74] They accepted those aspects of pagan philosophy that were compatible with their faith. Theirs is the exact opposite of the method of Synesius.

If their Trinity was based on soteriology, their cosmology and anthropology were based on allegorical interpretation of Scripture. The intelligible world and the eternal procession of reality from the One were transformed to fit the notion of a Creation in time. Man would return to the image of God in himself through a combination of Christian "grace" and "free will,"[75] not by climbing the ladder of dialectic to intuition of the Forms or uniting with the One through the purified divine soul's ascent through the Hypostases. Such a "return of the soul" could not be accepted by the Cappadocians, for it would negate the idea of the redemption.

As fourth-century philosophers, they were more aware of heretical possibilities than their Alexandrian predecessors. They accepted elements of Platonism, but uncompromisingly rejected those doctrines which the Christian revelation denied.[76] Among these doctrines were those which Synesius refused to give up, including the eternity of the cosmos, and the divinity of the soul as a separate and distinct substance. The Cappadocians' approach was diametrically opposed to Synesius'. They believed that the Scriptures, not philosophy or the platonized Chaldaean Oracles, were the Gnosis and Christian Oracles (*logia*) of God. This Gnosis is in the Old and New Testaments. They were revealed by the Holy Spirit through the *theologoi* or mouthpieces of God. For Synesius there were also a few autodidacts instructed by God, but these were to be found in all religious traditions. As a syncretist, Synesius had no trouble including Zoroaster and other pagan and Christian figures.

73. For a detailed discussion of the Cappadocian Fathers' philosophy, see Wolfson, *Philosophy* 141–232.

74. Sheldon-Williams, 425.

75. Greg. Naz. *Or.* 38.11, *PG* 36.321C; Ruether, *Gregory* 130–134; Otis, *DOP* 12.94–124.

76. Sheldon-Williams, 426.

As bishop, Synesius did attempt scriptural allegory. He does speak of the Gnosis of both Testaments.[77] But he soon reveals only a sketchy knowledge of Christian tradition and speaks as a Neoplatonist. One has the feeling that Synesius was experimenting with scriptural allegory simply as a man of letters and philosophy who had learned something of Alexandrian exegesis from his Christian friends.

Synesius put philosophy before revelation; the Cappadocians, and others, put revelation first: their ideas and spiritual awareness were determined by scripture and its interpretations developed within the Christian community. Their way of life was determined by the practices of the Christian community. To the Christian world, Synesius was an outsider in the process of working out a compromise. His ideas and spiritual awareness were determined by philosophy. His metaphysical poetry and discussions of spiritual experience reinforced the way of Philosophy, not that of Christian religion.

The *On Dreams*; Dualism; Chaldaean Oracles; Resurrection of the Body

Synesius' work *On Dreams* (405–406) provides an interesting contrast with the *Dion*; in some ways they are opposites. *On Dreams* is a work on the nature of the soul, its constituent elements, and its destiny, as well as a study of the phenomenon of dreams. It embodies a theory of allegory, together with a theory of the efficacy of dreams for the art of divination. The Chaldaean Oracles also play an important part in it. Most interesting for us is Synesius' analysis of the *ochema-pneuma* or "vehicle of the soul,"[78] which formed an important part of the psychology and anthropology of the astral religion of late antiquity. This vehicle was said to accompany the soul when it entered the cosmos, join it to the body and later accompany it on its return journey.

Synesius' use of allegory in this work has much in common with the methods of Sallustius, Julian and other later ancient thinkers. This method, which had a long history,[79] explained away the "falsehoods" and

77. Synesius, *Homily* I, 295D–269A (ed. Terzaghi, 280).
78. For a general discussion of this doctrine, see Dodds in his edition of Proclus, *The Elements of Theology*, appendix II, "The Astral Body in Neoplatonism," 313–321; also Kissling, *AJP* 43.318–330.
79. For a good analysis of the allegorical method in late antiquity and its historical roots, see Pepin, *Mythe et allégorie*; cf. Sallustius, *Concerning the Gods and the Universe*, which was written to present an outline of systematic theology for the members of Julian's pagan church; also Julian, *Or.* V.

harshness of the old myths by special methods of interpretation. In *On Dreams*, Synesius gives us an example in his conception of Zeus:

> But if anyone is persuaded by other passages to conclude that the hegemony of Zeus is one of physical force, because the poet says . . . "he was superior in force" (*Od*. XVIII 234), that man has a vulgar acquaintance with poetry, and is unaware of the philosophy therein, which says that the gods are nothing else but Nous. In this way, again, he connects his superiority in strength with his greater age, meaning that Zeus has greater primacy with respect to Nous. And what else is strength of mind, but wisdom? Whatever god, therefore, is deemed worthy to rule the gods, holds sway through an abundance of wisdom, since he is a noetic being, so that the passage "he was superior in force" is a circumlocution which comes to mean the same thing for us as the phrase "he has greater knowledge." [80]

There is further evidence of Hellenic beliefs in *On Dreams*. Discussing the sympathy of the whole and the harmony of opposites that brings unity to the cosmos, Synesius mentions an offering "to some god of those who are within the cosmos," [81] implying that there is a divine hierarchy in which some gods are encosmic and dwell within this universe, while others are hypercosmic and dwell beyond it. [82]

Although Synesius might not have been a ritual theurgist, he certainly did believe—as did almost everybody in late antiquity—in the efficacy of dream interpretation as a sound method of reading the future

80. *De Ins*. I, 131C–D (ed. Terzaghi, 145; Migne, *PG* 1284): εἰ δέ τις ὑφ' ἑτέρων ἐπῶν ἀναπείθεται τὴν ἡγεμονίαν τοῦ Διὸς χειρῶν ἰσχὺν εἶναι λογίζεσθαι, ὅτι, φησί,

βίη δ' ὅγε φέρτερος ἦεν, (*Od*. 18.234)

οὗτος φορτικῶς ὡμίλησε τῇ ποιήσει, καὶ ἀνήκοός ἐστι τῆς κατ' αὐτὴν φιλοσοφίας, τοὺς θεοὺς οὐδὲν ἄλλο ἢ νοῦς λεγούσης. ταύτῃ τοι προσπερονᾷ πάλιν τῷ κατ' ἀλκὴν περιεῖναι, τὸ καὶ γενεῇ πρότερος, τὸν Δία νοῦν λέγων ἀρχεγονώτερον· νοῦ δὲ ἰσχὺς τί ἂν ἄλλο ἢ φρόνησις εἴη; καὶ ὅστις οὖν θεὸς ὢν ἄρχειν ἀξιοῦται θεῶν, νοῦς ὤν, σοφίας περιουσίᾳ κρατεῖ, ὥστε καὶ τὸ βίη δ' ὅγε φέρτερος εἰς τ'αὐτὸ ἡμῖν τῷ πλείονα οἶδεν ἀνακάμπτει καὶ περιίσταται. Cf. *Enn*. III.5, 8, 9 and IV.4.9.

81. *De Ins*. II, 132D (ed. Terzaghi, 147 = *PG* 1285). This whole passage is filled with Hellenic religious piety; e.g. οὐ γάρ ἐστιν ὁ κόσμος τὸ ἁπλῶς ἕν, ἀλλὰ τὸ ἐκ πολλῶν ἕν. The exact passage quoted (in the text) suggests that Synesius believed, at least here, in chains of emanation, sympathy and correspondence; contrary to what is often said, his criticism of magic would be understood by Iamblichus as applicable only to lower forms of divination; also, Synesius might have had some kind of mystical-magical practice in mind here: καὶ δὴ καὶ θεῷ τινι τῶν εἴσω τοῦ κόσμου λίθος ἐνθένδε καὶ βοτάνη προσήκει, οἷς ὁμοιοπαθῶν εἴκει τῇ φύσει καὶ γοητεύεται, κτλ (132D).

82. For the orders of gods summarized, see Sallustius, *Concerning the Gods* 6; for a more complex and complete description, see Procl. *Elem. Theol.* prop. 113–165; guides to Proclus' complicated and detailed descriptions of the divine orders in the *Theol. Plat.* have been summarized by Lewy, 483; cf. Proclus, *Théologie Platonicienne* ed. Saffrey and Westerink, 1.lxv–lxvii.

and as protection against hostile magicians and their powerful demons. In his work *On Dreams*, Synesius describes how the latter helped him when he was on his diplomatic mission to Constantinople on behalf of his native Cyrene:

> My life has consisted of literary pursuits and hunting, except for the time I served as an ambassador. Would that I had not seen three un-speakable years taken out of my life! Yet, even then I enjoyed the greatest profit from divination. For it neutralized attacks launched against me by spirit-raising magicians, revealing them and saving me from all of them. It also helped me in public administration, so that the finest things were accomplished on behalf of the cities. Finally, now more confident than any Greek ever was, it brought me into close association with the emperor.[83]

It seems that, in the case of Synesius, dream interpretation acted as a safety valve for the anxiety caused by real or supposed attacks on him by magicians who were working for his political rivals. If Synesius could read the future, he would be able to ward off all possible mischances by antic-ipating them.

Lacombrade (following Synesius' own claim) sees an element of originality in Synesius' theory of the *pneuma*. He believes that it brought Synesius close to the Christian doctrine of the Spiritual Body, at least in an allegorical sense. He goes so far as to assert that the sole purpose of the work, despite digressions, parentheses, etc., is focused on the question: "To what extent does the individual consciousness, made up of a con-glomerate of sense impressions peculiar to a given soul, survive the anni-hilation of the body?"[84] But it is important to remember that this question was also addressed by Porphyry, Proclus and other pagans. Thus it can be understood as a problem within the tradition of pagan Neoplatonism.

The doctrine of the *pneuma* is a difficult one and this is not the place to go into it in detail.[85] Suffice it to say that it acts as the vehicle of the soul on which the latter rides, as on a boat, when it enters the physical cosmos from the intelligible realm. This soul-envelope makes union with body

---

83. *De Ins.*, PG 1309A: ἐμοὶ μὲν οὖν βίος βιβλία καὶ θήρα; ὅτι μὴ πεπρέσβευκά ποτε. ὡς οὐκ ὤφελον ἀποφράδας ἰδεῖν ἐνιαυτοὺς τρεῖς ἐκ τοῦ βίου. καὶ μέντοι τότε πλεῖστα δὴ καὶ μέγιστα ὠνάμην αὐτῆς. ἐπιβουλάς τε γὰρ ἐπ᾽ ἐμὲ ψυχοπομπῶν γοήτων ἀκύρους ἐποίησε, καὶ φήνασα καὶ ἐξ ἁπασῶν περισώσασα, καὶ κοινὰ συνδιῴκησεν, ὥστε ἄριστα ἔχειν ταῖς πόλεσι, καὶ ἐς τὴν βασιλέως ὁμιλίαν τῶν πώποτε Ἑλλήνων θαρ-ραλεώτερον παρεστήσατο. The reference to Hellenes here is to those who believe in the Hellenic religion rather than simply Greeks.

84. Lacombrade, *Synésios* 160; cf. *Ep.* 154, 1556B.

85. For a good discussion of the theory of the *pneuma* in Porphyry, Synesius and others, see Smith, *Porphyry's Place* 152–158.

possible, and, in the condition of union with body it becomes the faculty of imagination (*phantasia*), which functions as a connecting link between the spiritual realm and the coarser realm of sense.[86] As such, it is the basis of sense perception and consciousness: a halfway house between spirit and matter, as it were, which makes communication between the two realms possible:

> The soul . . . carries the *eidolon* with it. In fact, when it has departed from the physical body, the *pneuma* which it put on among the spheres accompanies it. And since, on account of its propensity to become embodied, it yielded to the latter the reason allotted to it so long as it was in relation with this body during its existence, on account of that inclination, the imprint of the imagination was stamped on the *pneuma*, and it is in these circumstances that the soul carries the *eidolon* with it.[87]

It is this Porphyrian idea of the imprint of imagination upon the *pneuma* liberated from earthly existence which Lacombrade claims will be transformed by Synesius and understood as the survival of the unique individual personality after death.[88] But it is also probable that this notion of Porphyry's was inspired by the Chaldaean Oracles, for his work *De Regressu Animae*, which deals with the liberation of the soul, drew heavily on Chaldaean sources.[89] Synesius' unique contribution was the identification of the *eidolon* or image with the thinking subject, thereby redefining the *eidolike psyche*; here *eidolon* has the double sense of (a) image and (b) phantom, or spirit: "The *eidolike psyche* is implicitly defined in the text under discussion as the subject which continues to preserve, in the beyond and under the form of a phantom (*eidolon*), the images of objects which it received during its life through the intermediary of the faculty of representation."[90]

Under the influence of Christian ideas, according to Lacombrade, Synesius took this Porphyrian idea one step further by means of an original interpretation of some verses from the Chaldaean Oracles. He was, in fact, seeking a solution that would safeguard the survival of the person-

---

86. Cf. *Oracles Chaldaïques*, ed. Des Places, frr. 29; 35, 4; 61; 104; 123, 1; 216, 1, and notes to all of these fragments. Smith points out that Porphyry connected the *pneuma* with *phantasia*. He added the Stoic idea, following Aristotle, which says the soul is itself *pneuma*. As the background for Porphyry's *anima spiritalis*, it is important for Synesius' theory: *Porphyry's Place* 155.

87. Lacombrade, *Synésios* 167; the following section includes a summary and criticism of Lacombrade's position.

88. For Synesius' similarity to Porphyry here see Smith, *Porphyry's Place* 156.

89. Cf. *ibid.*; Fitzgerald, *Essays and Hymns* 464 and n. 405; *Oracles Chaldaïques*, 18–24.

90. Lacombrade, *Synésios* 160.

ality in the beyond: "In this case, he dares to oppose the doctrine of the Chaldaean Oracles to the traditional teaching of Hellenism."[91] The passage from the Oracles is as follows:

> It shall not leave behind the residue of matter on the precipice [i.e., Tartarus or the material world]; but the *eidolon* also has a portion in the realm surrounded by light.[92]

Synesius' commentary on the Oracles constitutes the main evidence for his theory of the *pneuma*:

> This is the antithetical place to Tartarus.[93] But one can be even more sharpsighted here. For it seems not only to carry up to the spheres the nature which has come from them, but if it snatches something from the summit of fire and air, when it descends into the *eidolic* nature, before donning its earthly shell, it is this, the Oracle declares, that it leads above with its superior part. For the residue of matter could not be the divine body. And one could rationally hold that things which have a common nature and contribute to a unified end cannot be altogether dissociated.[94]

Thus, Synesius argues, the soul combines with the "summit" or "perfection" of the superterrestrial physical elements, fire and air, on its descent into the *eidolic* nature, i.e., the *pneuma*. These elements also accompany it on its return journey.[95] For the "spiritual body" could not be the earthly "residue of matter" spoken of by the Oracle, but rather (as we shall see)

91. *Ibid.* 168.

92. *De Ins. PG* 1297B; *Oracles Chaldaïques* fr. 158; for further discussion see *ibid*. 35–36. Lacombrade translates (168): "Et tu ne laisseras pas retourner à la terre la souillure de la matière, car il y a une place aussi pour l'eidolon dans la vaste région de lumière." Des Places translates: "Tu ne laisseras pas au précipice le résidu de la matière; mais l'image aussi a sa part au séjour baigné de lumière."

93. On the *amphiknephes*, or dark lower realm which is opposed to the light, see *Oracles Chaldaïques*, 16 and fr. 163, 3; *De Ins.*, 1293D.

94. *De Ins.*, 1297B; (ed. Terzaghi, 140D–141A): οὗτος δὲ ἀντίθεσιν ἔχει πρὸς τὸν ἀμφικνεφῆ. καίτοι τι καὶ πλέον τις ἂν ἐν τούτοις ὀξυωπήσειεν· οὐ γὰρ μόνην εἰς τὰς σφαίρας ἀνάγειν ἔοικε τὴν ἐκεῖθεν ἥκουσαν φύσιν, ἀλλὰ εἴ τι καὶ τῆς πυρὸς καὶ τῆς ἀέρος ἀκρότητος εἰς τὴν εἰδωλικὴν φύσιν ἔσπασε κατιοῦσα, πρὶν τὸ γήϊνον ἀμφιέσασθαι κέλυφος, καὶ τοῦτο, φησί, τῇ κρείττονι μερίδι συναναπέμπει· ὕλης γὰρ σκύβαλον οὐκ ἂν εἴη τὸ θεσπέσιον σῶμα. καὶ λόγον δ' ἂν ἔχοι τὰ κοινωνήσαντα φύσεως καὶ εἰς ἓν συντελέσαντα μήτοι παντάπασιν ἄσχετα εἶναι. On the summit of the elements, see *Oracles Chaldaïques*, frr. 76 and 82. Synesius (*PG* 1297C=141A Terzaghi) says that the elements of fire and air are next to heaven (κύκλῳ σώματι), unlike earth, which is the farthest away of all existing things.

95. Cf. *De Ins.* 1293C, where Synesius, speaking of the *pneuma*, says that it would be a shameful thing for souls to leave elements behind on earth which they had borrowed from above; i.e., from the spheres; αἰσχρὰ δ' ἂν ἐπάνοδος γένοιτο μὴ ἀποδιδούσαις τὸ ἀλλότριον, ἀλλὰ περὶ γῆν ἀπολιπούσαις ὅπερ ἄνωθεν ἠρανίσαντο. (*De Ins.* 1293C= 138B–C Terzaghi).

there will be a place for this residue in the realm of light *as eidolon*, i.e., after it has become transformed and spiritualized. Here the "residue" could refer to irrational elements of the personality, or sense impressions that arise as part of the natural process in the material world.[96] In turn, they will be converted to the "imagination" through the activity of the *pneuma*, and thus become "image" (*eidolon*) or spiritualized elements of the empirical personality—and there is a place for image *eis topon amphiphaonta*, "in the realm surrounded by light."

Andrew Smith has shown that Porphyry's theory of the *pneuma* was slightly different from that of Synesius.[97] Porphyry (*Sent.* XXIX) claims that the *pneuma* attacks an *eidolon*, but in Synesius the *pneuma* actually becomes an *eidolon*. The rest of the Synesian theory follows from this distinction. It is likely that for this reason Synesius claimed to have made an original philosophical contribution in this work. Otherwise, the *On Dreams* is heavily indebted to Porphyry's theory of the *pneuma*.[98]

Having established, then, that the soul which has entered the *pneuma* can combine with the "summit" of air and fire which are encosmic, but not earthly, Synesius pushes the argument a step further. But if, he argues (141 A–B), superior elements can yield to inferior ones, and a *pure body* can contribute to the lower material realm (εἰς ἰλὺν συνετέλεσεν σῶμα ἀκήρατον), then inferior elements (i.e., irrational or material) can, in their turn, accommodate themselves to the spiritual nature. Having accomplished this, they become aetherialized (as the summit of air and fire) and accompany the soul on its upward journey, at least as far as the "summit" of the cosmic elements,[99] if not the noetic itself. According to this interpretation, the Oracle might mean: you will not completely leave empirical elements of personality to dissolution in the material realm. When still in their raw or "hylic" form, they are not the "spiritual

---

96. Lacombrade seems to think that Synesius in this passage (1297B) is speaking of elements of the personality which unite with the soul and accompany it on its return journey; thus he interprets τὸ θεσπέσιον σῶμα to mean νοῦς. But Synesius seems to mean that the *"spiritual body"*—why call νοῦς σῶμα?—is made up of purified elements (i.e., like fire and air), therefore the Oracle refers to its not being left behind because it has been transformed. It is not until 1297C that Synesius implies that earthly elements can also unify with the pneumatic envelope under the soul's hegemony. Pure Nous is ἀφάντ<u>αστον</u>.

97. *Porphyry's Place*, Appendix II, p. 156.

98. *Ibid.*

99. According to Synesius in some part of τοῦ κυκλικοῦ (1293C); he is apparently referring to the cyclical body of Heaven; (Ar., *De Caelo*, 289a30). This conclusion is reinforced in 141C where Synesius declares that nothing hinders the somatic substance, which has arisen out of the elements, from rising out of its fallen condition—along with the natural ascent of the soul—and becoming harmonized with the spheres, (i.e., as if rising into its proper nature).

body," but transformed into *eidolon* they can be unified with it. Thus the Oracle might be translated: "It will not forsake the residue of matter on the crags of Tartarus; nay rather as image (*eidoloi*) it has a portion in the realm of light." [100]

In order to clarify the obscurity of the Oracle, then, Synesius has interpreted it logically and according to Neoplatonic doctrine on cosmology. He has attempted to demonstrate that the *pneuma* acts as a quasi-physical transformer of matter into spirit. Through this process something of the "residue of matter" is appropriated to the *eidolon*, which becomes part of what a Christianizing Platonist might try to interpret as the "resurrected body" of Christian doctrine. But not even this theory must necessarily be interpreted as primarily Christian: [101] True, the doctrine of the "subtle body" *pneuma* would be (and was) the most logical starting point for any Neoplatonist about to approach the question of the Resurrection. But, in fact, certain other fragments of the Chaldaean Oracles, in addition to statements by other Neoplatonists, seem very close to this idea of Resurrection—at least if it is understood as a "body of light" or some such thing, rather than the return of man's gross physical body. The devoutly pagan Hierocles, for instance, speaks of man as a ψυχὴ λογικὴ μετὰ συμφυοῦς ἀθανάτου σώματος; i.e., a rational soul with a cognate immortal body. [102] Proclus himself admits that the vehicle of the soul "rises with the soul when it is purified of matter and has returned to its own shape, as in the same degree the soul makes use of it." [103]

100. Cf. Smith, *Porphyry's Place* 62, with *Oracles Chaldaïques*, 163–164. Psellus, *Comm. in Orac. Chald. PG* 122.1125B–C, associates the "residue of matter" with the *body itself*, which the Oracles say can be resurrected along with the soul and become incorporeal or at least ethereal; I have taken this into account; but identifying the "residue of matter" with irrational elements of personality or sense impressions seems to be more consistent with the Neoplatonic doctrine of the *pneuma*. Otherwise Psellus' ideas are very close to those of Synesius. No doubt this and other oracles speak of the salvation of the body; it is a question of how the body becomes transformed and spiritualized. Synesius also claims originality in this work (*Ep.* 154 *ad fin.*); since the Oracles already contain a doctrine akin to the Christian resurrection of the body, it is probable that Synesius' originality lies in the way he interpreted that doctrine. I have accordingly suggested the above interpretation on the basis of Synesius' passages in *De Ins.* (1297B–C).

101. It is interesting to note that Psellus affirms this as a Chaldaean doctrine but claims that Gregory of Nyssa *denied* it in his doctrine of the soul and its constituent elements. Psellus, *Comm. in Orac. Chald.* 1125B (*Oracles Chaldaïques* 163).

102. Cf. Fitzgerald, *Essays and Hymns* 456 and 462. Hierocles is interesting because he believed in creation of the world in time, but claimed this was Plato's (and some Neoplatonists') real doctrine; Wallis, *Neoplatonism* 142, believes Hierocles merely misunderstood the doctrine; this is hard to believe and other possible explanations must still be explored.

103. Procl. *Elem. Theol.* prop. 208; cf. Dodds' commentary in his edition of the *Elements*, 306–308.

Two other fragments of the Chaldaean Oracles speak of a doctrine
that has some relationship to that of the Resurrection:

ἐκτείνας πύριον νοῦν
ἔργον επ' εὐσεβίης
ῥευστὸν καὶ σῶμα σαώσεις.

If you extend your mind inflamed
with the work of piety,
you will even save the body which is in flux.

Σώζετε καὶ τὸ πικρᾶς ὕλης περίβλημα βρότειον.

Save also the mortal garment of bitter matter.[104]

The latter is from a *Hymn* of Julian. There is no question, then, that many
pagans, through Chaldaean doctrine, maintained some kind of belief allegorically akin to the Resurrection. But, as Synesius says (*Ep.* 105), it was
to be understood as *hieron ti aporreton*. Thus Synesius did not have to
alter this idea very much to approach certain contemporary Christian
doctrines of purification and salvation "of the composite elements of the
human being."[105] Indeed, Hadot connects the idea of salvation found in
Marius Victorinus' work *Adversus Arium* with the Chaldaean notions of
salvation:

> Moreover, salvation according to Victorinus does not appear to be
> purely intellectual (58-*Adv. Ar.*, I, 62, 37): 'The material soul is in
> the material body, which must be purified with the three others in
> order that it receive eternal light and eternal life. . . . *The notion
> of purification of man's inferior elements seems to come from the
> Oracles.*'[106]

Finally, Wallis points out that Proclus accepted two vehicles of the soul:

> one immortal, the other perishable. With this goes a *compromise on
> the irrational soul's immortality*, for according to Proclus the immor-
> tal vehicle is the seat of certain roots of 'irrational life,' which the soul
> always retains, and which provide the initial stimulus behind her de-
> scent into this world.[107]

And again on the attempt to harmonize the pagan with the Christian conception of Resurrection:

104. *Oracles Chaldaïques*, ed. Des Places, frr. 128 and 129. For a brief discussion of
the "astral body," salvation, the cosmos and theurgy in the Oracles, see the edition of Des
Places, 15–17; for further references to frr. 128 and 129, see Des Places *ad loc*. For other
Oracles (or probable Oracles) quoted by Synesius in *De Ins.*, and commentary, see *ibid.*, *ad
frr.* 118 and 218.
105. Hadot, *Porphyre et Victorinus*, 343 n. 11.
106. *Ibid.*   107. *Neoplatonism*, 157f.

This concept [*of the pneuma*] seemed to offer hope of bridging the gulf. But the contrast between that body and man's gross terrestrial body was still too sharply drawn by the pagans to be acceptable to Christian orthodoxy and, while a standing temptation to Platonizing thinkers, the doctrine was condemned as Origenism at the Council of Constantinople in 553.[108]

The Greek idea of immortality was not completely impersonal in this period. Even Plotinus, at some point in his life, seems to have believed in Forms of individuals.[109] Proclus and many other Neoplatonists had conceptions of immortality that included personal elements.[110] Finally, it is not possible to separate the Oracles from philosophy, since all Neoplatonic thinkers, theurgic or otherwise, were influenced by them.[111]

108. *Ibid.*, 104.

109. *Enn.* V. 7.1–3 (this is a point of contention among scholars); of course, even these Individual Ideas would be general (in a sense—or so it seems to me), and each individual would have to fill in the details, i.e., *actualize* the potentialities of his own proper Idea, which would include each soul's tendencies rather than map out and determine each of its everyday actions throughout a lifetime. "Non-telic accidents" should also be possible; e.g., each of us is born with certain tendencies, but environment and historical conditions could alter these a little or a lot. Some potentialities may not even be actualized.

With these things taken into consideration, I see no reason why this notion is inconsistent with general Neoplatonic metaphysics.

110. Cf. Wallis, *Neoplatonism* 157.

111. But cf. Hadot, *Porphyre et Victorinus*, 343–344 n. 11, who says: "Le *De regressu animae* parle d'une purification de l'âme intellectuelle par détachement du corps (fr. 11, Bidez; *De civ. dei* X, 30 et XII, 27), d'une purification de l'âme pneumatique, c'est-à-dire de l'imagination par les rites chaldaïques (fr. 2, 3, 4, Augustin *De civ. dei* X, 9, 27)." This is a distinction between Chaldaean and purely philosophical notions. With respect to the way Synesius (and Victorinus) used these ideas Hadot observes: "Les Oracles semblaient envisager également un salut et donc une purification pour les parties inférieures de l'homme. C'est du moins ainsi que les néoplatoniciens les comprenaient, car Synésius, *De insomn.* IX, p. 162, 2, Terzaghi, après avoir cité (p. 161, 16, P.G. t. LXVI, 1297B) l'Oracle: 'Il y a aussi pour le reflet une place dans le lieu rempli de lumière.' (ἀλλὰ καὶ εἰδώλῳ μερὶς εἰς τόπον ἀμφιφάοντα entend cet εἴδωλον comme désignant le véhicule de l'âme, composé de feu et d'air (cf. H. Lewy, *Chaldaean Oracles*, p. 219, n. 168; qui pense que cette interprétation de Synésius n'est pas conforme à la lettre des *Oracles* pour qui le véhicule se dissout dans l'ascension de l'âme). Un autre *Oracle* (cf. Psellus, *Expositio in orac. chald.* P.G. t. 122, 1140B; Kroll, *De orac. chald.* p. 54; H. Lewy, *Chaldaean Oracles*, p. 169, n. 387): σῶμα σαώσεις (tu sauveras ton corps) semble affirmer un salut du corps. Selon H. Lewy, *The Chald. Orac.*, p. 213 et sq., il ne s'agirait que d'un salut médical, d'une pureté et d'une hygiène à observer en cette vie. Mais il est possible que les néoplatoniciens aient pensé, comme Synésius, à une sorte de métamorphose des éléments du corps au sein du corps cosmique de l'âme divine (Synésius, *De insomn.* IX, p. 162, 19, Terzaghi=PG t. 66, 1297C): ἐν τάξει τινὶ τοῦ κυκλικοῦ γίνεται (sc. τὸ εἴδωλον). La fin du texte de Victorinus, 58 = *Adv. Ar.* 1, 62, 38–39: 'Ut accipiat lumen aeternum' semble d'ailleurs correspondre à une conception chrétienne de ce salut des éléments du composé humain."

Finally Hadot applies this idea to a Christian context: "Dans le développement 'chrétien', il y a un choix entre les éléments sauves et le vieil homme qui est abandonné. Ici, tous les éléments sont purifiés; il n'y a pas de choix."

In addition, Synesius' statements present difficulties and the question must remain problematical. The vehicle, which contains the now aetherialized elements, does *not* accompany the soul all the way, but only goes to the "summit of the elements" and "tastes of the light." It therefore remains *encosmic* even if it is immortal, at most like the stars and the other heavenly bodies which lie below the divine hypostases and remain at the summit of the spatio-temporal order.[112] Ironically, the more carefully worked out theories of the pagan Proclus can be more easily harmonized with the ideas of the Resurrection and Ascension.

If Synesius thought that he was being somewhat innovative here, he was also careful to discuss this work—as well as the *Dion*—with Hypatia, and to send her a copy before it was published.[113] The student of ancient religion should also note that Synesius claims that the work was written in a single night under the inspiration of a religious experience.[114]

112. According to Smith, *Porphyry's Place* 53, Porphyry reconciled the problem in a similar way: the *lower* soul continues after death to subsist in a celestial body. Thus it is still able to contemplate the noetic realm. Therefore, the two functions of soul—soul as pure essence, and embodied soul—can be reconciled.

113. *Ep.* 154 *ad fin.*

114. *Ibid.* This is also true of Julian's *Hymn to King Helios*. Both of these claims are difficult to believe. Surely they are rhetorical. Perhaps a first rough draft was written down in a state of ecstasy, but the polished works we have were later carefully refined.

VII

On the Eve of the Episcopate (A.D. 410)

In the year 410, Theophilus proclaimed Synesius Bishop of Ptolemaïs. Synesius' private spiritual struggle during a period of some eight months at Alexandria may provide us with a key to his complicated personality and difficult historical position. Having analyzed Synesius' works and determined to some extent his spiritual development from about 393–395 to 409, we must now examine his *Ep.* 105 to bring to a focus what we have already said, and to define Synesius' relationship to the Church more precisely. In *Ep.* 105 Synesius explicitly states his position on Christian dogma. He gives several reasons why he feels unworthy to become a bishop: he wishes to remain married; he is morally imperfect; he desires a leisurely life of study and recreation, spent in contemplation of divine matters and in sport and dialogue with friends; he insists (contrary to fact) that he has no political ability; and he desires intellectual pleasures which no priest can allow himself. Finally, in addition to claiming that this position would not give him time enough to work out his own salvation,[1] he brings up his most serious argument.

It is difficult, if not completely impossible, for opinions to be shaken which the soul has received as true knowledge through dialectical demonstration. You know that philosophy vigorously opposes those opinions which are generally discussed and adhered to by the majority. Indeed, I will never consent to the belief that the soul comes into being after the body. I will not affirm that the cosmos—and all of its parts—is going to be destroyed. As for the current belief in the Resurrection, I am far from agreement with the notions of the majority on the subject, for I consider it a holy and ineffable mystery. The philosophic mind, although it perceives truth, consents to the use of falsehood. For light is to truth as the eye is to the mind:[2] as enjoyment of an excess of light could hurt the eye, and as darkness is of

1. *Ep.* 105, 1484C: τῷ γὰρ οἰκείους εἶναί μοι καὶ πάλαι μολυσμοὺς καὶ τὸ τυχὸν μέρος ἐπιγινόμενον εἰς προσθήκην μέγα συμβάλλεται.

2. Migne reads δῆμον, Hercher νοῦν; the former might be justified as follows: light is necessary to truth as is the eye to the common man; i.e., he who lives by sense and ὀρθῂ δόξα; (but one would expect αἴσθησις in that case): νοῦν seems closer to Platonic analogies, but is also problematical because *sunlight* should illuminate the eye unless, of course, the "inner eye" is meant. Is ἥλιον another textual possibility?

greater benefit to those who suffer from opthalmia, so also I believe
that the false is beneficial to the people, and truth is harmful to those
who have not the strength to gaze intently upon the clear manifestations of reality. If the laws of our priesthood allow me these reservations, then I can become a priest; one who philosophizes in private,
but 'mythologizes' in public; [so that] if I do not teach, then at least I
will teach no new doctrine and thus I will allow people to retain their
previous notions. But if anybody says that I too must be moved in this
direction, that the priest must hold the same opinions as the common
people, then I will reveal my true feelings very quickly. For what has
philosophy to do with the people? The truth about divine things is of
necessity ineffable; but the multitude has need of another system.
. . . If I am called to the priesthood, I will make no pretense about
dogma. I testify to these things before God and man. Truth is proper
to God, before whom I wish to be without guilt in all things. In this
one thing alone I will not practice deception.[3]

Synesius, for all the changes he has undergone, reveals himself to
be basically the same man who had been the enthusiastic student of
Hypatia. He still holds views originally revealed in his correspondence
with Herculian, his friend from Alexandria. He still believes that the dialectical demonstration of the philosophers is the soul's canon for true
knowledge. His Platonist statements show a Platonist's aversion to philosophizing among the common people, for whom the sacred subject
must remain a mystery;[4] for those who are not strong enough to look upon
Reality would be better off if they believed in a diluted version of the
truth. The masses, for their own, as well as the general good, are to be

---

3. *Ep.* 105, 1485A–1488B: χαλεπόν ἐστιν, εἰ μὴ καὶ λίαν ἀδύνατον, εἰς ψυχὴν τὰ
δι' ἐπιστήμης εἰς ἀπόδειξιν ἐλθόντα δόγματα σαλευθῆναι. οἶσθα δ' ὅτι πολλὰ φιλοσοφία
τοῖς θρυλουμένοις τούτοις ἀντιδιατάττεται δόγμασιν. ἀμέλει τὴν ψυχὴν οὐκ ἀξιώσω
ποτὲ σώματος ὑστερογενῆ νομίζειν. τὸν κόσμον οὐ φήσω καὶ τἄλλα μέρη διαφθεί-
ρεσθαι. τὴν καθωμιλημένην ἀνάστασιν ἱερόν τι καὶ ἀπόρρητον ἥγημαι, καὶ πολλοῦ δέω
ταῖς τοῦ πλήθους ὑπολήψεσιν ὁμολογῆσαι. νοῦς μὲν οὖν φιλόσοφος ἐπόπτης ὢν τ'ἀ-
ληθοῦς συγχωρεῖ τῇ χρείᾳ τοῦ ψεύδους· ἀνάλογον γὰρ ἔστι φῶς πρὸς ἀλήθειαν καὶ
ὄμμα πρὸς νοῦν. ᾗ οὖν ὀφθαλμὸς εἰς κακὸν ἂν ἀπολαύσειεν ἀπλήστου φωτὸς καὶ ᾖ τοῖς
ὀφθαλμιῶσι τὸ σκότος ὠφελιμώτερον, ταύτῃ καὶ τὸ ψεῦδος ὄφελος εἶναι τίθεμαι δήμῳ
καὶ βλαβερὸν τὴν ἀλήθειαν τοῖς οὐκ ἰσχύουσιν ἐνατενίσαι πρὸς τὴν τῶν ὄντων ἐνάρ-
γειαν. εἰ ταῦτα καὶ οἱ τῆς καθ' ἡμᾶς ἱερωσύνης συγχωροῦσιν ἐμοὶ νόμοι, δυναίμην ἂν
ἱερᾶσθαι τὰ μὲν οἴκοι φιλοσοφῶν τὰ δ' ἔξω φιλομυθῶν· εἰ μὴ διδάσκων, ἀλλ' οὐδὲ μέντοι μεταδιδάσκων, μένειν δ' ἐῶν ἐπὶ τῆς προλήψεως. εἰ δέ φασιν οὕτω δεῖν καὶ κιν-
εῖσθαι, καὶ δῆμον εἶναι τὸν ἱερέα ταῖς δόξαις, οὐκ ἂν φθάνοιμι φανερὸν ἐμαυτὸν ἅπασι
καθιστάς. δήμῳ γὰρ δὴ καὶ φιλοσοφίᾳ τί πρὸς ἄλληλα; τὴν μὲν ἀλήθειαν τῶν θείων
ἀπόρρητον εἶναι δεῖ, τὸ δὲ πλῆθος ἑτέρας ἕξεως δεῖται. αὖθις δὲ καὶ πολλάκις ἐρῶ,
μηδεμιᾶς ἀνάγκης παρούσης οὔτ' ἐλέγχειν σοφὸν οὔτ' ἐλέγχεσθαι. καλούμενος δ' εἰς
ἱερωσύνην οὐκ ἀξιῶ προσποιεῖσθαι δόγματα. ταῦτα θεόν, ταῦτα ἀνθρώπους μαρ-
τύρομαι. οἰκεῖον ἀλήθεια θεῷ, ᾧ διὰ πάντων ἀναίτιος εἶναι βούλομαι. ἐν τοῦτο μόνον
οὐχ ὑποκρίνομαι.

4. Cf. *Epp.* 137 and 143.

taught a "fiction" that is not really a lie, but rather a mythicized version of the truth palatable to them: ταυτῇ καὶ τὸ ψεῦδος ὄφελος εἶναι τίθεμαι δήμῳ, κτλ. Behind the myth, properly understood, lies the truth which only the initiated philosopher can discern. In both his way of thinking and the language he employs, Synesius reminds us of Plato himself. One need only think of the relationship between the philosopher and the rest of society in the *Republic*. Socrates considers it legitimate for the philosophical elite to tell the masses a fiction which will make them better citizens—the well-known *gennaion e kalon pseudos*.[5]

The first philosophical objection to Christian dogma stems directly from the Platonic and Neoplatonic traditions, in which the soul—itself *naturally* immortal, and not, as in Christian thought, a created thing *immortalized* by divine Grace—is related to the eternal world of Ideas and is therefore ontologically prior to the body. And, in the Platonic tradition, that which is ontologically prior is superior. Therefore, a soul created "after" the body would be inferior.[6] Marrou claims that Synesius was not really in opposition to the Church on this point, because dogma was not yet firmly fixed:[7]

> This is the typical question discussed at the time—*difficillima quaestio*, as St. Augustine would call it; and when in 419–420 he devoted to it a long treatise in four books, *De Anima et eius origine*, he was still loath to commit himself. In the East, another bishop, Nemesius of Emesa, who may well have been writing at the same time as Synesius and had an equally Neoplatonist background, proposed openly the doctrine of the pre-existence of the soul.[8] . . . in any case Nemesius' example shows that the dogma on this particular point was not yet fixed. He was objecting to the theories naively formulated by Methodius of Olympus to refute Origen's well-known teaching on the pre-existence of souls. These are difficult for a Platonist, for if the soul were created after the body, as Methodius alleged, the spiritual nature of man would be in some way inferior to his corporeal nature.[9]

But there are more important criteria than an analysis of the individual issues. Two things must be taken into consideration: firstly, Sy-

---

5. Cf. Plato, *Rep.* 376E–392C and 414B–415E.

6. For a discussion of Christians who held this view, see Marrou in *Conflict* 146. For discussions of Greek v. Patristic ideas of immortality see Jaeger in *Immortality and Resurrection* 97–114 and Wolfson in *Immortality* 54–96.

7. Marrou in *Conflict* 146ff.

8. Marrou, *ibid.*, continues: "a later translation of his work *On the Nature of Man* was widely read in the West during the middle ages when it was attributed to Gregory of Nyssa, and under cover of his authority caused many qualms among the scholastics."

9. *Ibid.*, cf. n. 3, "Gregory of Nyssa had already criticized this theory of Methodius in his *De hominis opificio*, 229B–233B."

nesius' *overall view of reality* was that of a pagan Neoplatonist. He
believed that the human soul and the uncreated cosmos were divine. Secondly, for him philosophy and not revelation remained the measure of religious truth. Having said this, an analysis of Marrou's criticism, point by
point, is in order.

First of all, it must be kept in mind that Augustine accepted the
creation of the world by God *ex nihilo*. He attempted in the *Confessions*
to refute the pagan doctrine of the eternity of the world by demonstrating
the paradoxical nature of the problem: the pagan objection is wrong, the
Creationist theory does not end in an *aporia* which implies that a perfect
and immutable God changed somehow, by creating time and the world
arbitrarily. St. Augustine asserts that there "was no time before time;"
i.e., that there was no time before the Creation, for time itself came into
being with the world—more than this we cannot know. The pagan objection misses the point. It is in this context that Augustine's work on the
soul must be understood. Being a Christian who understood and explained his faith in Platonic terms, it was necessary for him to attempt to
preserve the spiritual nature of the soul. Somehow this doctrine had to be
made compatible with Creationism. Perhaps a theory of Creationism in
which the divine mind creates a hierarchy of substances (i.e., Angels,
spiritual matter, souls, then bodies and the material world) would be the
best solution to the problem. According to this theory, everything in the
universe, except God, would be a creature; nevertheless, the ontological priority of some substances over others would be maintained—although the more spiritual substances would still be entirely *dependent* on
their Creator's will for their subsistence, immortality and other qualities.[10] At any rate, in the case of Augustine, as well as that of Nemesius
and other Christians of this type, this problem was a perennial one.
Surely nobody—even those now largely discredited, like Alfaric, who
have tried to demonstrate that Augustine actually was a convert to Neoplatonism before he was a convert to Christianity—would maintain that
Augustine was still hovering at the brink of a lapse into paganism as late as
419–420! Marrou has demonstrated a perennial difficulty of Platonizing
Christians and not the fact that Synesius was not in opposition to the
dogma of the Church at this point. For the case of Synesius is different

10. This is close to Neoplatonism in one way because, strictly speaking, all things
exist only because they have unity which they ultimately derive from the One (Procl., *Elem.
Theol.* prop. 1); but the philosopher who must purify his soul by causing the originally pristine mirror to become clear once again, is much less dependent on grace than the Christian
who can "lose his own soul" by the Creator's fiat. The later Neoplatonists never made as
sharp a distinction between the world and its Creator as the Semitic religions; cf. Wallis,
Neoplatonism 148.

from that of the other thinkers that Marrou discusses. It seems to me that the main question has still been left unanswered: why did Synesius himself feel compelled to bring up his objection to a doctrine of the prior existence of the soul as one of his differences with the Church? It might be argued that his real purpose was to set himself off from the mass of the faithful who were unable to rise to a philosophical appreciation of this doctrine. Perhaps also he saw some of the implications of the dogma, where it might lead, and wanted to make it very clear on which side of the issue he would take his stand. Most important of all, if conceived of together with a Neoplatonic belief in an eternal cosmos, the soul must be seen as part of an eternal order, immortal and therefore divine. This is a pagan perspective.

This leads us to Synesius' second objection: "I will never affirm that the cosmos—and all its parts—will be destroyed." This objection stems from the old Platonic and Aristotelian notions of the eternity of the world. In Neoplatonism, the One is ontologically prior to everything else, but no temporal relationship is implied. The hierarchy "always was" and "always will be": there is no time when the cosmos was not—because there "never was" any specific act of creation: a *creatio ex nihilo* was considered an absurdity by Greek philosophers.[11] How, then, can that which does not begin in time end in time? Marrou claims that Synesius, by not discussing the creation, was already making important concessions to the Church.[12] But I fail to see how the notion of an uncreated, eternal world which "proceeded" out of the One was not the unspoken assumption which led Synesius to his conclusion.[13] How can a Platonist possibly object to the idea that the cosmos is destructible and nevertheless believe that it was created in time? Synesius might not have approached Plotinus' powers as a thinker, but how could anyone who considered himself an initiate into the mysteries of philosophy fail to see the contradictions here? Marrou continues: "as the Cappadocian Fathers had already pointed out, those who admitted that the world had a beginning would soon be led to conclude that it must also have an end."[14] So much by logic. But Synesius never did admit this. On the basis of the evidence, both of Neoplatonic thought and

11. For the idea of the eternal cosmos in which matter is perpetually given form through the ruling intelligence of the universe and in which the heavens are indestructible, cf. e.g. Ar. *De Caelo* 1.10 and 11. Matter was always there in an abstract way, and so was Form: Matter taken in itself is indefinite according to Aristotle: we only experience it in combination with Form: *Metaphysics* VII.17, 104A–B; cf. *Enn.* II.1.1 and II.9 *passim*.

12. *Conflict* 147.

13. Since the visible world is in time, the terms *emanated* or *proceeded* and *perpetual* would actually be more accurate.

14. P. 147 n. 1: "St. Basil in Hexaëmeron, 1, 4B; Gregory of Nyssa, *op. cit.*, (*De hominis opificio*) 209B."

what we know about Synesius, we must conclude that he brought up this objection not as a literary posture, but because of the difficulty he found in dealing with this dogma. He was simply an honest man who could not take a position as bishop without warning his superiors of his theological independence or heterodoxy. It seems to me, then, much more likely that Synesius maintained the belief, in some form, of the eternity and divinity of the cosmos. When he stated his position succinctly, he expected that all its implications would be understood.[15]

It must also be admitted that many Greek Fathers were unclear on this issue. For example, Basil carefully distinguished creation *ex nihilo* from emanation, whereas Gregory of Nyssa attempted to reconcile the two ideas.[16] In the sixth century, the Christian philosopher Philoponus was still an isolated figure when he tried to prove by *philosophical argument* that the world had a beginning. But Synesius maintained the traditional Greek philosophical position on all the individual issues, and this added up to a Neoplatonic world-view.

The third objection of Synesius focuses on the Resurrection itself. Synesius obviously cannot take it literally, although apparently he does see the symbolic representation of a "sacred ineffable mystery" in the story; an interpretation of the Resurrection which is perfectly consistent with the "gnostic" aspects of Christ expressed in the *Hymns*.[17] To a Greek philosopher like Synesius this myth taken literally seemed to be a vulgar metaphysical absurdity. Any doctrine which dealt with contact between

15. Marrou, *ibid*. 147, also says: "The words καὶ τ' ἄλλα μέρη appear to be redundant, but the destruction of at least some parts of the world is difficult to accept—the stars, for instance. This is a major difficulty arising from the permanence of the laws of nature; is it necessary to recall that in the middle of the thirteenth century St. Thomas Aquinas himself was to admit that 'there is no evidence to demonstrate that the creation of an eternal world is impossible?'" But this is also standard Neoplatonism: the whole cosmos is indestructible not its parts (which come and go, or are always changing)—at least those in the sublunary realm. Plotinus himself goes to some lengths to demonstrate why the stars are perpetual even though they are parts. Marrou does not deal with this. However, as he says, "though the whole cosmos and all its parts" seem to imply this, on the other hand, it might simply be a redundancy used for dramatic and awesome effect: "I cannot believe that the world and everything in it will ever be destroyed, etc."

16. Gersh, 21, discusses these theories, scholarly opinions on them, and their implications for Christian Neoplatonism. Following Wolfson, he states that "Basil distinguishes pagan emanation from Christian creation by three criteria: first, emanation is from God while creation is *ex nihilo*; secondly, emanation is an eternal process while creation takes place in time, and finally, emanation is natural while creation is a deliberate act of will. The pagan and Christian approaches cannot be distinguished by these simple criteria alone, for . . . Gregory of Nyssa evolved a theory which effectively combines the two." Synesius, of course, did neither of the above. For him, "pagan emanation" was the only possibility; cf. Wolfson, *HTS* 63.53–60.

17. Cf. above on the *Hymns* and the Incarnation, pp. 98–111.

nous and the material world had to be somehow understood *immaterially* by a philosopher.

Marrou concludes that Synesius brought up all the important theological problems that the Alexandrian Neoplatonists were to be concerned with until the sixth century.[18] In his view, Synesius was a transitional figure who did not totally give up his Hellenism, but was certainly attempting to blend it with Christianity. He was simply not in a historical position to resolve all the problems that would have yielded to someone living at a later time. But after this, while discussing Synesius' views with respect to the common people (i.e., his approval of the *gennaion pseudos*), Marrou says: "Here again it is not a pagan who is speaking, but a man of letters of the ancient world, with his prejudices, his intellectual pride, his contempt for simple souls, 'the populace, the vulgar.'"[19] But such a statement should not be taken out of context. The prejudices alluded to by Marrou were an integral part of Hellenism; indeed, to the extent that Christians believed in pass and honors grades in religion they were Hellenizing. As we have already seen, Synesius was too much of a philosopher and mystic to be considered a man of letters over and against these pursuits. Furthermore, he never abandoned his philosophical position. He accepted Christian dogma to the extent that it was compatible with philosophy. He did not attempt to use philosophy in order to prove the rational validity of Christian doctrine. This may be a subtle difference, but it is a difference nevertheless.

Finally, it is important to see Synesius' objections as forming one overall pattern. Was any Church Father unsure of *all* these points at the same time? Singly in isolation, they may be rationalized as being very close to Christianity—perhaps with the exception of Synesius' second objection, if I have understood it correctly. Collectively, they form a serious objection which cannot be overlooked. This is especially true of the first two objections which together, as we have seen, add up to a typically Hellenic view of the nature of man and the universe.

The real theological basis of "higher" polytheism is the idea of the divinity of the cosmos, which allows the High God to manifest himself under the form of a *multiplex numen*. Therefore, Synesius' willingness to accept Christian doctrine (as he understood it) and not worship the gods as gods did not alter the essential nature of his beliefs. He did not need the cults and rites of the gods, but he believed in a philosophical doctrine to which many sophisticated pagans adhered.

On the other hand, Synesius decided to accept Christianity as that

18. Pp. 148–150. 19. *Ibid*.

religion through which the divine would be mediated in the future. Thus he accepted the Christian system of symbols and hierarchy. Therefore, he must have made room for the idea of its legitimate replacement of paganism on the level of cult. To that extent he accepted the historical mission of the Church.[20] Only to that extent was he a Christian. There is simply no evidence that he was moving in the direction of orthodoxy when he became a bishop.

On the theological level Synesius' position may at best be thought of as a form of Christianity in which Neoplatonic–Chaldaean symbols have been equated with Christian symbols. Thus Synesius' Christianity is basically a means of expression for old ideas rather than an acceptance of new ones. The syncretistic bridges he built were really designed to make the new religion serve Neoplatonism: *theologia ancilla philosophiae!*

Marrou's contention that, had Synesius lived in the sixth century, he would have discovered orthodox solutions to his theological problems is, of course, not verifiable. Just because he was in the Alexandrian tradition does not mean that he would necessarily have done the same as John Philoponus and his contemporaries.[21] The one certainty is that by the sixth century, when Justinian closed the schools and mounted an ideological campaign against paganism, some Alexandrians were able to find philosophical rationales for orthodox Christianity. Synesius did not try to do so, and we are forced to settle for the historical (not philosophical) ambiguities of his position. There is no evidence that justifies a clear prediction of his future development. Even after he became a bishop he did not change very much. The problems he brought up were perennial throughout the Middle Ages. It is as valid to say that he would have been Averroist had he lived about 1250 as to say that he would have been an orthodox Christian philosopher had he lived about 550.[22]

Having resolved any lingering doubts he might have had about the pagan gods *per se*,[23] as well as convincing himself that the bishopric might be a step upward to the realm of philosophy, rather than descent from it

20. Cf. above on *De Providentia*, pp. 70–73.

21. Cf. Marrou, 148. Two tracts of Philoponus (among others) *On the Eternity of the World against Proclus* and *On the Resurrection* were attempts to answer difficulties posed by Greek philosophy.

22. See e.g. Haskins, 348. The Averroists believed that matter was eternal and denied personal immortality.

23. Cf. *Ep.* 57, 1389A–B, in which the daemons are referred to as struggling with God. Synesius is reporting what a group of old priests told him; for *them* the gods were daemons. This is also one place where Synesius clearly calls the Holy Spirit *pneuma* rather than πνοία (unless we accept *Hymn* X as authentic), he calls it τὸ πνεῦμα τὸ ἅγιον; but again, he is reporting what some priests said to him, and *pnoia* is a poetic word.

as he had feared,[24] Synesius "under divine guidance"[25] decided to accept ordination. He began to think of himself as a philosopher-bishop, one who is the moral and spiritual leader of his flock, but who understands and interprets the tradition through an esoteric mystical theology based on Neoplatonism. This conception of leadership is nothing less than a new and original form of the Platonic idea of the philosopher-king of the *Republic* and the man who has a real understanding of the principles of things—and therefore is able to rule the state properly—presented in the *Politicus*, the "Republic" of Plato's *Republic*.[26] These doctrines, of course, he now understood in terms of the episcopal office and all of its peculiar functions and obligations. Synesius had chosen Christianity historically and existentially, if not philosophically, and he would have to live with that decision. Such was the nature of Synesius' accommodation with the Church.

24. Cf. *Ep*. 96, 1165A: . . . ὡς μὴ φανῆναί μοι τὸ πρᾶγμα φιλοσοφίας ἀπόβασιν, ἀλλ' εἰς αὐτὴν ἐπανάβασιν.

25. Cf. *ibid*.: τοῦ θεοῦ δὲ ἐπενεγκόντος οὐχ' ὅπερ ᾔτουν, ἀλλ' ὅπερ ἐβούλετο, . . . The idea of divine will was not unknown in paganism; e.g., Julian felt that he had been "chosen" by Helios. (He also regarded the Greeks and Romans as "chosen people"); cf. also *Ep*. 57, 1339A, where Synesius states that he was overcome by god just before he accepted the episcopate.

26. *Rep*. 471C–474B: *Politicus* 293D–E; Synesius transfers these ideas to accommodate them to his new role as the philosopher-bishop; cf. Cramer, *Röm. Quartalschrift* 72.43ff.

VIII

The Later Years (A.D. 410–414?):
The Philosopher-Bishop

The *Homilies*

Let us now investigate the available evidence for the period when Synesius acted as bishop of Ptolemaïs, to see if we can discover any trends in his thought that might indicate whether he moved closer to orthodox Christianity, or simply maintained and developed the position he had reached by the year 410.

The two extant homilies delivered by Synesius are extremely interesting if considered in the context of his resolve to mythicize in public but philosophize in private. The first, an allegorical exegesis of a portion of a psalm, reads like an exercise from the catechetical school of Alexandria. It is one of the few occasions when he actually explicates a Christian text.

> There is a cup of unmixed wine in the hand of the Lord, filled with a mixture, and he pours from this one into that one, but the dregs of it have not been drained.[1]

He attempts to make the contradictions of this passage intelligible. It does not seem to make sense, but this is only the case if the text is understood literally. "If unmixed, how is it filled with a mixture, and if it is one, how did he pour from this one into that one?"[2] These problems are to be resolved through a symbolic and allegorical interpretation of the passage.[3] The cup is the Word of God freely offered to men in the Old and New Testaments, "for the soul is watered by this drink":[4]

1. *Homily* I, 295C (ed. Terzaghi, 279): "Ποτήριον ἐν χειρὶ κυρίου οἴνου ἀκράτου πλῆρες κεράσματος, καὶ ἔκλινεν ἐκ τούτου εἰς τοῦτο, πλὴν ὁ τρυγίας αὐτοῦ οὐκ ἐξεκενώθην" (*Ps*. 75:8).

2. *Ibid*. (ed. Terzaghi, 280).

3. *Ibid*. 295D; the allegorical method will demonstrate true harmony behind apparent discord: παντάπασιν ἀτόποις ἐόικε τὰ λεγόμενα· οὐ μὴν τὰ γε νοούμενα· οὐδὲν μέλει τῷ θεῷ θεοφορήτου λέξεως. πνεῦμα θεῖον ὑπερορᾷ μικρολογίαν συγγραφικήν. σὺ δὲ βούλει τὴν ἐν τῇ διαφωνίᾳ συμφωνίαν θεάσασθαι; κτλ.

4. *Ibid*. 295D–296A (ed. Terzaghi, 280).

Inasmuch as it is a word, each is unmixed. Yet it is mixed as a double word. For the unity which is formed from the two is a perfection of gnosis. The Old [Testament] held the promise; the New brought forth the Apostle. And the passage "he poured from this one into that one" speaks allegorically of the succession of the teachers of the Law of Moses and the Lord. And the cup is one. For one Spirit inspired the prophet and the apostle, and after the fine ancient painters, He drew in outline and then subsequently portrayed in exact detail the features of the gnosis. "But the dregs of it have not been drained."[5]

The Logos is separate in each testament and so unmixed. But being a "double" word compounded out of the two, it is mixed. The unity formed out of the unmixed mixture of both Testaments is a perfection of gnosis.

Synesius also sermonizes and interprets passages in close accord with his own Neoplatonic preferences:

Our god is wisdom and reason. A cup which disturbs philosophical thought and disrupts the process of rationality does not befit reason.[6]

The terms herein employed are philosophical; the passage displays an ethic under Greek influence in which error equals a disturbance of reason. Indeed, as Synesius proceeds, his interpretation becomes more openly Neoplatonic.

Some of the things he says are in accordance with Pythagorean–Platonic doctrines about the relationship of body to soul; e.g., "when a body is well-nourished and fleshy, it prevents the soul from discerning things properly."[7] And speaking of the cup in the hand of the Lord: "that cup is *aristopoion*, filled with wine, and having been sought after is able to raise us up to Mind (Nous)."[8] Imagine the expressions on the faces of the people of Synesius' congregation as they ascend with their bishop, by means of a symbolic understanding of Scripture, to the realm of Pure Intellect! And the *bishop* here employs the term Nous rather than

5. *Ibid*. 296A–296D: ὅτι μὲν λόγος ἐστίν, ἄκρατός ἐστιν ἑκάτερος. κιρνᾶται γὰρ καὶ διττὸς ὤν. ἐν γὰρ τὸ ἐξ ἀμφοῖν συνιστάμενον τελείωσις γνώσεως. ἡ μὲν παλαιὰ τὴν ὑπόσχεσιν ἔσχεν, ἡ δὲ νέα τὸν ἀπόστολον ἐξήνεγκεν. τὸ δὲ «Ἔκλινεν ἐκ τούτου εἰς τοῦτο» τὴν διαδοχὴν τῶν διδασκάλων αἰνίττεται τοῦ νόμου τοῦ Μωσαϊκοῦ καὶ τοῦ Κυριακοῦ· καὶ τὸ ποτήριον ἕν· ἐν γὰρ ἔπνευσε πνεῦμα καὶ εἰς προφήτην καὶ εἰς ἀπόστολον, καὶ κατὰ τοὺς ἀγαθοὺς ζωγράφους πάλαι μὲν ἐσκιαγράφησεν, ἔπειτα μέντοι διηκρίβευσε τὰ μέλη τῆς γνώσεως· « Πλὴν κτλ. *Pneuma* also is Spirit here, but it is not a *Hymn*.

6. *Homily* I, 295B (ed. Terzaghi, 279): ὁ θεὸς ἡμῶν σοφία καὶ λόγος ἐστίν. κρατὴρ ὁ παρακινῶν τὸ φρονοῦν, ὁ ταράττων τὸ λογιζόμενον οὐδὲν προσήκει τῷ λόγῳ.

7. *Ibid*. ὅταν εὐτροφῇ σῶμα περὶ σάρκωσιν, ἀποστρέφει ψυχὴν περὶ φρόνησιν.

8. *Ibid*. 295C: ἀριστοποιόν ἐστιν ἐκεῖνο τὸ ποτήριον, οἴνου πλῆρες, ὅγε καὶ μνηστευθὲν εἰς νοῦν ἡμᾶς ἀξιοῖ διεγείρεσθαι.

Logos! This is extremely complex, philosophical and abstruse for a popular sermon. It seems that Synesius not only mythicized in public, he also succumbed to the temptation of publicly philosophizing behind the myths. The Hellene and initiate into the mysteries of philosophy shows through the ecclesiastical *persona*.

This method of interpretation should not surprise us very much. *Homily* I displays an attempt on the part of Synesius to deal with Scripture in the Alexandrian manner: this is, after all, a perfectly logical activity for a Neoplatonist who would be a philosopher-bishop. But his thoughts demonstrate that he still retained his Hellenic values and his Greek philosophical orientation.[9] His method is only superficially similar to that of Clement and Origen.

Homily II is an Easter Eve sermon to the newly baptized members of the congregation. In it Synesius employs language that virtually transforms the Easter ceremony into a Neoplatonically interpreted mystery initiation: it is a holy night on which the light (*phos*) is made manifest to the purified (*tois katheramenois*). It is a light far surpassing that of the sun, for even the fairest thing on earth cannot be compared to the Demiurge. This light, which illuminates souls and the visible (*aistheton*) sun, is not a created thing.[10] He warns the newly baptized concerning the danger of incurring a pollution (*molysma*) after purification (*katharsis*). This accords with the late pagan theory of sin as a stain or pollution brought about by contacts with the material world.[11] Synesius portrays Christ as saving mankind from the pollution incurred through prolonged contact with matter. This is pagan language.

Perhaps it will be objected that the language used here by Synesius could be made to fit either a pagan or a Christian interpretation. Because of the ambiguity of language, the terms *demiourgos* and *demiourgema* (among others) could be interpreted as referring either to a theory of

9. Cf. Isidore of Pelusium's *Ep*. 5, 281: τῆς θείας σοφίας ἡ μὲν λέξις πεζὴ, ἡ ἔννοια δὲ οὐρανομήκης.

10. *Homily* II, 297A–B (ed. Terzaghi, 281): Νὺξ ἱερά, φῶς ἐνεγκοῦσα τοῖς καθηραμένοις ὅσον οὐδ' εἰς ἡμέραν ἔλαμψεν ἥλιος· οὐδὲ γὰρ οὐδ' ὅσιον ἐξετασθῆναι τῷ δημιουργῷ κἂν τὸ κάλλιστον ἐπὶ γῆς· ἀλλ' οὐδὲ δημιούργημα ἐκεῖνο τὸ φῶς, ὃ φωτίζει ψυχάς, καὶ τὸν αἰσθητὸν ἐφώτισεν ἥλιον ὁμολογίᾳ τῆς παρούσης μακαριότητος. Even a biblical paraphrase used by Synesius (297B–C) may be seen as one which has "Orphic" overtones and might very well have its origin in the context of a Hellenistic mysticism which has been seen as part of the background of Judaism in the Hellenistic-Roman age, as well as that of Christianity: ἐπὶ γῆς ὄντες καὶ ἐν οὐρανῷ τὸ πολίτευμα ἔχοντες (*Phil*. III.20), which is similar to the "Orphic" slogan "I am a citizen of earth and starry heaven, but my origin is heavenly."

11. *Ibid*. 297C: φοβήθητε τῆς ἀξίας ἀποπεσεῖν· δυσέκνιπτον τὸ μετὰ κάθαρσιν μόλυσμα.

Creation or one of emanation.[12] The use of mystery language in order to facilitate the presentation of Christianity to the Greek world was nothing new. For example, Paul called Christianity a *mysterion*,[13] and Clement of Alexandria promised the Greeks that he would show them the mysteries of the Logos in terms they could understand.[14] Yet Christianity was not just another mystery. It was something new and unique for which the Logos had partially prepared the way by means of the spread of mystery religions and philosophy throughout the Greco-Roman world. Thus the way had been made ready for the true Mystery: that of the redemption of the whole world through the Crucifixion and Resurrection of Jesus Christ. Just as the *pax Romana* had created the ecumenical conditions that heralded the birth of the world's Savior, so also the Hellenistic mysteries of the Greeks, Egyptians, Asiatics, etc., helped to prepare mankind's understanding for the revelation of the True Mystery of Salvation. When the right time (*kairos*) arrived, the old pagan mysteries were to be rejected as profane and replaced by the Christian mystery. In short, the mysteries were part of the education of mankind under the tutelage of the Logos—to the extent that the language and imagery of the mysteries could clarify Christian concepts, they could be legitimately used by Christian thinkers, teachers, priests and laymen.

Thus it might be asserted that Synesius in *Homily* II was merely following what had become a traditional pattern for Christians since the second or even the first century A.D. Yet unlike Clement, for example, who clearly distinguished Christianity from the other mysteries, not only the terms Synesius uses but also the meanings these express indicate an interpretation in harmony with Neoplatonism and Hellenistic syncretism. *Homily* II sounds more like the speech of a pagan hierophant addressing new initiates than it does the Easter sermon of a bishop.[15] Although the light spoken of by Synesius might be equated with the Logos, there is no specific mention of Christ in this Easter sermon. Synesius himself, in a letter (*Ep.* 13) to one Peter the Elder, speaks both of the coming Easter festival and his own incompetence (due to lack of scriptural knowledge) to preach a proper sermon. Synesius does not openly contradict the Christian myth here, but his sermon is something that could be accepted—

12. Even the pagan Hierocles, for instance, understood the Platonic demiurge as a *creator god.*

13. *Rom.* 16:25ff, I *Cor.* 2:7–10, *Col.* 1:26ff, *Eph.* 1:8–10 and 3:3–12.

14. Clement, *Protrepticus* XII. 119; for a discussion of the specifically Christian usage of the term μυστήριον in St. Paul, Clement and other Fathers, see Rahner, 337–401, esp. 355–369.

15. Lacombrade, *Synésios* 264 n. 66, gives all the references to the handful of biblical citations in the works of Synesius. Cf. *Ep.* 67, 217A.

with slight variations—by all contemporary religions. It is as if Synesius telescoped the religious content of all the old cults into the Christian ritual, while remaining a universalist at heart—somewhat like his opposite numbers in the Renaissance (e.g., Pico, Ficino, Cusanus) who recognized the value and truth of other religions, even polytheism, while still remaining Christians.[16]

The Catastases

Two speeches (or perhaps letters), which describe conditions in Libya and are known as the Catastases,[17] reveal something about Synesius' activities as a bishop. The first one, optimistic in tone, praises Anysius, a good officer who managed to repel the barbarians temporarily. His praise of Anysius as a soldier is typically Roman, while his ethical and political statements imply the possibility of achieving harmony between the values of Greek philosophy and the Christian religion; e.g. 305A:

> Since I have not chosen to adhere to an apolitical philosophy, and since the most philanthropic religion urges us to develop a character in sympathy with the common lot, I have responded to your call.[18]

However, this brief respite of 411 due to the success of Anysius was not to last, and the second Catastasis sounds a profoundly pessimistic note. Fitzgerald thinks that it is not a speech but a personal letter (of A.D. 412–413) to someone who might be able to influence Anthemius, Praetorian Prefect of the East, to send help and attract the attention of the Imperial Council.[19] Synesius' appeal to save the Pentapolis as a province of the Empire reads like a miniature "Fall of Rome." The year is 412 or 413. Anysius, who only postponed the disaster, is gone. The military situation

16. On Neoplatonic pagan-Christian syncretism in the Renaissance, see e.g. Wind, 1–25; Seznec, 84–99; M. Ficino, *De sole*; Pico Della Mirandola, *De dignitate hominum*; Cusanus, *De docta ignorantia* 1, 25.

17. These works are called the Catastases because they refer to the state or condition of the province. They also plead the case for the province in the hope of restoring it to a settled state; for this range of meanings see *LSJ*, *s.v.* κατάστασις.

18. Catastasis I, 305A–B (ed. Terzaghi, 283). This passage unites Christianity with the Classical tradition; cf. *ibid.*, PG 1576=306D: τίνα δὲ ἔξεστι καλεῖν ἀδωρότατον; οὐ τὸν ὑπερορῶντα καὶ τῶν ἀπὸ τοῦ νόμου κερδῶν; ὁ θεοσεβὴς δὲ τίς ἂν γένοιτο μᾶλλον, ἢ ὅστις ἅπαντος ἔργου καὶ λόγου θεόθεν ἄρχεται;

(305 A–B): Οὔτε φιλοσοφίαν ἀπολίτευτον προελόμενος, καὶ τῆς φιλανθρωποτάτης θρησκείας ἐναγούσης εἰς ἦθος φιλόκοινον, ὑπήκουσά τε καλούμενος ὑφ' ὑμῶν, κτλ.

19. For this opinion as well as the problem of dating this work, see Fitzgerald, *Essays and Hymns* 476–478 (412–413 A.D.).

has become desperate. Synesius, now under tremendous pressure, calls on the old Roman spirit in his hour of desolation:

O for the spirit of the ancient Romans, who were victorious in all of their battles, wherever they fought; they who joined together the continents through their victories, now are in danger of losing at the hands of a wretched race of nomads their Libyan with their Greek possessions and even Alexandria in Egypt.[20]

The Pentapolis is finished and Synesius has fantasies of escape to the island of Cythera, opposite the Peloponnesus, where he will live as a stranger, unknown his famous ancestry, which he claimed could be traced back to the Heraclids in the public tablets:

Alas for Cyrene, where the public tablets have recorded the pedigree of my ancestors from Heracles down to myself. For I would not be considered simple, if I mourn among those who are aware of the decline of my noble line. Alas for the tombs of my Doric ancestors in which I shall not find my rest![21]

So much for the despair of Synesius the Hellene, citizen of an ancient polis. But Synesius the bishop also expresses his despair:

Alas for Ptolemaïs, where I was the last ordained priest. But this terrible fate has come to me. I am no longer able to speak. Tears have stopped my tongue. I have reached the point of imagining the abandonment of sacred things. It was already necessary for the fleet to sail away; but when someone calls me to take ship I will beg to remain for a little while. For first I will go to the shrine of God. I will move around the altar. I shall dampen the most precious floor with my tears. I will not flee before I bid farewell to that entrance and that throne. O how many times will I invoke the name of God and turn to Him; O how many times will I throw my two hands against the latticed gates. But necessity is an overpowering thing. I desire to give my eyes a sleep undisturbed by the bugle-call.[22]

In a later passage (304A–B), he tearfully resolves to die at the altar if necessary. The fact that the last two passages quoted follow one another in

20. Catastasis (II) III, 301B (ed. Terzaghi, 288): ὦ τοῦ πάλαι Ῥωμαίων φρονήματος· οἱ πάντα πανταχοῦ νικῶντες, οἱ τὰς ἠπείρους τροπαίοις συνάψαντες, νῦν ὑπὸ δυστήνου καὶ νομαδίτου γένους κινδυνεύουσι ταῖς Ἑλληνίσι Λιβύας προσαποβαλεῖν καὶ τὴν παρ'Αἴγυπτον Ἀλεξάνδρειαν.

21. Catastasis (II) V, 303A (ed. Terzaghi, 291): Ὦ μοι Κυρήνης, ἧς αἱ δημόσιαι κύρβεις μέχρις ἐμοῦ κατάγουσι τὰς ἀφ' Ἡρακλέους διαδοχάς. οὐ γὰρ ἂν εἴην ἀρχαῖος, ἐν εἰδόσιν ὀλοφυρόμενος τὴν καταβεβλημένην εὐγένειαν. ὦ μοι τῶν τάφων, ὧν οὐ μεθέξω, τῶν Δωρικῶν.

22. Ibid., 303A–C: ὦ μοι Πτολεμαΐδος, ἧς ἀνεδείχθην ὕστατος ἱερεύς. ἀλλὰ προσέστη μοι τὸ δεινόν· οὐκέτι δύναμαι λέγειν· ἐπιλαμβάνεταί μου τῆς γλώττης τὰ δάκρυα· γέγονα πρὸς τὴν φαντασίαν τῆς τῶν ἱερῶν ἀπολείψεως. ἔδει μὲν οἴχεσθαι πλέοντας·

the text is one more indication that Synesius felt that it was possible to remain loyal to ancient classical ideals and still be a Christian bishop. Although he was under a tremendous emotional strain, it would be rash, it seems to me, to claim that he was confused or schizophrenic on this point. He is lamenting the imminent loss of everything he holds sacred in the world. Synesius had still not achieved or attempted the spiritual transformation of an Augustine or Gregory of Nazianzus.[23] His lamentations over the things he was attached to, and was about to lose, are understandably emotional. The Church and its objects are sacred to Synesius because popular Christianity now has absorbed everything that was sacred in popular paganism. Christianity in Synesius' view has virtually become the means by which the sacred is made manifest to the Greco-Roman world. Just as the pagan mysteries were appreciated by the vulgar on a different level than that of the philosopher, so it is with Christian symbols. The religious stance of Synesius is not contradicted by his self-revelations in the second Catastasis.

Some of his other acts and statements during his tenure in office also indicate that he was successfully playing his chosen role. As a bishop travelling around his province, he was called on to settle a dispute between Paul, Bishop of Erythrum, and Dioscurus, Bishop of Darnis. Paul demanded possession of an old fortress on the border of their respective dioceses. When Dioscurus refused, Paul sneaked in anyway, set up an altar, began to administer the sacraments, consecrated the place and refused to give it up. Synesius denied the validity of the consecration on the grounds that the *spirit* of the ceremony is more important than the *performance* of ritual; injustice cannot be connected with holiness.[24] Therefore an unjust fraud cannot be a true basis for claims of sanctification. Clearly at work here is the Platonic philosophical principle that holiness must be just.[25] This, then, is a perfect example of Synesius acting as a bishop without compromising himself. In this case he could feel that the priesthood

---

ἀλλ' ὅταν ἐπὶ ναῦν τις καλῇ, μικρὸν ἀναμεῖναι δεήσομαι· βαδιοῦμαι γὰρ πρῶτον ἐπὶ τὸν νεὼν τοῦ θεοῦ· κυκλώσομαι τὸ θυσιαστήριον· δάκρυσι βρέξω τὸ τιμαλφέστατον ἔδαφος· οὐκ ἀποδραμοῦμαι πρὶν θύραν ἐκείνην καὶ θρόνον ἐκεῖνον ἀσπάσασθαι. ὦ ποσάκις θεοκλυτήσω τε καὶ μεταστραφήσομαι· ὦ ποσάκις ταῖς κιγκλίσι τὼ χεῖρε προσμάξομαι. ἀλλ' ἰσχυρὸν ἀνάγκη πρᾶγμα καὶ βίαιον. ἐπιθυμῶ δοῦναι τοῖς ὀφθαλμοῖς ὕπνον ἀπερισάλπιστον. Lacombrade, *Synésios* 237, points out that Synesius uses both the Christian term θυσιαστήριον and pagan term βῶμος—which is scrupulously avoided by ecclesiastical authors—to designate the altar of his church. This would naturally tend to happen if Synesius saw the Church as the religion which had replaced all the other cults.

23. Cf. Misch, *Geschichte d. Autobiog.* 607.
24. Cf. Fitzgerald, *Essays and Hymns* 50.
25. This important issue is discussed in the *Euthyphro* 12D–E.

had not been a decline from the realm of philosophy, but, on the contrary, a step upwards to it.[26]

In a letter to a friend who had become a monk,[27] Synesius the bishop wrote encouraging things: although the white mantle of philosophy is clear and luminous to the eyes and would be better suited to the pure character, he whose motive is truly divine can even wear the black mantle of the clergy. What really counts is the spiritual quality of the person involved. The real justification of an action is its motive; virtue resides in the person's intention. This belief that intention counts more than office is another example of his philosophical religiosity.

As we have seen, he was worried that the office of bishop would distract him from his true pursuits. Synesius continued to believe that the philosophic life was still the most consonant with the divine. He hopes that his friend will be able to practice true philosophy in his new life. He also hopes that his own philosophizing will not be in vain and is somewhat envious of his friend, who has attained serenity and achieved the goal which Synesius has been seeking for so long.[28]

It should be noted that Synesius the bishop seems to have been more willing to accept monasticism than the Synesius of the *Dion*. He even helped to found a cloister.[29] As it is described here, however, monasticism does not seem to be in conflict with Synesius' original ideals.

The Eunomians

As bishop, Synesius was obliged to deal with the Eunomian heretics. They had come into the province on a pretext, but they were really there to cause trouble by preaching their heretical doctrine. Synesius did not hesitate to exile them, although he did not confiscate their property. Does this mean that he had become orthodox? In *Ep*. 5 (to the Elders) he calls the Eunomians diabolical, and in one of his rare "Biblical" moods speaks of them in a tone of Old Testament wrath.[30] Considering Synesius' theologically tolerant outlook, why did he not help rather than hinder the Eunomians?

First of all, Theophilus, with whom he had good relations, was vio-

26. See *Ep*. 11.
27. See above 136 and n. 44.
28. See above n. 26; Synesius tells his correspondent that he (the latter) has left his friends behind Ἄτης ἐν λειμῶνι κατὰ σκότον ἠλασκόντας; cf. Empedocles, fr. 121 DK.
29. See *Ep*. 126; cf. Wilamowitz, 288.
30. *Ep*. 5; on Synesius' OT wrath, cf. also *Ep*. 57 *passim*.

lently anti-heretical when he found it expedient; he was especially hypo-
critical when it came to Arians and Origenists, to whom the Eunomians
were related. He might tolerate such opinions held by a Synesius but not
held by a group of potential troublemakers. Synesius had also promised to
conform to the external policies of the Church. The Eunomians were dis-
rupting the smooth operation of the *kalon pseudos* and therefore had to
be expelled from the new Platonic City. Unity was necessary to the
Church: truth was to be arrived at by philosophic clergymen, who knew
how to handle it, not a group of heretical upstarts. The Eunomians were a
source of potential strife that could lead to political and social upheavals
within the Church. The Church was one of the few stable institutions left
in the Empire: if the Greco-Roman way of life was to be preserved, the
Church had to be preserved.

When Synesius became bishop he promised to work in the interests
of the Church; even if he felt that the Eunomians had a case, he might
very well have found it necessary to persecute them. Let us also keep in
mind that Synesius, as has been demonstrated, was not in conflict with
orthodoxy on the specific issue in question in this dispute, the relationship of the Persons of the Trinity.

More important than these considerations was the fact that the Eunomians were stirring up the numerous old Arian groups in the province.[31] Some Arianizing bishops had compromised at the Council of Nicaea and survived. There were only two Arian holdouts, one of whom was
Secundus of the Libyan Pentapolis. This is an indication that Arianism
was a powerful force in Libya. The Church historian Philostorgius claimed
that Libya gave more support to Arianism than any other province. Constantius II, in a letter to Arius himself, allowed the latter to act indepen-
dently in Libya where his supporters were numerous. Earlier, Constantine, seeing that Arius was in Libya, quoted from the Sibylline
Oracles a prophecy of doom for the province. Later in the century the
Arian churches demanded toleration in Libya and Egypt.

Synesius himself was aware of this state of affairs. His *Ep.* 67 to Theophilus describes a confusing ecclesiastical situation in the Pentapolis. He
had been sent to the villages of Palaebiscus and Hydrax. But, he says,
they do not traditionally constitute a See. The villagers had been subject
to the Bishop of Erythrum for a long time. They wanted this arrangement
to continue. For a short time there had been a bishop of Palaebiscus earlier in the fourth century; but he had been chosen because the bishop of

31. For a complete discussion of these fourth and early fifth century problems in Libya, see Chadwick, *HTR* 53. 171–195. This paragraph and the next are based on pp. 175–178
of his article.

Erythrum was weak. Thus the townspeople chose one Siderius as their bishop. He had been in the army of Valens, was locally influential and could act as their *patronus*. When he was consecrated Alexandria and the three bishops of the province were ignored; Philo of Cyrene acted on his own. Later, Athanasius, who found Siderius reliable, made him bishop of Ptolemaïs. The "See" of Palaebiscus was discontinued.

Synesius says that these dubious Church practices were a result of conditions in the local churches: "for at that time the multitude embraced heretical doctrines."[32]

Thus Arianism was a strong force in Libya well into the fourth century, if not beyond.[33] Obviously Synesius, as the agent of Theophilus, would help to extend Church authority in this area.[34] Given this historical background, the theology of the Eunomians was unimportant. Synesius had not become bishop to help preside over the dissolution of the Eastern Provinces of the Roman Empire.

What people turn to in times of crisis tells us much about their real beliefs. Indeed, it might be generally admitted that during such times, an individual's deepest religious orientation will reveal itself. When close to despair, Synesius turned to philosophy for consolation. When this failed, he attempted to find consolation in the performance of his duty. Finally, with some success, he turned to the Stoic philosophy of Epictetus. He also continued to confide in Hypatia. He did *not* attempt to find personal hope in Christ or Scripture.[35]

It is not uncommon to find people returning to the Church of their youth in a crisis of life or spirit, even if they had been extreme anticlericals, atheists, or agnostics. To what extent should any genuine conversion reach into the deeper layers of the personality and not be easily erased at the first real test? How much allowance should be made for the

---

32. *Ibid.*; Synesius, *Ep.* 67, 1413E and 1417A.

33. Chadwick, 178–179.

34. *Ibid.* 180; Theophilus was trying to use the Sixth Canon of Nicaea as a justification for his acts. This document divided ecclesiastical authority. Alexandria was given power over Libya; Synesius would not oppose Theophilus on behalf of the City. He also claimed innocence of Canon Law (*Ep.* 76).

35. *Ep.* 126, 1505C; *Ep.* 132; see also Wilamowitz, 288: "so hilft ihm kein Bibelwort, sondern er greift nach Epiktet." Yet as bishop, he still speaks of the foundation of a cloister. His despair has Greek tragic overtones, "mit dem euripideischen οἴμοι˙ τὶ δ'οἴμοι; θνητὰ γὰρ πεπόνθαμεν beginnt er, dann teilt er die Trauernich" (*ibid.*). It is interesting to note that Stephen MacKenna, the modern translator of Plotinus, also turned from Neoplatonism to Epictetus late in his life; see his *Journal and Letters* 70, 221, and 257. See also Geffcken, 221. Synesius also was still writing to Hypatia during this period; see e.g. *Epp.* 81, 124, and 16 (124 might be problematical.) For the general question of the authenticity and dating of the letters in this period, see Lacombrade, *Synésios* 249–250.

limit of human endurance? We know that Synesius had lost his children, and everything else he valued in the world was literally crumbling around him. That he could not even find solace in philosophy at first is an indication of the impact that his troubles had upon him. When he recovered, however, he did so by means of philosophy and not Christian doctrine. His continued confidence in Hypatia is also an indication that his primary attachment was still to philosophy.

Synesius made a historical decision to become a bishop. He accepted Christianity as the religion through which, in the future, the divine would be mediated to the mass of mankind, but did he ever view the pagan cults as anything other than this? This is a perennial stance of those within many religious traditions who place a very high value upon philosophical truth. As we have suggested, it is not unlike that of certain Islamic philosophers.[36]

Thus, unless we accept the almost certainly spurious *Hymn* X as not only genuine, but also, considering the above, as the very last statement of Synesius, a statement that would indicate a complete spiritual conversion through Christ, we are led to conclude on the available evidence that Synesius never abandoned his original notion of the philosopher-bishop. He must be given credit for arriving at a brilliant and workable solution to a most difficult religious problem. The transformation of the old idea of the Platonic philosopher-king into a "philosopher-bishop" was an ingenious idea: one which made it possible for a Synesius to live with the great changes taking place about him and still play an active role in the life of his times.

Synesius as Bishop: Political Implications

In addition to spiritual responsibilities, the bishop in the late Empire had political, judicial and social functions to perform.[37] He was often chosen by the ecclesiastical administration for his experience and influence in the world of politics and by the local masses as a new kind of *prostates tou demou*. For this reason, it is important to take into consideration

36. As late as the sixth century, Boethius, an apparent Christian educated in pagan philosophical "schools," turned to philosophy in his time of greatest need; see *De consolatione philosophiae*. The question of his position is still open to interpretation. De Vogel, however, in *Vivarium* 9.44–66 and 10.1–40, reviews all work on Boethius and finds certain statements in the *Consolation* that she believes to be specifically Christian.

37. For the political role of bishops in the late Empire, see Lacombrade, *Synésios* 217; for the different roles of Synesius as bishop, *ibid*. 299.

the political side of Synesius' experience with the Church. Theophilus, the wily bishop of Alexandria, an opportunist politician, must have followed the career of Synesius with interest. Shortly after his return from a successful visit to Constantinople, Synesius married a Christian with the blessing of Theophilus: it is reasonable to assume that a friendship developed between the two men at this point. Theophilus could use a dependable man like Synesius—especially since he would never partake of the kind of doctrinal controversy that might cause trouble for the bishop.[38] In this sense, Synesius' religious views could be advantageous to a political manipulator. Theophilus also saw Synesius operate very effectively in his own home of Cyrene, taking the initiative in leadership against barbarian tribes and continually struggling against the excesses of corrupt administrators. In his correspondence, Synesius continually complained about the misdeeds of these men and he was certainly not averse to fighting them.[39] Nor was he averse to praising those with whose ability and performance he was pleased.[40]

Theophilus was correct in his assessment, for when Synesius became bishop, his bold excommunication of the tyrannical provincial governor Andronicus probably checked Andronicus' ambitions and suppressed potential trouble.[41]

It is obvious that such bishops operating in sensitive areas could be useful to the emperors: they could act as a check on members of the imperial administration over whom the emperors had very little control. Perhaps the Church could help lighten some of the administrative burdens of the late Empire and render otherwise ineffective legislation occasionally enforceable.

In addition to his obvious political abilities, Synesius had from his Constantinople days a list of important friends well placed in the bureaucracy; these included Aurelian, Praetorian Prefect of the East, and Simplicius, who was supreme commander of the armed forces.[42] Certainly Theophilus was also well aware of the distinction which an aristocrat like Synesius would give to the inner circle of the Church. Many pagans who held a liberal position on the Christian issue might be convinced to come over to the Church if so distinguished, noble and learned a man would

38. Cf. Wilamowitz, 281.   39. Cf. e.g. Epp. 37 and 47.

40. Cf. Ep. 62; a case in point is Marcellinus, the Comes who saved Ptolemaïs from near disaster.

41. Ep. 57; this is one of the few places where Synesius demonstrates any knowledge of Scripture. For further discussion of the implications of Ep. 57 (against Andronicus), see Lacombrade, Synésios 240–243.

42. For a partial list of his friends, their offices and rank, see Coster, 16.

accept an episcopate. Theophilus certainly strengthened his own and the Church's position with the recruitment of Synesius: this kind of propaganda had its effect.[43]

Synesius himself was well aware of the profound changes that had taken place in the last century and even in his own lifetime. Although anti-pagan legislation had been promulgated for some time, the situation only now, during the last decade of the fourth century, became even more difficult for pagans in the East.[44] He realized that the days of Julian were long past and that the only way to save the best of Hellenism was to incorporate it into the Church. Synesius, as part of the Church, could help pour the old Hellenic wine he loved so well into new Christian bottles. He was not orthodox, but he sincerely wanted a Christian Church that would maintain Hellenic values and ideas, if not Hellenic cults.

43. Cf. Socrates, *HE* VI. 6.7, 9, 12, 15–17; VII.7, who relates some of the opinions and doings of Theophilus. He held the views of Origen on the incorporeality of the divine nature. When a group of monks, known as Anthropomorphists because they believed God had human features, threatened him, he is reported to have said: "In seeing you I see the face of God," and then denouncing the Origenists, whose beliefs he supposedly shared, worked up the monks' hostility. He himself continued to read Origen after he denounced his teachings. Sozomen (*HE* VIII.14) judges him in a similar fashion. Theophilus was always involved in disputes and power struggles, including one with St. John Chrysostom that ended in the latter's downfall. Synesius, however, seems to have gotten on quite well with Theophilus.

44. See the Introduction, n. 3. The most eloquent pagan protest in the West was, of course, Symmachus' *Relatio* III.

Conclusion

i

"It is almost always a futile attempt to estimate the relative importance of outward events and of inward tendencies in determining the course of any man's life and the development of his character," says Alice Gardner in attempting to evaluate Synesius.[1] Yet we must undertake this task insofar as it is possible. With this in mind, let us first briefly review and criticize some of the main theories about Synesius.

Evagrius, the Church historian, sees Synesius as a brilliant philosopher and good man who stood in relation to the Church as a sympathetic outsider. He believed that divine grace, "since it is never content to leave its work unfinished," completed the conversion of Synesius.[2] This is also the opinion of Photius, who thought that the dogma of the Resurrection became an article of faith with Synesius after his elevation to the episcopate.[3] Among the most interesting of all is the Byzantine *Pratum Spirituale*, which depicts Synesius as a devout man who convinces a learned pagan, Evagrius, of the very dogmas in which, as we know, he himself did not believe.[4] This is an interesting reversal, to say the least. As we mentioned earlier, some early modern scholars such as Pétau (who uses Portus, a Renaissance humanist), follow this pattern, but employ more careful scholarly methods to demonstrate their thesis. Synesius himself, however, wrote a letter after he had become a bishop, in which he states:

> If I am unable to say any of the things which you are used to hearing,
> I am to be forgiven and you are to be blamed in this matter; because
> you have chosen a man who does not have knowledge of God's Scrip-
> tures instead of one of those who are acquainted with them.[5]

1. Gardner, *Synesius* 91.   2. Evagrius, *HE* 15.
3. Phot. *Bibl.* 1.26.   4. *Pratum Spirituale* in *PG* 66.1043–1046.
5. *Ep.* 13, 1349C: εἰ δὲ μηδὲν ἔσχον εἰπεῖν, οἵων ἀκούειν εἰώθατε, συγγνώμη μὲν ἐμοὶ τοῦτο, ἔγκλημα δὲ ὑμῖν, ὅτι τὸν οὐκ εἰδότα τὰ λόγια τοῦ θεοῦ τῶν εἰδότων ἀνθείλεσθε.

But any real conversion to orthodoxy, unless it occurred at the last moment, would surely have led the newly baptized and ordained Christian bishop to a more careful and thorough study of the Scriptures.

As we have already pointed out many times, Synesius' ignorance of Scripture, his failure to mention Christ where one would expect otherwise, his approach to dogma and exegesis, all bear witness to his uniqueness. In these places we have often implicitly made use of an *argumentum ex silentio* in an attempt to establish his originality, spiritual isolation, and lack of familiarity with the Christian tradition. Such an argument is compelling because we can trace the original way in which he approached Christianity on those very points where one would most expect him to base his arguments on the New Testament and the Fathers.

Other scholars as Marrou and Lacombrade approach the subject more cautiously and are careful about their conclusions. As we have seen, Marrou and Lacombrade tried to fit Synesius into the mold of a transitional figure who was both devoted to the Hellenism of the past and looking forward to the orthodox Christianity of the future. But the pattern which they try to impose on Synesius' spiritual development is somewhat artificial; e.g., they largely ignore elements, such as Chaldaean theology, which make a different interpretation highly probable—one which allows him to remain a Neoplatonist.

Wilamowitz's assertion that Synesius remained a *de facto* pagan has much validity. In general, his views are a necessary criticism of his predecessors. His great contribution was the discovery that *Hymn* X is a spurious work. This did much to undercut any argument that claimed Synesius finally underwent a total conversion to orthodox Christianity through Christ.

Geffcken takes a balanced view, for which there is much to be said. As we have noted, he sees Synesius as a pagan who was not hostile to Christianity *per se*, but only to certain forms of the Christian life that seemed barbarous to him. His conversion was a slow process without any sudden or drastic change. Christianity never became the living reality for him that it did for Marius Victorinus. But Geffcken does not attempt to analyze Synesius' method or to resolve all of the contradictions presented by the evidence in the short space he devotes to him. Nor does he deal with his relationship to the Oracles—but this was not a real possibility before the work of Lewy and Theiler was completed.

Gardner tries to work out the conversion of Synesius in religious and philosophical terms.[6] She claims that after the pagan temples closed,

6. Gardner, *Synesius* 89.

Synesius satisfied his religious needs by celebrating Christian mysteries in churches, that philosophically he believed the gods to be forms of Nous as did Julian and Iamblichus, that he eventually associated these with angels and ceased to look on them as objects of worship. But there is no evidence of this: on the contrary, we have seen that Synesius maintained his cosmos-piety. In addition, we know that angels (as distinct from "gods") form part of the Neoplatonic and Chaldaean scheme of emanation, so that Synesius' hypothetical shift from gods to angels cannot be the one-level process that Gardner envisions. She also feels that he began to identify Christ and the Christian Logos with the Neoplatonic Nous. This is correct, but not unique to Synesius: it is one of the natural theological meeting-points between pagan and Christian Neoplatonism.

Fitzgerald has given us a fine, annotated translation of the works of Synesius, but I believe that his views both of Neoplatonism and of Synesius prevent him from fully understanding some of the issues. He is drawn to Synesius and sees in him the attractive figure of a learned gentleman in a semi-barbarous age. As for Neoplatonism, he thinks it a weak, final attempt to revitalize a philosophy that was once a living reality and that ends in the very antithesis of rational Greek philosophy: it is irrational, oriented toward magic and theurgy, merely an escapist attempt to achieve ecstasy without the use of reason. After thus oversimplifying and distorting the Neoplatonic position, he claims that Synesius, who was neither an escapist nor an otherworldly mystic, cannot be a true Neoplatonist.

Having started out with these now very dated assumptions, Fitzgerald tries to prove his hypothesis. At best he oversimplifies, at worst he is simply wrong. Quite often, both the text he is translating and evidence he introduces into his notes provide a refutation of his theories. For instance, Fitzgerald tries to prove that Synesius is a "Platonist" rather than a Neoplatonist by showing how much he quotes Plato, but every Neoplatonist thought of himself as a Platonist and quoted and commented on Plato's works extensively. Synesius himself would find this argument unintelligible.

Let us now attempt, in conclusion, to establish the nature and significance of Synesius' spiritual development.

First, we must ask exactly how Synesius viewed the historical mission of Christianity. If it was to replace all the other cults with the religion of Christ, was it not necessarily the prophesied new dispensation and not merely the one new cult *par excellence*, which had absorbed all the others? This is a very difficult question to answer, for Synesius does not deal with it directly, so that we must attempt to infer the answer from his behavior and his writings. One possibility is that Synesius saw the success of the Church as the result of historical circumstances (*tyche*) to which it was necessary to accommodate himself. However, given his stated providential theory of history, this is not likely. Nor did Byzantine historians use the word *tyche* in the way Thucydides, or even Polybius, used it: simply as Fortune, cosmic or otherwise. What was Chance to us here below was, if not predetermined, at least eternally known by God through his providence (*pronoia*).[7] Given Synesius' views of these matters, it is quite possible that he considered the Church's success as somehow connected with providence.

The Christian religion did not entail a "transvaluation of all values" for Synesius, but it was to be the historical means for the preservation of the old values in a somewhat altered setting. The new world could not maintain the old cults. Neoplatonic philosophy, the religion of the few, would continue within the Church, presumably among the ranks of the higher clergy and perhaps philosophically inclined monks. For a Hellene in a fragile empire, this certainly could seem providential.

Synesius' beliefs were, for the most part, esoterically compatible with and analogous to some Christian ideas: he identified the innermost Chaldaean-Neoplatonic triad with the Persons of the Trinity: he equated the Chaldaean "seal" of Nous with the Christian seal of baptism; he accepted the Incarnation and Resurrection allegorically and symbolically; he allowed for divine intervention in the economy of providence. He also might have assumed that the philosophical schools would be permitted to continue even if cults and mysteries were outlawed. Indeed, the Neoplatonic school at Alexandria did continue as a Christian institution until the Arab invasion of 641. Needless to say, its graduates could have become excellent philosopher-bishops.

As bishop, Synesius was obliged to dispense the sacraments, excommunicate, persecute heretics and perform the other spiritual and temporal functions inherent in his office. If we accept his piety and sincerity as genuine, he truly believed that the divine could be mediated to the people through Christian ritual and symbolism. The meaning of these rituals and symbols was another matter. So was the source of their authority: philosophy.

Although he did not partake in the external conflict between paganism and Christianity, in a sense that conflict took place within his own

---

7. On early Byzantine historiography and the ideas of *Tyche* and *Pronoia*, cf. Evans, *GRBS* XII.81–100, esp. 93–100. For an excellent study of how the early Church historians transformed and adapted these ideas to their Christian interpretations of history, see Chesnut, 61–189.

soul. His personal attempt at resolution of the conflict within himself and his subsequent resolution of the problem is of the greatest significance for the study of the Christianization of the aristocracy of the East in the late Roman Empire. Some sympathizers of Julian and the circle of Symmachus and Praetextatus would think of him as a "collaborator." Indeed, he was an ally of Theophilus, the man who had destroyed the Serapeum. There can be no doubt that Synesius was well aware of this fact. It was also fortunate that he probably did not live to see the murder of Hypatia. But the result of that might have been increased hostility toward certain "barbaric" forms of the Christian life rather than towards the Church itself.[8] Had he been able to watch the development of the Christian Church for the next thousand years, he would have approved of some things while disapproving of others; the Church, after all, did not go in a direction entirely unfavorable to those with the beliefs of a Synesius. He would have been fascinated by the writings of Pseudo-Dionysius the Areopagite, a man whose Christian mysticism was so strongly influenced by Proclus that it has been called a system of Christian theurgy.[9] Characteristically, Dionysius' doctrine narrowly escaped condemnation; and fortunate it was for the mystical theology of the high Middle Ages that it did escape. Synesius would have also been perfectly at home with Renaissance mystics and philosophers such as the Florentine Platonists and Nicolas of Cusa.

It has been said of the circle of Symmachus that they were noble but myopic men who clung to the past without understanding the future.[10] The same cannot be said about Synesius. Whatever else is true, he opened a philosophical path into the Church for aristocrats of the old classic Greco-Roman mold. For this reason, he is of great importance for the history of late Roman culture and society. Synesius, and others like him, were the Church's best answer to the movement of Julian and his followers.

Thus Synesius must remain a complex and interesting figure. The best we can do is to bring out as many of his characteristics as possible in the hope of continually gaining new insights. He was able to live in an era

8. Indeed, Socrates, *HE* 7.15, condemns the deed in no uncertain terms, saying that it was both harmful to the Church and most un-Christian.

9. Cf. Sheldon-Williams, 457–459. But see now Gersh, *From Iamblichus to Eriugena*, who discusses certain Cappadocian influences on Pseudo-Dionysius and Christian aspects of his thought. According to Gersh the dominant influence on Pseudo-Dionysius is theurgic Neoplatonism, but he is not *simply* a "Proclus baptized" (p. 20); see also especially pp. 4, 21, 138, 152–190, and 283. Synesius, on the other hand, might at most be called a "baptized Porphyrian."

10. For this opinion see McGeachy, 192.

of profound change without compromising his philosophy. Perhaps the one thing that most makes him a fitting subject for study is, as we pointed out earlier, that he was a remarkable combination of all eras of classical antiquity in one person. He was the noble descended from the hero Eurysthenes, the classical Greek who wrote in late Attic and Doric and was proud of his Lacedaemonian heritage, the Neoplatonic philosopher who was initiated into the Hellenistic mysteries of Alexandrian thought by Hypatia, the Roman provincial of the curial class who was able to speak eloquently before the emperor and make important friends at court, and finally the Christian bishop, ordained as if by some divine artist to make this portrait complete.

ii

This work has attempted to demonstrate that Synesius was primarily a philosopher. He never confessed a creed such as the Nicene, nor did he believe in redemption through Jesus Christ the Logos. He was not a convert who appropriated classical *paideia* for religious purposes. He did not equate the *theoretikos bios* with Christian theology or the Christian life. For him, philosophy was Neoplatonism, of the non-theurgic Porphyrian variety taught by Hypatia. All of his work points toward the Way of Philosophy, not the Way of Christian Religion.

His ideas of salvation were basically those of Plato and the "Orphics" as interpreted by the Neoplatonists. The Savior figure he presents in his *Hymns* as Jesus is much closer to the *theios aner* of mystical Hellenistic syncretism than the Jesus of the Gospels, and closer to Apollonius or Pythagoras as man-god than the Jesus of Logos-theology (except to the extent that that theology was influenced by Platonism). One senses that Synesius would have been much more comfortable discussing eschatology and related questions with the Socrates of the *Phaedo* than discussing the coming kingdom with Jesus and his disciples.

Historical circumstances led him into the Church. He had common interests with orthodox Christians against the barbarian Arian Goths. The orthodox feared an Arian Empire as much as a barbarian one. But for Synesius, the issue was barbarism versus Greco-Roman civilization. He found allies among orthodox Christians (educated in the manner of the Cappadocians) who supported his policies. The Theodosian age had taught him that paganism as cult and mystery was on the decline. He realized that the best in Hellenism would have to be saved in a Christian Empire, and he acted accordingly. Thus, he created the idea of the philosopher-bishop. In this we see his brilliance and originality.

Plotinus had said that the gods should come to him, not he to them.[11] Yet at times he does admit that cult was somehow divinely inspired. Porphyry interpreted pagan religion philosophically. Both of these philosophers understood that philosophy itself was the "true mystery": this was already an old tradition. Later Hellenes were syncretists who thought that all religions were "true," and that their truth was best understood in philosophical terms.

Synesius brought this tradition to its logical conclusion: living in an age when a re-valorized paganism was in decline, he fully understood the independence of philosophy. It could be used to interpret Christian myths and mysteries as well as pagan ones. It could still claim preeminence. Herein lie his real originality and flexibility.

We have suggested that among thinkers within the revealed traditions, his ideas resembled those of Islamic philosophers such as Al-Fārābī more than those of any contemporary Christian: he interpreted religion *as* philosophy and affirmed the primacy of reason. But Al-Fārābī and the others lived in a world where Islam was an established fact; indeed, Avicenna found no problem in simply equating Islam and philosophy. Synesius could not do this: he was part of a world in which a conflict of religions was taking place. He was forced to make a choice.

After he became a bishop he did not change. His Christian allegorical exegesis and sermonizing are the work of a Neoplatonist who still preferred the term Nous to Logos. He maintained contact with Hypatia philosophically as well as socially. In difficult times, he read Epictetus rather than the Gospels: philosophy was his salvation. His social and political connections, his perception of his age: these ultimately led him into the Church. Such things happened often in the world of late antiquity. But Synesius was too serious a Neoplatonist to care more about his social connections than about his ideas and view of the One, Man, and the Universe. If we take the long view, it seems to me that Synesius, and those like him, did more for the future of philosophy as an independent force than for philosophy as the *ancilla theologiae*.

Thus, finally, we see Synesius as a late antique man in his unique historical position. For him Zeus was Nous: the second term in the equation was the one that mattered. Quietly the pupil of Hypatia moved into the Church. But we can only say that he was a Christian insofar as he

11. Porphyry, *Vit. Plot.* X.36–37.

accepted the title of bishop and performed the functions of his office. For him the Church was a new type of Platonic republic in which religion had the same status as it did in Plato's *Laws*. This is what the philosopher-bishop believed—and ideally a Synesian church would be ruled by philosopher-bishops! He did not believe that the Church was the True Israel, nor did he expect the New Jerusalem to descend from Heaven. Indeed, in a somewhat different spirit from that of Tertullian, were it possible, one would like to ask Synesius what Athens has to do with Jerusalem. Nor did he ever say *credo ut intellegam*. If he had been confronted with the ontological proof, he would have judged it on philosophical grounds. He would not have accepted it as something which reinforced a revelation in which he *already* had faith. For Synesius believed not in the God of Abraham, Isaac and Jacob. He believed in the God of the philosophers.

Bibliography

I. Ancient Works

Augustine, Saint. *De Civitate Dei*. Edited and translated by W. M. Green, W. C. Greene, P. Levine, G. E. McCracken, E. M. Sanford, and D. S. Wiesen. 7 vols. Cambridge, Mass., 1957–1972.

———. *Les Confessions*. Edited by M. Skutella. Paris, 1962.

Averroës. *On Plato's Republic*. Translated by Ralph Lerner. Ithaca, N.Y., 1974.

Basil of Caesarea. *Opera*. Edited by J. P. Migne. *PG* vol. 31. Paris, 1858.

Callistratus. In *Philostratorum et Callistrati Opera*. Edited by A. Westermann. Paris, 1849.

Clement of Alexandria. *Opera*. Edited by J. P. Migne. *PG* vol. 8. Paris, 1857.

Corpus Hermeticum. Edited by A. D. Nock. Translated by A. J. Festugière. Paris, 1945–1954.

Damascii successor. *Dubitationes et solutiones de primis principiis*. Paris, 1889.

Damascius. *Vita Isidori reliquiae*. Edited by C. Zintzen. Hildesheim, 1967.

Eunapius' *fragmenta*. In *Fragmenta Historici Graeci Minores*. Edited by L. Dindorf. Part 1, pp. 205–274. Leipzig, 1870–1871.

———. *Vitae sophistarum*. Edited by J. F. Boissonade. Paris, 1849.

Evagrius Scholasticus. *Historia Ecclesiastica*. Edited by J. P. Migne. *PG* vol. 86. Paris, 1860.

Gregory of Nazianzen. *Opera*. Edited by J. P. Migne. *PG* vol. 37. Paris, 1858.

Gregory of Nyssa. *Opera*. Edited by J. P. Migne. *PG* vols. 44–46. Paris, 1858 and 1863.

Hermetica. Edited and translated by W. Scott. 4 vols. Oxford, 1926.

Iamblichus. *De Mysteriis*. Edited by E. Des Places. Paris, 1966.

———. *De Mysteriis*. Edited by S. Parthey. Berlin, 1857. Reprint, Amsterdam, 1965.

———. *De Vita Pythagorica*. Edited by A. Nauck. St. Petersburg and Leipzig, 1884.

———. *Iamblichi Chalcidensis in Platonis Dialogos Commentariorum Fragmenta*. Edited and translated by J. M. Dillon. Leiden, 1973.

———. *Life of Pythagoras*. Translated by Thomas Taylor. London, 1818. Reprint, London, 1965.

———. *Les mystères d'Egypte*. Edited and translated by E. Des Places. Paris, 1966.

Juliani epistulae et leges. Edited by J. Bidez and F. Cumont. Paris, 1922.

———. *Oeuvres Complètes*. Edited by J. Bidez, C. Lacombrade, and G. Rochefort. Paris, 1924–1972.

———. *The Works of the Emperor Julian*. Edited and translated by W. C. Wright. 3 vols. New York, 1913–1923.

Macrobius. *Commentary on the Dream of Scipio*. Translated by W. H. Stahl. New York, 1952.

———. *Saturnalia*. Translated by Percival Vaughan Davies. New York, 1969.

Olympiodorus. *Olympiodori philosophi in Platonis Phaedonem Commentaria*. Edited by William Norvin. Leipzig, 1913.

Oracles Chaldaïques. Edited by E. Des Places. Paris, 1971.

Orphicorum fragmenta. Edited by O. Kern. Berlin, 1922.

Philostorgius. *History of the Church*. Translated by E. Walford. London, 1855.

———. *Kirchengeschichte*. Edited by J. Bidez. Leipzig, 1913.

Philostratus. In *Philostratorum et Callistrati Opera*. Edited by A. Westermann. Paris, 1849.

Philostratus and Eunapius. *Lives of the Sophists*. Translated by W. C. Wright. New York, 1922.

Photius. *Bibliothèque*. Edited and translated by R. Henry. Paris, 1959.

Plotinus. *Enneads*. Edited by P. Henry and H. R. Schwyzer. Museum Lessianum, 1959–1973.

———. *Enneads*. Translated by S. MacKenna. Revised edition. New York, 1969.

———. *Enneads* I-III. Translated by A. H. Armstrong. Cambridge, Mass., 1967.

Porphyry. *Porphyrii Opuscula Tria*. Edited by A. Nauck. Leipzig, 1860.

Pratum Spirituale. Edited by J. P. Migne. *PG* 66.1043–1046. Paris, 1859 and 1864.

Proclus. *Elements of Theology*. Edited by E. R. Dodds. Oxford, 1933.

———. *In Timaei*. Translated by Thomas Taylor. London, 1820.

———. *Procli Hymni*. Edited by E. Vogt. Wiesbaden, 1957.

———. *Théologie platonicienne*, I-III. Edited by H. D. Saffrey and L. G. Westerink. Paris, 1968.

———. *Timée*. Edited by A. J. Festugière. Paris, 1966–1968.

Rhetores Graeci. Edited by L. Spengel. 3 vols. Leipzig, 1894.

Sallustius. *Concerning the Gods and the Universe.* Edited and translated by A. D. Nock. Cambridge, Mass., 1926.

Scriptorum Paganorum I-IV Saec. de Christianis Testimonia. Edited by W. Den Boer. Leiden, 1948.

Socrates Scholasticus. *Historia Ecclesiastica.* Edited by J. P. Migne. *PG* vol. 67. Paris, 1859.

Sozomen. *Historia Ecclesiastica.* Edited by J. P. Migne. *PG* vol. 67. Paris, 1859.

Sozomen and Philostorgius. *History of the Church.* Translated by E. Walford. London, 1855.

Synesius of Cyrene. *The Essays and Hymns of Synesius of Cyrene.* Translated by A. Fitzgerald. 2 vols. Oxford, 1930.

———. *Hymnes.* Edited by C. Lacombrade. Paris, 1978.

———. *Les Hymnes de Synésios de Cyrène.* Translated by M. Meunier. Paris, 1947.

———. *Synesius Cyrenensis Hymni.* Edited by N. Terzaghi. Rome, 1939.

———. *Letters.* In *Epistolographi Graeci.* Edited by R. Hercher. Paris, 1879. Pp. 638–739.

———. *The Letters of Synesius of Cyrene.* Translated by A. Fitzgerald. Oxford, 1926.

———. *Synesius Cyrenensis Opera Omnia.* Edited by J. P. Migne. *PG* vol. 66. Paris, 1859 and 1864.

———. *Synesius Cyrenensis Opuscula.* Edited by N. Terzaghi. Rome, 1944.

Theodoretus. *Historia Ecclesiastica.* Edited by J. P. Migne. *PG* vols. 80–84. Paris, 1859–1860.

Zosimus. *Historia Nova.* Edited by B. G. Niebuhr. Bonn, 1837.

II. Modern Works

Anastos, M. "Pletho's Calendar and Liturgy." *Dumbarton Oaks Papers* 4 (1948) 183–305.

Angus, S. *The Mystery Religions and Christianity.* 1925. Reprint New York, 1966.

Armstrong, A. H. "Plotinus." *Cambridge History of Later Greek and Early Medieval Philosophy.* Part III, 193–268. Cambridge, 1967.

Asmus, J. R. "Synesius und Dio Chrysostomus." *Byzantinische Zeitschrift* 9 (1900) 85–151.

Aubin, P. *Le problème de la conversion.* Paris, 1963.

Barns, J. D. "Shenute as a Historical Source." *Actes du X. congrès international de papyrologues.* Warsaw, 1964. Pp. 151–159.

Bidez, J. *La vie de l'empereur Julien*. Paris, 1930.

———. *Vie de Porphyre*. Ghent, 1913.

Bizzochi, C. "Gl' inni filosofici di Sinesio interpretati come mistiche cele-brazioni." *Gregorianum* 32 (1951) 347–387.

Bloch, H. "The Pagan Revival in the West at the End of the Fourth Century." In *The Conflict Between Paganism and Christianity in the Fourth Century*. Edited by A. Momigliano. Oxford, 1963. Pp. 193–218.

Böll, F. *Kleine Schriften*. Leipzig, 1950.

Boyancé, P. *Le cult des muses chez les philosophes grecs*. Paris, 1937.

Brown, Peter. *The Making of Late Antiquity*. Cambridge, Mass., 1978.

———. "The Philosopher and Society in Late Antiquity." *Center for Hellenistic and Hermeneutical Studies*. Graduate Theological Union, Berkeley, Ca. *Colloquium #36*, 1980.

———. *Religion and Society in the Age of St. Augustine*. London, 1971.

Cameron, Alan. "The Last Days of the Academy at Athens." *Proceedings of the Cambridge Philological Society* 15 (1969) 7–29.

———. "Notes on Palladas." *Classical Quarterly* 15 (1965) 215–229.

Chadwick, H. E. "Faith and Order at the Council of Nicaea." *Harvard Theological Review* 53 (1960) 171–195.

Cherniss, Harold. *The Platonism of Gregory of Nyssa*. New York, 1930.

Chesnut, Glen. *The First Church Histories*. Paris, 1977.

Cochrane, C. N. *Christianity and Classical Culture*. New York, 1957.

Coleman-Norton, P. R. *Roman State and Christian Church*. 3 vols. London, 1966.

Coster, C. H. *Late Roman Studies*. Cambridge, Mass., 1968.

Cramer, Winfrid. "Zur Entwicklung der Zweigewaltenlehre: Ein unbeachteter Beitrag des Synesios von Kyrene." *Römische Quartalschrift* 72 (1977) 43–56.

Crawford, W. S. *Synesius the Hellene*. London, 1901.

Cudworth, R. *The True Intellectual System of the Universe*. London, 1678.

Cumont, F. *After Life in Roman Paganism*. 2nd ed. New York, 1959.

Dagron, Gilbert. "Aux origines de la civilisation byzantine: langue de culture et langue d'État." *Revue historique* 241 (Jan.–Mar. 1969) 23–56.

———. *L'empire romain d'Orient au IV*ᵉ *siècle et les traditions politiques de l'Hellénisme*. Travaux et mémoires du centre de recherche d'histoire et civilisation byzantines 3. Paris, 1968. Pp. 1–242.

Daniélou, J. *A History of Early Christian Doctrine*. Vol. I: *The Theology of Jewish Christianity*. Translated by J. Baker. London, 1964.

———. *Platonisme et théologie mystique: essai sur la doctrine spirituelle de saint Grégoire de Nysse*. Paris, 1944.

Delatte, L. *Traités de la Royauté d'Ecphante, Diotogène et Sthenidas.* Liège and Paris, 1942.

Dillon, J. M. *The Middle Platonists: 80 B.C. –220 A.D.* Ithaca, New York, 1977.

Dodds, E. R. *The Greeks and the Irrational.* Berkeley, 1957.

———. *Pagan and Christian in an Age of Anxiety.* Cambridge, 1965.

Dölger, F. J. *Sphragis, eine altchristliche Taufbezeichnung in ihren Beziehungen zur profanen und religiösen Kultur des Altertums.* Paderborn, 1911.

Downey, G. "Themistius and the Defense of Hellenism in the Fourth Century." *Harvard Theological Review* 50 (1957) 259–274.

Encyclopedia and Dictionary of Religion. Philadelphia, 1979.

Encyclopedia Judaica. Jerusalem, 1971.

Evans, J. A. S. "Christianity and Paganism in Procopius of Caesarea." *Greek, Roman and Byzantine Studies.* 12 (1971) 81–100.

Evans-Pritchard, E. *The Sanussi of Cyrenaica.* Oxford, 1948.

Evrard, É. "A quel titre Hypatie enseigna-t-elle la philosophie." *Revue des études grecques* 90 (1977) 69–74.

Festugière, A. J. *Personal Religion Among the Greeks.* Berkeley, 1954.

———. "Proclus et la religion traditionelle." In *Mélanges André Piganiol* 3. Paris, 1966.

Findlay, J. N. *Ascent to the Absolute.* London, 1970.

———. "The Logic of Mysticism." *Religious Studies* 2 (1967) 145–162.

Fitzgerald, A. *The Essays and Hymns of Synesius of Cyrene.* Oxford, 1930.

———. *The Letters of Synesius of Cyrene.* Oxford, 1926.

Fowden, B. "Bishops and Temples in the East Roman Empire." *Journal of Theological Studies.* n.s. 29 (1978) 53–78.

Gardner, A. *Synesius of Cyrene, Philosopher and Bishop.* London, 1886.

Geffcken, J. *Der Ausgang des griechisch-römischen Heidentums.* Heidelberg, 1929. Reprint, Darmstadt, 1963.

Gersh, S. E. *From Iamblichus to Eriugena: An Investigation of the Prehistory and Evolution of the Pseudo-Dionysian Tradition.* Leiden, 1978.

Gibbon, Edward. *The History of the Decline and Fall of the Roman Empire.* Modern Library Edition. New York, 1966.

Gilliard, Frank D. "The Social Origins of Bishops in the Fourth Century." University of California dissertation. Berkeley, 1966.

Glover, T. R. *Life and Letters in the Fourth Century.* Cambridge, 1901.

Goodenough, E. R. "The Political Philosophy of Hellenistic Kingship." *Yale Classical Studies* 1 (1928) 55–102.

———. *The Psychology of Religious Experiences.* New York, 1965.

Grande, C. del. "Composizione musiva in Sinesio." *Byzantion* 33 (1963) 317–323.

Grützmacher, G. *Synesios von Kyrene, ein Charakterbild aus dem Untergang des Hellenentums.* Leipzig, 1913.

Hadas, M., and Smith, M. *Heroes and Gods: Spiritual Biographies in Antiquity.* London, 1965.

Hadot, Ilsetraut. *Le problème du néoplatonisme alexandrin: Hiéroclès et Simplicius.* Paris, 1978.

Hadot, P. *Porphyre et Victorinus.* 2 vols. Paris, 1968.

Haskins, C. H. *The Renaissance of the Twelfth Century.* New York, 1957.

Henry, P. "The Adversus Arium of Marius Victorinus." *Journal of Theological Studies.* n.s. 1 (1950) 42–55.

Hulen, A. B. *Porphyry's Work Against the Christians.* New Haven, 1933.

Inge, W. R. *Christian Mysticism.* London, 1899. Reprint New York, 1956.

Jaeger, W. *Early Christianity and Greek Paideia.* Cambridge, Mass., 1961.

––––––. "The Greek Ideas of Immortality." In *Immortality and Resurrection.* Edited by K. Stendahl. New York, 1965. Pp. 97–114.

James, William. *Varieties of Religious Experience.* The Gifford Lectures, 1901–1902. New York, 1958 (Mentor edition).

Johnson, Douglas I. *Jabal al-Akhdar. Cyrenaica: A Historical Geography of Settlement and Livelihood.* Chicago, 1973.

Jonas, Hans. *The Gnostic Religion.* 2nd ed. Boston, 1963.

Jones, A. H. M. "Constantinople." *Oxford Classical Dictionary.* (2nd ed.). Oxford, 1970. P. 281.

––––––. *The Later Roman Empire.* Oxford, 1964.

––––––, Martindale, J. R., and Morris, J. *The Prosopography of the Later Roman Empire* I, A.D. 260–395. Cambridge, 1971.

Kelly, J. N. D. *Early Christian Doctrines.* 2nd ed. New York, 1960.

Kerenyi, K. *Die Mysterien von Eleusis.* Zurich, 1962.

Kissling, R. C. "The ὄχημα-πνεῦμα of the Neoplatonists and the *De Insomniis* of Synesius of Cyrene." *American Journal of Philology* 43 (1922) 318–330.

Labriolle, P. de. *La réaction païenne.* Paris, 1934.

Lacombrade, C. *Le Discours sur la Royauté de Synésios de Cyrène à l'Empereur Arcadios.* Paris, 1951.

––––––. *Synésios de Cyrène: hellène et chrétien.* Paris, 1951.

Ladner, G. *The Idea of Reform.* Cambridge, Mass., 1959.

Laistner, M. L. W. *The Platonism of Gregory of Nyssa.* New York, 1930.

Lampe, G. W. H. *The Seal of the Spirit.* London, 1967.

Lang, Wolfram. *Das Traumbuch des Synesios.* Heidelberger Abhandlungen zur Philosophie 10. Heidelberg, 1926.

Lemerle, P. Review of Lacombrade, *Synésios de Cyrène: hellène et chrétien. Revue de philologie* 79 (1953) 228–230.

Lewy, Hans. *The Chaldaean Oracles and Theurgy.* Cairo, 1956.

Lindner, Kurt. *Beiträge zu Vogelfang und Falknerei im Altertum.* New York and Berlin, 1973.

Lloyd, A. C. "Later Neoplatonism." *Cambridge History of Later Greek and Early Medieval Philosophy.* Part IV, 269–325. Cambridge, 1967.

McGeachy, J. A. *Quintus Aurelius Symmachus and the Senatorial Aristocracy of the West.* Chicago, 1942.

MacKenna, S. *Journal and Letters of Stephen MacKenna.* Edited by E. R. Dodds. London, 1936.

MacMullen, R. "Constantine and the Miraculous." *Greek, Roman and Byzantine Studies* 9 (1968) 81–96.

————. *Enemies of the Roman Order.* Cambridge, Mass., 1966.

Marrou, H. I. "Le 'conversion' de Synésios." *Revue des études grecques* 65 (1952) 474–484.

————. *S. Augustin et la fin de la culture antique.* Paris, 1938.

————. "Synesius of Cyrene and Alexandrian Neoplatonism." In *The Conflict Between Paganism and Christianity in the Fourth Century.* Edited by A. Momigliano. Oxford, 1936. Pp. 128–150.

Matthews, J. F. *Western Aristocracies and the Imperial Court.* Oxford, 1974.

Mattingly, H., and Warmington, B. H. "Constantine." *Oxford Classical Dictionary.* (2nd ed.). Oxford, 1970. Pp. 280–281.

Mazzarino, Santo. *Aspetti sociali del quarto secolo.* Rome, 1951.

Meijerling, E. P. *Orthodoxy and Platonism in Athanasius: Synthesis or Antithesis?* Leiden, 1966.

Merlan, P. "Plotinus and Magic." *Isis* 44 (1953) 341–348.

————. "Religion and Philosophy from Plato's Phaedo to the Chaldaean Oracles." *Journal of the History of Philosophy* 1 (1963) 163–176.

Misch, G. *Geschichte der Autobiographie.* Leipzig and Berlin, 1907.

————. *A History of Autobiography in Antiquity.* Translated by E. W. Dickes. 2 vols. Cambridge, Mass., 1951.

Moles, J. L. "The Career of Dio Chrysostom." *Journal of Hellenic Studies* 98 (1978) 79–100.

Momigliano, A., ed. *The Conflict Between Paganism and Christianity in the Fourth Century.* Oxford, 1963.

Nestle, W. "Die Haupteinwande des antiken Denkens gegen das Christentum." *Archiv für Religionswissenschaft* 37 (1941–1942) 51–100.

Nicolosi, Salvatori. *Il "De Providentia" de Sinesio di Cirene.* Padua, 1959.

Nock, A. D. *Conversion.* Oxford, 1933.

O'Brien, E. *Varieties of Mystic Experience.* New York, 1965.

Otis, B. "Cappadocian Thought as a Coherent System." *Dumbarton Oaks Papers* 12 (1958) 94–124.

Pelikan, Jaroslav. *The Christian Tradition*. I: *The Emergence of the Catholic Tradition*. Chicago, 1971.

Pépin, J. *Mythe et Allégorie: les origines grecques et les contestations judéo-chrétiennes*. Paris, 1958.

Petit, P. *Les étudiants de Libanius. Un professeur de Faculté et ses élèves au Bas-Empire*. Paris, 1956.

Petry, Ray C., ed. *Late Medieval Mysticism*. Philadelphia, 1957.

Rahner, H. "The Christian Mystery and the Pagan Mysteries." *Papers from the Eranos Yearbooks*. Edited by J. Campbell. Translated by R. Manheim. New York, 1955.

Raine, Kathleen. "Thomas Taylor et le mouvement romantique anglais." *Le Néoplatonisme*. Paris, 1971. Pp. 475–483.

———. "Thomas Taylor in England." *Thomas Taylor the Platonist*. New York, 1969. Pp. 3–48.

Rist, J. M. *Plotinus and the Road to Reality*. Cambridge, 1967.

Rosàn, L. J. Art. "Proclus." *Encyclopedia of Philosophy* 6.479–482.

———. *The Philosophy of Proclus*. New York, 1949.

Rostovsteff, M. I. *Social and Economic History of the Roman Empire*. 2nd ed. Oxford, 1957.

Ruether, Rosemary R. *Gregory of Nazianzus: Rhetor and Philosopher*. Oxford, 1969.

Ruggini, Lellia C. *Simboli di battaglia nel tardo ellenismo*. Pisa, 1972.

Schramm, M., and Vogt, J. "Synesios vor dem Planisphaerium." In *Das Altertum und jedes neue Gute. Festschrift für Wolfgang Schadenwalt zum 15.3.1970*. Stuttgart, 1970. Pp. 265–311.

Seeck, O. "Studien zu Synesios." *Philologus* 52 (1894) 442–483.

Seznec, J. *The Survival of the Pagan Gods*. 2nd ed. New York, 1953.

Sheldon-Williams, I. P. "The Greek Christian Platonist Tradition from the Cappadocians to Maximus and Eriugena." *Cambridge History of Later Greek and Early Medieval Philosophy*. Part VI, 421–533. Cambridge, 1967.

Smith, A. *Porphyry's Place in the Neoplatonic Tradition. A Study in Post-Plotinian Neoplatonism*. The Hague, 1974.

Smith, Jonathan Z. *Map Is Not Territory*. Leiden, 1978.

Stein, E. *Histoire du Bas-Empire*. Paris, 1949–1959.

Stramondo, Giuseppina. "A Peonio sul dono." *Miscellanea di studi di letteratura cristiana antica* 14 (1964) 5–79.

Theiler, W. *Die Chaldäischen Orakel und die Hymnen des Synesios*. Halle, 1942.

———. *Forschungen zum Neuplatonismus*. Berlin, 1966.

Tillich, Paul. *A History of Christian Thought*. Cambridge, Mass., 1956.

Treu, K. *Synesios von Kyrene, ein Kommentar zu seinem Dion*. Berlin, 1958.

Trexler, R. "Florentine Religious Experience: The Sacred Image." *Studies in the Renaissance* 19 (1972) 7–41.

Trouillard, J. *L'un et l'âme selon Proclos.* Paris, 1972.

Villard, U. Monneret de. *Le leggende orientali sui Magi evangelici.* Studi e Testi 103. Vatican, 1952.

Vogel, C. J. de. "Boethiana I." *Vivarium* 9 (1971) 44–66.

——. "Boethiana II." *Vivarium* 10 (1972) 1–40.

Walker, J. "The Tolerability of Metaphysics." *International Philosophical Quarterly* 13 (1973) 5–23.

Wallis, R. T. *Neoplatonism.* New York, 1972.

Walzer, R. "Early Islamic Philosophy." *Cambridge History of Later Greek and Early Medieval Philosophy.* Part VIII. Cambridge, 1967.

——. *Greek into Arabic, Essays on Early Islamic Philosophy.* Cambridge, 1962.

Wilamowitz-Moellendorff, U. von. "Die Hymnen des Synesios und Proklos." *Sitzungsberichte der Königlich Preussischen Akademie der Wissenschaften* 14 (1907) 272–295.

Wind, E. *Pagan Mysteries of the Renaissance.* Revised ed. London, 1967.

Wolfson, H. A. "The Identification of *Ex Nihilo* with Emanation in Gregory of Nyssa." *Harvard Theological Review* 63 (1970) 53–60.

——. "Immortality and Resurrection in the Philosophy of the Church Fathers." In *Immortality and Resurrection.* Edited by K. Stendahl. New York, 1965. Pp. 54–96.

——. *The Philosophy of the Church Fathers.* Cambridge, Mass., 1956.

Index

Designer: Sandy Drooker
Compositor: G & S Typesetters, Inc.
Text: Linotron 202 Caledonia
Display: Phototypositor Caledonia
Printer: Thomson-Shore, Inc.
Binder: John H. Dekker & Sons